Flying Models

Rubber • CO_2 • Electric & Micro Radio Control

Tips & Techniques for Beginner & Expert

DON ROSS

The author of RUBBER POWERED MODEL AIRPLANES

BOOK 2

An *AViation Publishers* Book
Published by *Markowski International Publishers*
Hummelstown, PA USA

Published by:
Aviation Publishers
Markowski International Publishers
One Oakglade Circle, Hummelstown, PA 17036 USA
(717) 566-0468

Publisher's Cataloging-in-Publication Data
(Provided by Quality Books, Inc.)

Ross, Don
Flying models: rubber, CO_2 electric & micro R/C: how to build adjust and fly rubber, CO_2, electric or compressed air powered model airplanes for sport, scale or endurance/Don Ross.—1st ed.

p.cm.
Preassigned LCCN: 98-66740
ISBN: 0-938716-54-9

1.Airplanes—Models 2. Airplanes—Models—Motors.I. Title
GV760.R67 1998 796.15'4 QBI98-911

On The Cover
Don Ross designed Evolution Micro RC Electric model developed from Peck One Niite 28, flown by Matthew Silbermann, photo by Don Ross, edited by Robin Marin. Cover designed by Leo McCarthy and Tony Peters.

Contents

Dedicated To

Henry Nelson who could make anything fly and Marty Taft who could make anyone want to.

Introduction

I had a great deal of help of many kinds in writing this book. Besides the news letter and magazine editors who work hard to bring new ideas to the modeling public, there are people you meet at a flying site who are happy to take time to explain and explore every nuance of their particular area of the hobby. And then there is the Metropolitan Sport Squadron, a bunch of guys who not only tolerate my company but have stretched themselves way beyond courtesy to help.

Leo McCarthy and Tony Peters created the cover. Robin Marin did the photo and my grandson, Matthew Silbermann posed. Jim Kaman's great graphics make everything clear. Walt Schwarz and again, Tony Peters who broke rubber motors for the cause and Martin Millman who codified the data. Rich Fiore, Gene Scheppers, Fred Dippel, Dom Antonelli and Gene Sellers who proof read and helped with building and test flying. Larry Sribnick whose "Techniques" publication gave me much electric information. Bob Bender and Henry Nelson who helped with flight trimming. Hangar Flying with Walt Balcer, Ken Bassett, Art Collard, Loren Dietrich, Tom Fennell, Mark Fineman, Rich Gorman, Paul Kaufmann, Charley Kriete, Kent LeMon, Bill Nesbitt, Al Rametta, Carl Steinberg, Joe Beshar and Sergio Zigras added many fine ideas. I got some fresh ideas from Jeff Anderson, Mike Parker and Tony Searle in England and Lawrie Kelsall in South Australia and even Jose Modejar in Peru. Certainly, Johanna and Max Sturm who made the neat text wrap computer formatting possible. Final editing was done by Mike Markowski and **Flying Models** Magazine editor Frank Fanelli. If I have left anyone out, you know who you are.

Also, both this book and I owe a big debt of gratitude to Mike Markowski of **Aviation Publishers** who got me started on this whole project by publishing my first book, **"Rubber Powered Model Airplanes."** RPMA is a good foundation for this or any advanced model book.

My wife, Doris and the rest of our family provided a secure nest in which I could gestate this book for 3 years.

1

TOOLS, MATERIALS AND CONSTRUCTION

While most books on construction seem to concentrate on **technique**, I'm going to start off about **tools** because without a wide selection of proper tools, certain techniques are almost useless. The tools I will discuss first are not complex power devices or super accurate measuring instruments. Rather, they are the very simple items everyone has in his shop and even around the house. The difference is that I feel you need to have a wide assortment of these items because they serve many different purposes.

Note: *This book is intended to be a companion to "Rubber Powered Model Airplanes". Since, it is not always possible to repeat background information you may want to get a copy . Specific references are made to "**RPMA**" pages where they apply to subject matter in the following chapters.*

Pins

It will take more than a few straight pins and "T" pins to do a good job, **Fig 1-1** shows 6 different kinds and *sizes* of pins with and without special heads. There are also devices that allow you to use pins to hold strips *without* piercing the strip. You can bend a pin to hold a strip **Fig 1-1A**. Most craft and hobby suppliers have many choices. You will be clamping or holding an infinite variety of assemblies in your modeling life and nothing will be more frustrating than holding something with 7 fingers and trying to stay still until the glue dries. You will get much better and stronger joints if you can hold the parts in *close* contact while they are glued.

Fig 1-1

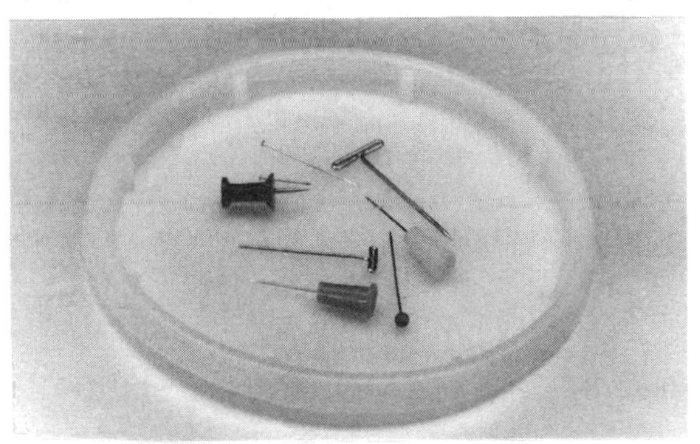

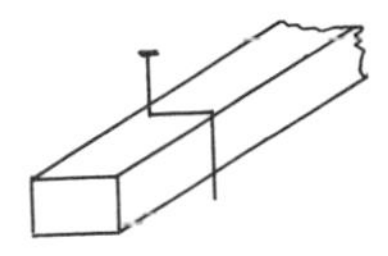

Fig 1-1A

Clamps

The same things said above about pins goes double for clamps. The very best construction comes when you can hold your assembly **absolutely square** and with **full surface contact** while glue dries. This not only assures straight, square alignment but it also insures against warps that can creep in just because the assembly is under stress from being glued while not in full contact.

Fig 1-2 shows the strains imparted on to two sheets that are glued with a gap. You can avoid this by cutting the two sheets while they are overlapped. There are clamps actuated by rubber bands, screw pressure and off- center locking. They come in a multitude of shapes and sizes and can also be modified by simply gluing a square of balsa or hard rubber to the clamping faces. **Fig 1-3** shows some of my collection. Keep your eyes open in hardware stores and craft shops for any new kind of clamp. A full inventory of clamps and pins and some clever use of rubber bands and masking tape will make building easier and finished models stronger and better looking.

Fig. 1-3

Another source for useful small clamps is the local dollhouse and accessories store. Recently, a friend sent me a collection of dollhouse clothespins ranging from about one inch to 2-1/2 inches in length. These are great for small clamping jobs. When you are in a doll store, look around for other tiny devices that can be used in model construction. You will be surprised at what a little imagination will reveal. Substituting a rubber band for the spring in a full-sized clothespin will reduce the chances of scarring Balsa parts.

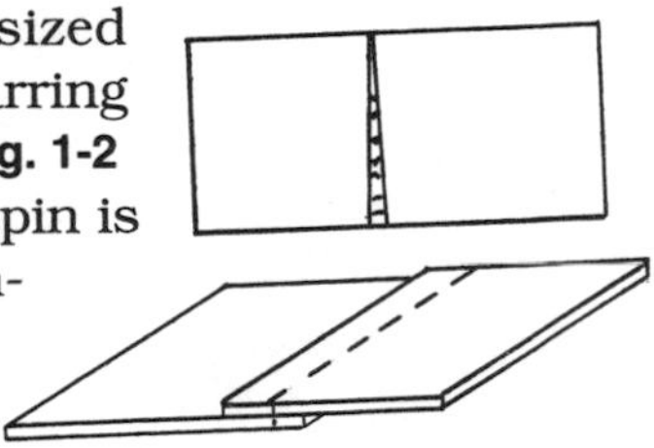

Fig. 1-2

A neat way to use a standard clothespin is to *reverse* the spring so the two holding fingers become the *long* sides. **Fig 1-4 A-C**.

A simple popsicle stick or tongue depressor can become a clamp to hold the rear of a fuselage when the sides are put together. Cut a tapered slot in the wooden clamp to fit the top view of the joined fuselage **Fig 1-5**.

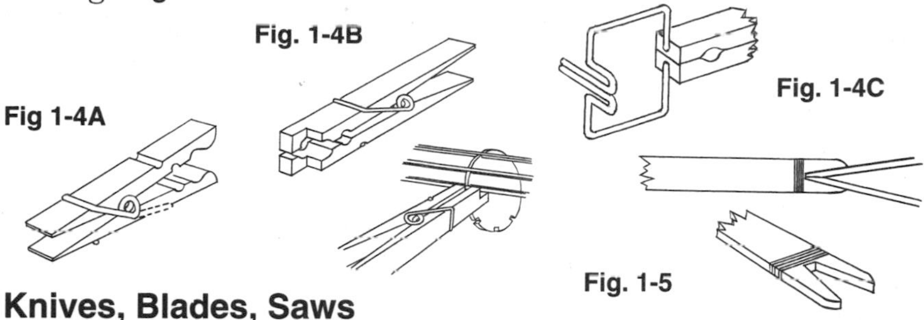
Fig 1-4A

Fig. 1-4B

Fig. 1-4C

Fig. 1-5

Knives, Blades, Saws

You can't have enough blades of enough different sizes and types. Remember, you will be cutting wood that varies in density from 4 pounds (per cu.ft.) Balsa to 16 pound spruce and ply. You will be cutting *with* the grain, *across* the grain and all kinds of combinations in between. You will be slicing, shaving, scooping and doing just about everything but chopping. Now, does that sound as if you can do it all with a used, single-edged razor blade ?

The integrity of your structures will depend on how closely and cleanly your cut edges fit. No amount of glue can efficiently fill a bad joint and, as said before, the shrinking of the glue when it dries will distort the joint and add strains that can lead to later warps. Notches in ribs and formers *must* be sharp, crisp and correct in size. These are almost always across the grain and near an edge so they tend to crack.

Of course, the number 11 Exacto type blade will become your most used cutting tool. However you *must* make sure you have a lot of them. The average 30-36 inch span model will require three or four blades during construction. The easiest way to operate is to buy them in boxes of 100 and be generous with replacements.

You can also sharpen these blades with an **Edger** which is quite efficient and easy to use. Besides the other size Exacto blades, you will need an X-acto® carving set for the "scooping" blades of different sizes. I also use a long X-acto blade® for prop carving and the fine saw blade for slots, etc. Another useful blade that requires careful handling is a pointed **double** edged razor blade.

Use the old, steel blades <u>not</u> the stainless kind. Leave the blade in the paper sleeve and grasp it with a pliers while breaking it in half, then breaking off two corners to leave it shaped as shown in **Fig 1-6**. Keep your eye open for kitchen type, small (4-5-inch) paring knives with narrow, thin blades that can be sharpened to a fine edge. These are very good for carving shapes in Balsa, Pine or foam. A brand new, very sharp potato peeling knife, (with the slot in the middle of the blade) can also be a useful carving tool for prop finishing. leading edges and wing tips.

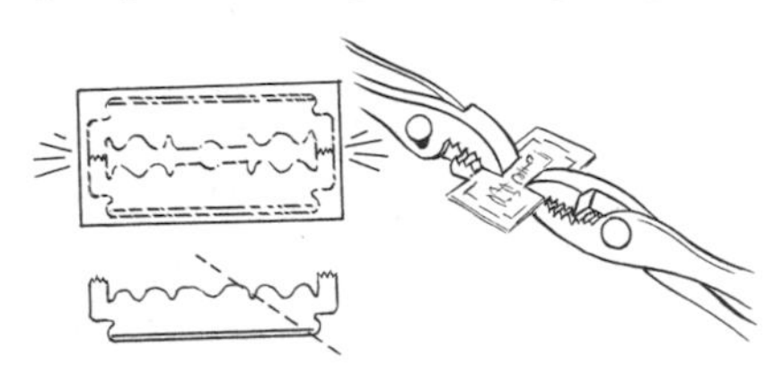

Fig 1-6

Diamond Machining Technology of Marlborough, Mass. makes an entirely new type of sharpening tool. It comes in sizes small enough for your field box or larger for your workshop. These whetstones employ a diamond compound bonded to a steel or brass plate which also has plastic dots embedded in the surface to help clear chips and accurately support your blade. I have found that a few passes before carving a noseblock or prop will return the blade to like-new sharpness and will preserve the edge.

Imagine that your rubber motor has just broken at 90% of total turns, suddenly you're faced with removing the tight rubber strands, cutting away tissue or Airspan, then cutting through glue, wood and carbon fiber to clean up the broken area. Next you have to *neatly* create new mating joints where you can splint longerons and re-attach wire landing gear. Does that sound like one type of cutting tool can do the whole job in a way that won't embarrass you next time at the field ? I have made such repairs **at the field** during a contest and, while not winning any Concours D'Elegance awards, have returned within an hour with a model capable of continuing to compete. Of course, you can avoid all that by using a winding tube but that belongs in another chapter.

Saw blades also deserve a few words. There are two different things to know about saw blades. First, the size of the teeth will affect the quality of your cut. This is usually expressed in "**Teeth per inch**". Tooth size ranges from about 24 to 54 teeth per inch with the higher number (54) indicating a finer cut. Again, you need to have a range of blade types to handle your range of applications. I use the **X-acto® Razor Saw** type as well as the fine saw blades that fit in the standard handle. With these, I have a Jeweler's Saw (a small coping saw) and a small hacksaw. For many years,

I did all my sawing by hand and it was quite adequate. Of course, a Dremel- type bandsaw or vibrating saw will work much faster, more accurately and will require less effort, but for the beginner almost all work can be done with a group of hand tools whose total cost is **less than $30.00**.

Drills

Again, the wider your assortment of this particular tool, the better and easier your construction will be. Start with #80 (.0135 in. diameter). You may want to drill a hole that is tight on 1/64" wire (.015in. dia.) and this will do it properly. Sizes through #60 (.040 in. dia.) which is just under 3/64" wire size, come in sets with 20 drills packed in a neat holder that dispenses one drill at a time and retains the rest in numbered slots. The next size set starts at #60 and usually runs through #1 (.228" dia.) Only after you have used the *exactly* right drill or gradually expanded a hole by successive drilling can you appreciate the advantages in having a wide drill assortment.

Do not look for bargains in drills. Some cheap imported sets are not properly hardened and will wear or break quickly. You will keep and use a good drill set for the rest of your life. Drills are the perfect gift request to make to your family. They are small, easy to pack and transport and cost just enough to represent a thoughtful gift without busting someone's budget.

Next, when you stop in at the dentist as we all do, ask him for some of his worn out carbide or diamond drills. These are usually discarded. He will have them in many sizes and various grades of roughness. He will also have grinders and polishers that can be very useful. A small carbide drill is great for removing that blob of excess epoxy that dripped out of your landing gear assembly. Some dentist drills can be used as routers to shape parts or holes or even grind right through music wire to make repairs. Also, you will get a lot of pleasure hearing a dentist's drill whirring away and doing something that doesn't hurt.

Of course, once you have all these drills, you need an assortment of tools to hold and use them. Add a right angle attachment and a variable chuck to your **Dremel**. Buy a **Pin Vise** for detail hand drilling and practice with it until you can drill a 1/64 in. hole through 1/16 in.ply. Also, get hold of a drill and screw size chart from your local hardware store. This will give you the fraction and decimal equivalents of your numbered drills as well as the tap drill sizes for various screws.

A **tapered reamer** is a handy tool available in most hardware stores. It is simply a tapered, fluted cutting tool that will allow you to enlarge a hole *slowly* as you twist the reamer into it. With a little practice, you can drill an undersized hole, then ream to a tight fit on a dowel, tube or any other insert. This works well when making a hole for the rear rubber peg through Balsa and thin ply. Tapered reamers range from .015" through .093". and are sometimes called "broaches".

I see that I have mentioned dimensions in both **fractions** and **decimals**. For the beginner, it's worth a moment to explain. We are all familiar with fractions of an inch and with manipulating them. We can kind of " feel" that 1/4" is about half of 1/2 " and it takes 4 of those tiny 1/64" pieces to make up 1/16in. But when it comes to decimals many can't quite feel them. Did you ever hear the story of the apprentice machinist who was asked "How many thousandths are there in an inch ?" He replied. "I dunno but they're so damn small there must be a million of them."

Note: wherever practical, (") designates (inches).

Well, a human hair is about two one- thousandths of an inch thick (.002). A 1/64" thick balsa sheet is .015 or 15 one- thousandths thick. 1/32" sheet is 31- thousandths (same as 31 one-thousandths), = .031. 1/16" sheet is 62 and a half .0625 thousandths and 3/32 = .093 = 93 thousandths. You can get these answers by simply dividing the fraction denominator into the numerator. From here on, I will use " to signify inch.

1/16 " equals 1.000 <u>divided</u> by 16 = .0625 or you can put a decimal equivalent chart on the wall along with your Balsa Density, Rubber Turns and a Standard Screw Thread chart. However, I feel very strongly that you need to spend just a few minutes "playing" with the numbers to develop a "feel" for decimals vs. fractions. This will become valuable in estimating the strength of a screw mounting, deciding on a wire size and a "million" other areas where you would rather have a number to go by than a guess. For instance, the rubber hook on a peanut can be .020" or .025" wire, which is between 1/64" (.015) and 1/32" (.032). This would be at least 30% lighter than going right to 1/32 diameter. That's how the pros win contests.

Work Boards

Now that you have an adequate set of tools, you will need someplace to use them. Probably the best and simplest work board is the warp free one made by **Guillow's.** It is one inch thick and made from blocks rather than laminated sheets. It comes in several sizes. I prefer the 16 x 36" size for most work. If used with reasonable care, it will last almost forever. Also, I use several boards made from ordinary ceiling tile material available in any lumber yard. These are cut to 12 x 24". I prefer to work with several smaller boards rather than a single large one. That way, I can set up a fuselage on one and, while it is drying, build a stab on another.

Others have recommended old doors, plywood with cork on top, and for fragile indoor wood, a sheet of glass. The main thing to remember is to be **sure** your board is **flat and warp free**. There's almost no other way you can end up with uniform flying surfaces. I have friends who "build in the air" and I admire their skill but have no desire to imitate them. A sturdy board will also serve as a base for clamps as well as pins when you assemble fuselages, etc.

Now, a few hints that will make your building a bit less frustrating:

- **1**. When pins or small metal parts drop to the floor, put a **strong** magnet inside a glass jar. Pass the jar over the pile of pins. Place the jar over your pin holder and remove the magnet.
- **2**. Tuck a lint free towel into your belt so it covers your lap. When small parts fall off the table they will end up in the towel.
- **3**. To hold small parts on your table, split a sheet of corrugated card board to show the honeycomb. Lay the parts in a trough and they will stay put.

Sanding

No matter how neat and careful the construction, what the observer (and the air) sees is the surface finish. Whether your model is all balsa or foam sheet, structure covered with tissue, silk or Monokote, or an ARF that you have covered, the final appearance will be governed by the smoothness and uniformity of the surface under the covering. Professional painters **always** concentrate on the substrate **before** the finishing steps.

The best way to control the surface conditions before covering is with sandpaper and sometimes sealing. Good sanding work takes little time and actually makes the covering job a lot easier.

First, you need at least 4 grades of sandpaper. The grades indicate the roughness of the grit. Usually, 180, 220, 400 and 600 will cover the range you will need. Some vendors **SIG** for instance, call this Fine, Very Fine, Super Fine and Ultra. Buy the stuff in whole sheets 12" x 12" so you can cut pieces any size. Always cut sandpaper from the back of the sheet with a razor blade and a straight edge unless you want to ruin a whole lot of scissors.

Next, glue a sheet of 220 grit paper to a board at least 12"x 12" You will find this an **invaluable** aid in holding flat parts to be sanded. Now promise me on your honor that you will **never** sand without using a block and **never** "in the air" without backing the work up on a board or other solid base. Just imagine the resulting airfoil after sanding the tops of the ribs with a folded sheet held in your hand while holding the wing up in the other hand. Then try to figure out why my model flies a lot better than yours.

There's a legend about Rembrandt who, when instructing a class of budding artists, dipped a brush in paint and **free hand** drew a perfect circle on a canvas. He then said, "When you can do that, you are an artist". Well, we want to be airplane builders and flyers, not artists. Therefore, we'll use any aid we can get and **avoid** all the free hand techniques.

The next step is to gather a supply of **Sanding Blocks**. There are many commercial blocks and all are quite good. **Fig 1-7** shows some of mine. Have at least one block for **each grade** of paper and, preferably several different shapes for each grade. For instance, you will need a block at least 6 inches long to sand wing structures because you need to sand in a chord wise direction (from L.E. to T.E. and back) and to do that you must span several rib bays. You will need flat blocks and curved ones, round and angular ones as well as thin wands and strips. In the beginning, don't try finish sanding with anything motorized like a Dremel or a sanding disk. These things will remove material much faster than you can control them.

Get a can of 3M #77 spray adhesive or a bottle of rubber cement., These are **very flammable** substances so use and store them with care. Stick your sanding sheets to the blocks with these unless you are using a commercial block with a wedge or other clamping device. Sandpaper that shifts while you are working can gouge and tear your work. When too worn you can glue another sheet on top or remove the sheet with a steady pull and a bit of solvent.

Sand **with** the grain whenever possible and use more strokes rather than more pressure.

Fig. 1-7

When working on both sides of any structure like a right and left wing, I actually *count* strokes so I remove approximately the same amount of material from both sides. Another technique is to **listen** while you are sanding. Soon, you will begin to hear hard or high spots as you pass over them. You will also hear the difference in pressure that you are applying and will be better able to sand more uniformly. Sanding for me is good therapy while listening to music or even watching TV. Since you aren't using sharp cutters, no blood will appear on the upholstery when your eye is diverted.

3M also makes a "Feathering Disk Adhesive" that is very good for gluing sandpaper to dowels. You can drill a hole 1/2" or 3/4" diameter or larger in a block, split the block and glue paper to the inside of the curve for sanding leading edges wing tips, etc. Another method is to buy 80 grit Carborundum powder in a craft store, coat a dowel with white glue and roll it in the powder.

An interesting item that may help in sanding when two parts have to fit smoothly together as with a nose block is some stuff called "Articulation Paper". If you visit the dentist a lot (as I do) then this is the stuff he puts between your teeth and asks you to "rub together please". It leaves a black mark where the surfaces touch first. This works even with wet surfaces. It's very cheap and your dentist will give you a package that will last 5 years.

Perma Grit is a steel sheet with Silicon Carbide brazed to the surface. For rough sanding, this can be a real winner. If properly cleaned it will last almost forever and will cut hardwood as well as Balsa. (Bob Barnes)

Often when you are sanding either a new or rebuilt structure, you will find or cause a dent in the surface. With soft balsa this can even happen by accidentally gripping too hard with a fingernail. Just put a few drops of white vinegar on the dent and it will raise level with the surface most of the time. I have even worked some saliva into a dent then heated it with an iron to raise the surface. This avoids complicated filling techniques.

Although there are many balsa fillers available to handle larger dents and fill in breaks, the easiest and cheapest material is ordinary **Spackling Plaster.** It comes in a plastic can and spreads like cream cheese. It sands well when dry and can be doped.

Now, your eye comes into play right along with the ear that has been listening to the sanding sound. Hold the part that is sanded up to a strong light and sight along the surface. Look for shadows caused by depressions and highlights on high spots.

Once all the dents and rough areas have been eliminated, you are ready for "finish sanding".

Most of the basic sanding should be done with 220 grit. When to switch to 400 or 600 is largely a matter of practice. For surface sanding you can use an *orbital* motion with the block. Sort of move the block in an oval with the long dimension parallel to the grain. At this point, 400 paper will give you a very "silky" feel to the surface. For most models at this point you should "seal" the surface before going to final finish with 600 paper. A light coat of 50% dope, 50% thinner, well dried, will work. Also, **Balsarite** and **Balsaloc** are very good sealers. For those who are worried about adding weight, a light sealer and final sanding may even save weight by requiring less adhesive for the covering since the surface is no longer absorbent. Remember, the first coat of dope (which is largely absorbed into the surface) weighs *twice* as much as the second coat. If the surface is sealed, that first coat is 50% lighter due to evaporation.

Plans

With photocopy machines available everywhere there is no longer any reason to cut up a plan or even to use the original plan. For the usual small model, it's easy to copy the plan in separate parts to work on separate boards. Also, photo copies are dandy for transferring images from plans to Balsa for the scratch builder. Just lay the copy face down on the Balsa and iron on the image. You can also transfer from most copies by wiping a small amount of thinner or polish remover on the back of the copy while its face is pressed against the balsa sheet. **Chartpak** makes a **Blender** (clear solvent in a magic marker). (Bob Becroft)

Now that we have the tools and the board, let's put the plans down and get to work. Tape the plan *very flat* to the board, then pin it firmly with thumb tacks. Add any special markings, like angle measurements or extra gussets or sticks to the plan at this point, so you won't forget them during building. Lay plastic food wrap not wax paper (which can get into glue joints and soften them), over the plan. Some folks are using the clear plastic backing from Monokote or similar products, which also works well.

Prepare all the pins, clamps, parts and glue that you will need for this particular assembly neatly at hand, put on your binocular magnifier and get ready to actually start building something.

Cutting Board

This is a very important tool. A proper cutting surface will not only help you to get sharp, square, cut edges but will also add a lot to the life of your cutting blades. A really hard surface like glass is not recommended. I prefer the new, self healing mats sold by almost every mail order house. However, for a real bargain, stop into a sewing supply shop. They sell the same type of mat in even larger sizes and for about half the price. Remember, even these almost impervious materials eventually show cuts and gouges and wear out, so expect to buy a new one every season.

Glue

There's a lot of stuff around that will stick things together. There's *nothing* around that will stick *everything* together and also be convenient to use all the time and anyplace. The good news is that there are so many substances available that we can choose the best for any particular use at very little cost.

Instant Glue (Cyanoacrylate)

I am **not** a great proponent of the instant glues known as Cyanoacrylates. They have their uses but are not a universal answer. First, unless your parts are a very good (actually touching all along the area to be glued) fit, you won't get a very strong joint. The "Thin" types that dry very fast often penetrate the wood thus leaving less to form a joint. The "Thick" types, unless used by an experienced builder, still don't fill gaps too well. They are hard to sand and may end up forming a hard bump around a sanded joint. Certainly these glues have a multitude of good uses and choosing the right ones will add to your building speed and pleasure. When used properly, you can't beat CyA for field repairs. I always carry some "Activator" too so I can spray the area *first* before adding the CyA. Baking soda sprinkled on the joint just after applying the CyA will speed the drying and strengthen the joint. You can also make a fillet of baking soda **before** adding the glue. This helps insure a good joint and fast drying.

CyA is also very good for "tacking" parts together before adding a drop of epoxy for strength. I use it whenever I'm adding a hook to a part, like the small ones used to hold the nose block in. CyA is very important as a tool to harden balsa in areas where you expect lots of rubbing, wear and impact. These would be nose blocks, (both at the edges where they enter the fuselage and the center hole that holds the prop bearing), wing or stabilizer saddles, landing gear mountings and all **tapped holes**. Always have some Debonder nearby for the time when you scratch your eye with the same fingertip that just touched the CyA. Only a special few of the CyA glues can be used with foam so be careful to check the container. CyA'd surfaces don't take paint as well as bare or prepared wood, so be careful here too.

While this stuff hardens wood, it also helps to "stiffen" it where a stick has broken. I guess everyone has at some time grabbed a fuselage too tightly and cracked a longeron. Chuck Zimmerman sticks a pin through the paper at the corner, pulls out the longeron until it is straight, then puts a drop of CyA on the area to hold it in alignment. Many CyA glues give off an irritating vapor so **always** work in a well- ventilated area.

Acetone Glue

This is the stuff that smells from Acetone and may be called Sigment, Testors Model Glue, Duco or Ambroid. It's probably the universal model glue and has improved quite a lot from the time you got a tiny bottle in every kit. The stuff is stronger, penetrates deeper and dries faster than before. It is particularly useful with balsa because a lot of it will evaporate as it dries thus resulting in a lighter assembly. It can also be softened with thinner to re-glue a bad joint or even re-position a flying surface for flight trim. Most folks use the stuff right out of the tube but if you want to go to a bit more trouble, you will get much better results by thinning the glue about 50% with ordinary dope thinner or Acetone. Just assemble a small squeeze bottle and nozzle or glue gun from **SIG** (SH-627) or **K&B** (KB703), mix as required, and use the same way as a commercial glue tube.

Thinned Acetone glue will penetrate easily into balsa, particularly on end grain joints like fuselage uprights, cross pieces or rib ends. This makes "double gluing" simple and efficient. When gluing several pieces like ribs, just wet the ends with a drop of thinned glue while you assemble some other part. In 60 seconds the glue will have penetrated and you can add the second coat and assemble. This method of "double gluing" will add almost no weight but can double your strength. I believe more damage is done to models by sloppy gluing than almost any other condition.

When you move from rubber power into gas, electric or R/C, the weight of your model increases dramatically. Most small electric models weigh *twice* as much as the same size rubber model. Doubling the weight quadruples the impact force. Since a heavier model will also fly faster, impact which is *mass times velocity* increases *both* factors, sometimes to a disastrous level if your glue joints are weak.

Aliphatic Glue

Sometimes called "Carpenter's" glue, this type is white or yellowish and water soluble. **Sig** sells it as "Sig-Bond", other brands are "Quicksand"and "Titebond". This stuff is very good for bonding balsa to ply or spruce or other hardwoods. It is easily thinned with water to the consistency you prefer. I use it thinned about 50-50. Mix and store it in a plastic bottle or glue syringe. Some care is necessary in choosing the right Aliphatic glue. Some types have a lot more solids than others. For instance, the "Elmer's" glue you have in the kitchen drawer for gluing down torn shelf paper simply isn't strong enough for model work. The "Carpenter's" glue you buy in the local hardware store needs thinning before being used on balsa.

Aliphatics become tacky quickly, set up in about 1/2 hour and need several hours to dry hard. They are fuel proof and excess can be wiped off with a damp cloth. Since Aliphatic glue is water soluble, spreading large amounts on thin sheets of balsa can easily result in warps that stubbornly stay twisted because the glue has sealed the fibers in shape. Conversely, the stuff is perfect for foam. It builds a nice joint even though the foam cells are sealed with no grain to penetrate. One builder I know makes a small puddle of white glue on a piece of scrap and just dips the end of a stick in the puddle before gluing. Tony Peters does all his tissue covering with thinned white glue. He paints it on with a small brush on the edge of the area to be covered and lays the tissue on top. Then, he pulls the tissue as tight as reasonable and smoothes it against the glue with his finger. Cover a foam part with a few coats of thinned white glue so that you can color dope over it without dissolving the foam.

One of the most interesting properties of Aliphatic glue is that the stuff can be **heat activated** after it has dried !! This opens up a whole world of ideas. I regularly laminate Tyvek® sheet between two layers of balsa to make an almost bullet proof yet light structural material for fuselage tubes, firewalls, front formers and other critical parts. Spread a thin layer of glue on one surface, allow to dry, press the surfaces together and heat with an iron until fused.

Epoxy

Lots of modelers avoid epoxy because it has to be mixed before use and that seems a lot harder to do than just squeeze some stuff from a tube. Well, it is a tiny bit harder but the work is more than justified by the results. I use epoxy wherever I attach wire or metal to wood and many places where I need maximum strength and may not be able to get into the area for repairs once the model is finished and covered. Wing and stab saddles and landing gear mountings are good examples. Prop hub wrappings, prop blade inserts and wire hubs, wheel bearings, motor mounts and servo rails are just a few places where the extra weight and work of epoxy is very worthwhile.

Note that epoxy materials don't dry by evaporating solvents. They harden through a chemical reaction thus retaining most of their original weight, so use sparingly. Also, most epoxies are very hard to sand and will leave unsightly bumps on balsa areas. Mixing is not very critical. Just spread a thin "bead" of epoxy "A" about an inch long, then spread another bead of the same width and length of "B" right along side. Use a stick to mix the two for 30 seconds and you are ready to work. Some epoxies require different proportions but the process is the same for small quantities. Judge the length of the bead by the size of the job. Don't mix up too much. Each type of epoxy will show a "working time" on the package. This is **not** the drying time but the amount of time you can still work with a newly mixed batch. Epoxies come in various hardening intervals from 5 to 30 minutes. For the types of models discussed in this book, 5 minute epoxy will do almost any job.

Try mixing a few drops of alcohol with your epoxy batch. It will dry smoother and penetrate better. Also, if you find one of the ingredients has hardened somewhat in the bottle, set the whole bottle in hot water for a few minutes. That will soften the stuff so it will run better from the tube. Another neat trick for spreading any kind of glue on a thin strip, like the top of a rib, is to cut a little slit in the end of the cement tube. This allows you to run right along an edge with a very uniform bead.

While we're talking about cement tubes, let's discuss those pesky tips that clog up no matter what kind of glue you use. Fill a baby food jar with acetone (thinner) and another with water. Remove the tip from the glue tube, replace the cap and immerse the tip in the correct jar until you need it again. Use water for aliphatic glue and acetone for all others including CyA. Acetone will definitely unclog even CyA glue tips if soaked for a while. There are many brands of application tips you can buy to attach to your glue tube. These will help control the amount of glue you dispense. I have several sizes for each kind of glue at a cost of only a few cents. This is also a good way to save weight by using only the necessary amount of glue.

If you have access to any sort of medical products, or have a medical supply house nearby, look for "**Plastic Pipettes**". These are small plastic bulbs with long, thin, flexible necks, **Fig 1-8**. Squeeze all the air out of the bulb by rolling it up tight like a used toothpaste tube, insert the tip into the bottle of CyA glue and suck up a bulb full. You can carry this right in your field box for quick repairs. The long tube will clog after every use so just cut 1/8- inch off the end.

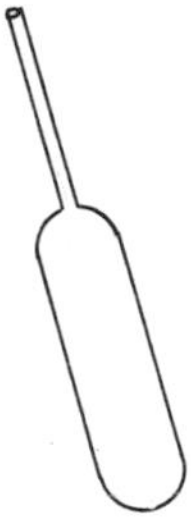

Fig 1-8

Glue Sticks

This is one of the newest and best ideas in adhesives. Available in almost any stationery store under many brands like **UHU** and **Dennison**, these sticks can be used to attach tissue or Mylar. They spread a thin coat of jelly like stuff that allows for some handling then dries hard. It takes only a bit of practice to be able to lay a sheet of tissue neatly on a wing and stretch most of the wrinkles out. This is covered in more detail in **COVERING**.

RC-56 - Canopy Glue

RC-56 is available in many hobby shops. Also, **Pacer**'s new "Formula 560" is just about the same stuff. This is a glue intended for attaching clear plastics to various surfaces. It works very well for canopies and will even adhere them well to Monokote. Another, perhaps cheaper, source is Vinyl Repair Glue available in upholstery and hardware stores. These glues may go on white or cloudy but they dry clear so a bit of overspill won't hurt. I usually let the stuff get tacky first before positioning the canopy or window. That eliminates a lot of sliding and spilling.

Contact Cements

The most popular is **3M Super 77**. These are either spray or paint- on glues that, when dry, become pressure sensitive. **Remember** that "Pressure Sensitive" means sensitive to pressure. That's not a play on words. It means that just mating the surfaces won't make the best bond. You have to actually apply pressure to activate a good pressure sensitive adhesive. Sometimes, that's not practical when dealing with fragile balsa structures. The best use for these adhesives is to attach a balsa or ply or Obichi skin to a foam part. Then you can apply pressure and clamp the parts together until set. 3M 77 is **very flammable** and **toxic** so it requires extreme care in use.

Heat Sensitive Adhesives

Sig, Stix-it, Balsarite and Balsaloc are all adhesives that can be brushed on, allowed to dry and re-activated with heat. These can be very useful in making laminates or applying some of the new covering materials like Polyspan, Airspan and Litespan. They also, when thinned by 40-50% with Butyrate thinner make very good wood sealer before doping or applying tissue, Silkspan or any other covering. As mentioned before, Aliphatic Glue can also be heat activated. This type of adhesive is particularly good for laminating sheets or strips.

Flexible Adhesives

Sold as "Zap-a-Dap-a-Goo" or similar names, these adhesives have limited applications in joining battery cells, attaching canopies or re-attaching Monokote. Also, they can be handy in your field box to attach balancing weights or even to hold a small electric motor in place while small thrust adjustments are made.

In general, you need several kinds of adhesive handy at your work table at all times. Use the best for each job to save weight and time. For beginners, I recommend using Cyano **very** sparingly while you learn to clamp, pin or hold parts together while other glues dry. This will enhance your skills and deliver much better flying models.

Cutting and Assembly

Many of the kits now available have laser cut parts which not only speed building but provide assemblies that are square, better fitted and much stronger as well as lighter. Perhaps the only problem with these parts is that in some cases you can see a faint brown burn line on the edge of the part. You can remove this with light sanding with 220 grit **or** with a solution of 1 part **Chlorox®** and 20 parts water. Just wipe it on with a **Q-tip®** and let the parts air dry or put them in the Microwave for 30 seconds.

Identical Rib Cutting

There are probably as many methods as there are modelers. Here are a few alternatives. Try some and choose the one that best fits your work habits:

1. a) Cut a rib pattern from an old leather belt or rubber sheet.
b) Glue it to a block and "rubber stamp" rib shapes to be cut.

2. 1/16" ply template, 250 grit sandpaper on rear and cut ribs.

3. Tack glue rectangular rib blanks with a 50-50 mix of thinner and acetone glue. Make sure blanks are square with each other and the table top. Glue **the exact** rib outline to the blank on **each** end the stack. Square them up with each other and with the stack. Cut and sand the stack to shape and put in **a sealed** plastic bag with a few drops of thinner. Wait an hour and ribs will separate .

Sliced Ribs

For smaller models, the very best way to create ribs is to slice them from a sheet. This allows you to construct a wing with the spar running **between** the ribs on top and bottom **Fig 1-9.** Most builders slice the ribs from a sheet of 1/32" or 1/16" thickness and fairly hard 8 lb. balsa **Fig 1-9A. Jim Jones** makes a swell gadget that helps you slice all the ribs the same width. One disadvantage of this type of sliced rib is that the grain of the balsa runs straight across the rib thus leading to cracks where the rib curves. A better way, pioneered by Tony Peters and Henry Nelson, is to first wet a sheet, then, with the grain running chordwise and (because of the forming) with the curve, form the rib shape over a block carved to the appropriate airfoil shape. For small models, particularly scale (up to 36" span), the exact airfoil shape is not too important, therefore, it's OK to create a 10 to 12% airfoil block that will accommodate any chord from 3-6 inches. The percentage figure indicates the proportion of height to chord, i.e.. a 6" chord at a 10% airfoil would have a (.10 x 6 = 0.6) = 6/10" **total** wing thickness including rib height and spars or ribs under the spar.

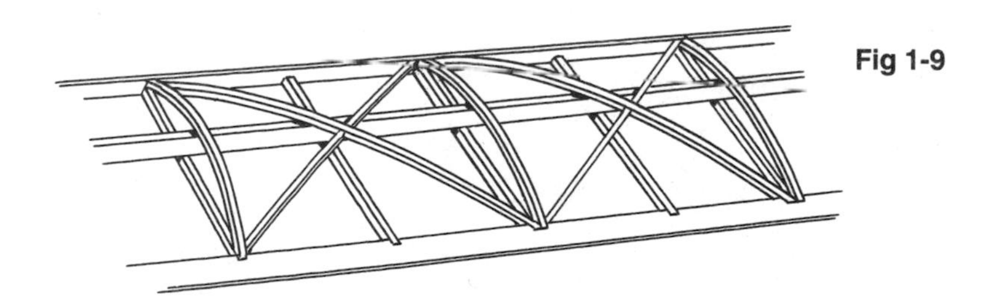

Fig 1-9

A typical block is shown in **Fig 1-10**. You can now control the rib thickness by simply choosing an appropriate sheet. Rib width can be controlled with a simple slicer **Fig 1-11 A or B**. or carefully done by hand with a flexible straightedge while still on the block. For tapered wings, just cut all ribs the same size, then cut off the back of each rib to fit the taper. This method lends itself well to complicated wing construction like slanted or even "Union Jack" ribs. **Fig 1-12** shows a conventional rib in a "Union Jack" (from the name of the English flag) configuration. This is much easier with sliced ribs.

Fig 1-10

A lower rib, (sliced flat or under cambered) can be laid under the spar on a diagonal thus adding strength. *Do not notch the spar to locate and hold the ribs. This will weaken it.*

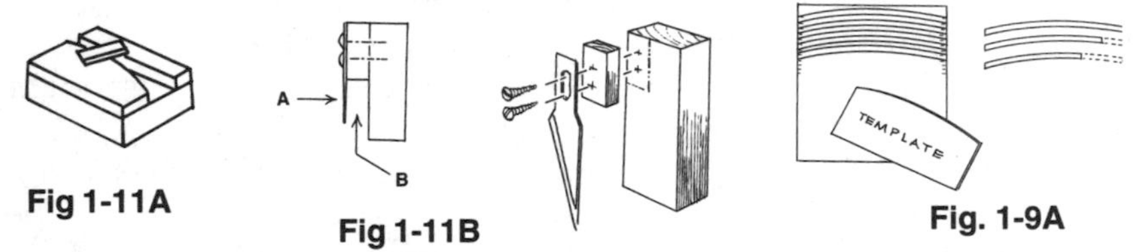

Fig 1-11A

Fig 1-11B

Fig. 1-9A

This is the time to build in "Washout" so the rear corner of the tip is higher than the rest of the wing. This is a **very important** step that can save you from a crash. Add a shim strip under the tip **at the rear only** while laying out the wing. Make sure this shim is in place when the wing is pinned down in the dihedral jig **and** while drying during water shrink or doping. If you cover with heat shrink material, re-check frequently. Both wings must have **equal** twist. Washout should be about 1/32" on each wing for each foot of total span. A 36" wing would use 3/32" to 1/8" shims.

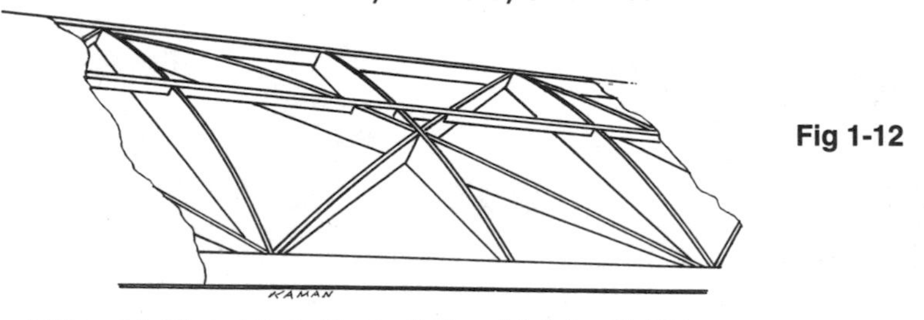

Fig 1-12

1-9A and 1-12 reprinted with permission of Aviation Publishers

Cracked Rib Wings

Possibly created by John Oldenkamp in his "Crackerbox" series of P-30 rubber models, the cracked rib wing may be the easiest and one of the strongest construction systems. Although we all think of airfoils as being important features of good flying models, the fact is that on a small stick and tissue model most airfoils will act the same within very narrow limits. Since the covering will sag and ripple somewhat between ribs, holding an exact airfoil shape is more wish than fact. Scratch builders will tell you that they were successful with an "Adidas 9" airfoil as long as they traced it from the outside, not the inside, curve of the sneaker.

One year at our One Design contest, Rich Fiore and I decided to survey whether a flat or under cambered airfoil performed best on the Jabberwock which was that year's entry. With 28 models entered in 6 events and rubber weight and prop all the same, we felt we had a good test group. It turned out that out of 28 models, there were 14 of each wing type. After 5 events, there was no obvious leader and we were down to 22 surviving models with the split still even. At the final event (Mass Launch) the **first 6 places were still evenly split !!**

Of course, for high performance competition models like Wakefields or towline gliders where the wings are solid balsa or aluminum covered, and even a small percentage improvement can put you in the winner's circle, an efficient airfoil becomes very important. But for the sport flyer, the cracked wing can be a real time saver and will produce an extremely strong wing.

To start, lay down your trailing edge which may be notched to receive the back end of each rib. Lay in your bottom ribs which can be either flat or under cambered. If the wing is to be under cambered you may want to block up the front of your trailing edge slightly to continue the curve. Use a metal straight edge to make sure the nose of **each** rib is the proper length to **exactly** reach the L.E. when assembled. If not, discard that rib and put in another. The ribs can be 8-10 lb. balsa strips 1/16" or 3/32" square depending on the size of the model . Use 3/32" square for anything over 22 inch span. Now, lay your spar over the bottom ribs about 1/3 back from the LE. A neat advantage of this type of wing is that you can use a tapered spar to make the wing **thinner** from center to tip. This will not only enhance flight but will make a stronger, lighter wing since the most stress is at the center. All ribs can be the same thickness, even in a tapered wing, since the spar will dictate the shape. Now, just "crack" each rib with a fingernail just at the place where it meets the spar. You can assemble the ribs perpendicular to the spar or at any angle making a truss or "Union Jack" design. These special shapes will add a lot of strength and almost no weight and will also give you a smoother covering job.

Once you have assembled the ribs, spars, leading edge, tips and built- in "washout", you can add a thin (1/16" square) strip to the **top** of the ribs running parallel to the spar **Fig 1-13**. This will cause the tissue to flow better over the ribs and create more of a curved airfoil shape, (**RPMA pg 45-46**).

Fig 1-13

A neat hint for those who want to form balsa for ribs is to get some "**B-Brite**" from a home brew store and mix 1 tablespoon per gallon with water to loosen the bond between the wood fibers.

Fuselage Construction

Most kits still call for two fuselage sides to be constructed as exactly the same as you can make them. To do this you **must** choose balsa strips that are as alike in weight and hardness as possible. See the chapter called, "**Compound Interest**."

Once you have the proper wood, here are a few ways to make identical sides.

1. Pin down the straightest longeron, either top or bottom. Then, cut the uprights **exactly** to the line on the plan, checking with a metal straight edge to make sure they all line up properly. **Cut 2** of each upright **exactly the same size**. Now, lay in your other longeron against the uprights. Pin all in place and glue in a few gussets to hold everything square.

2.When the first side is complete and **dry**, remove the pins. Don't worry, it will stay where it is held by the light adhesion of the glue to the plastic food wrap over the plan. Now lay another sheet of food wrap over the first side. Proceed with the second side by placing pins **in the same holes as before**, adding more where needed. The two sides should match perfectly with no razor cutting to separate them.

3. Another neat method is to cut a fuselage outline from art board (about 1/8" thick). Cut to the outside of the longerons. Save the surrounding art board outline, not the fuselage cutout. You can now build fuselage halves inside the cut outline and all will match.

Once you have two sides, assembling them with cross pieces

and formers so you avoid the dreaded "Banana" shape requires some preparation. If you are not one who builds jigs and fixtures for assembly lineup you need to start doing so. Nothing detracts from good appearance or stable flight more than a crooked fuselage. Obviously, this is going to affect the alignment of wings, thrust and tail group so you may as well correct it in the building instead of trying to warp corrections into the finished model.

Your fuselage sides should be built with sticks that match in weight and springiness, Then you need to locate the "box" that supports and directs the model's alignment. This is usually the area right under or over the wings and extends about the length of the chord. This is the box you have to brace with a block or sheet fixture supported by right angle triangles and **firmly** clamped to your flat board while the glue dries. A typical sheet fixture is shown in (**RPMA pg 40**). Now add 12- to -16 gussets at all the right angle corners of that box. The rest of the fuselage construction can practically be done "in- the- air" and still maintain alignment.

I suggest you disregard the plans a bit here and make all your nose openings 1 x 1-1/4" and add a 1/8" wide block between the tail posts. This will allow you to interchange nose blocks, props, and electric motors between models. The tail block holds a stab incidence adjusting screw and strengthens the tail assembly.

Keel Fuselage

Many new kits, particularly scale models, call for the fuselage to be built on a "keel" which is nothing more than a balsa strip cut to the outline of the top or bottom of the fuselage to which formers are glued to create the shape. One of the problems here is that gluing formers to both sides of the keel at different times can easily cause warping when the glue dries. The keel needs to be of very hard balsa or you can make two separate keels from thinner wood. Glue the formers to each *while they are pinned down* and assemble them later. Also, it's a good idea to go the gusset route with the front, rear and the formers around the "basic box" to make everything square.

Formers and Stringers

One problem with curved formers is that the grain doesn't follow the curve so they may crack just as you are cutting a stringer notch or even assembling the stringers. Try gluing a sheet of tissue to the back of the former sheet with the tissue grain perpendicular to the wood grain. This will add almost no weight and will help with the cracking problem. Chapter 6, "**Scale**" discusses reducing former size, notching for stringers or laying them on top. If you have stringer notches in die or laser cut formers, use sandpaper wrapped on a dowel to sand "scallops" in the formers between stringers so the formers don't show through the covering.

Here are some ways to cut stringer notches:

1. Two or three Dremel saw blades mounted together to the thickness of the notch with a disk to control depth **Fig 1-14**.

Fig 1-14

2. Sandpaper glued to the edge of a stick mounted on a block **Fig 1-15**.

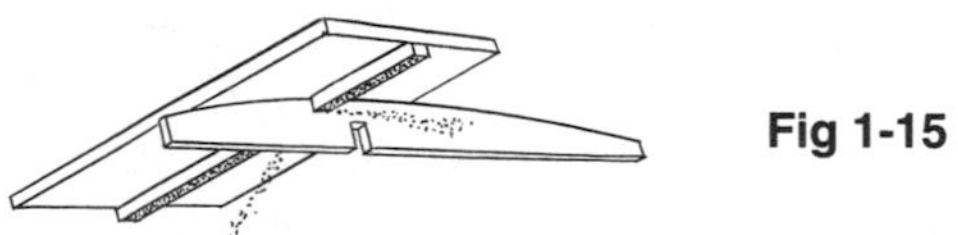

Fig 1-15

3. Square file used to cut <u>diamond</u> shaped notches **Fig 1-16**.

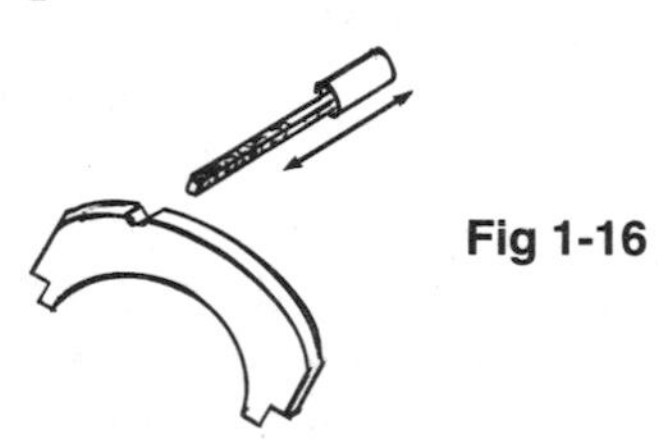

Fig 1-16

Here are some more hints that will make building easier and more accurate:

Drilling Balsa (Kay Larsen)

Put a couple of drops of CyA on the face and rear of the sheet *before* drilling. Press sheet against hard block and drill. If many holes are needed, lightly glue a sheet of thin ply to the rear. Remove with thinner when finished.

Cutting Metal or Carbon Fiber

Put a layer or two of masking tape over the area to be cut. Mark the required cut line on the tape and proceed. This will hold chips and prevent curled edges.

Tube Bending (Jeff Fredericks)

Fill Aluminum tube with salt. Plug both ends and bend slowly. **This prevents tube from kinking.**

Slicing Tubing (Leroy Saterlee)

You may want to slice rubber or plastic tubing for scale tires, cockpit coaming, de-icer boots, jet intake rims or windshield edges. You can get almost any size tube by stripping the insulation off various electrical wires or collecting grass stems and drying them. To get a straight slice through one side just drill a block for a tight fit on the tube, insert a # 11 blade in the block as shown and pull the tubing through **Fig 1-17** .

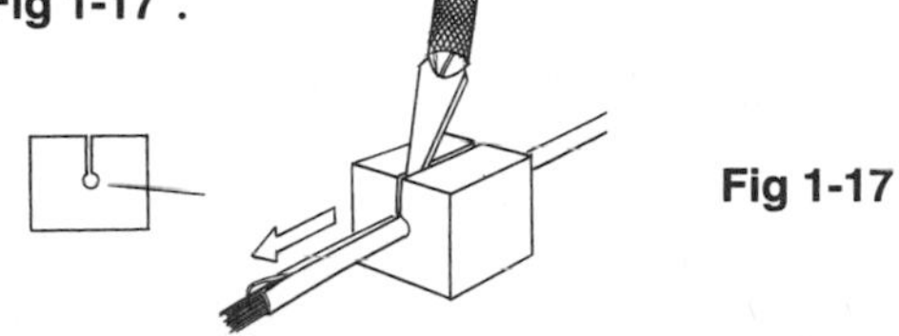

Fig 1-17

Making Sharp Bends in Thin Wire (Terry Kruger)

Put wire inside a brass tube whose ID is only slightly larger than wire OD. Place another tube along wire and bend where the tubes meet **Fig 1-18**

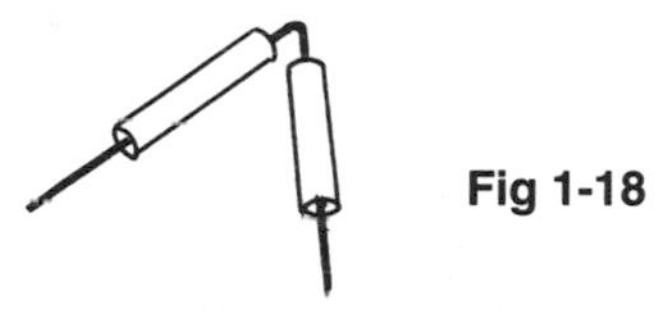

Fig 1-18

Drilling Tubing or Dowel

Here's one I really like. Notch a clothespin for the tubing size. Drill a hole through the clothespin perpendicular to the notch. Insert tubing and drill through again, **Fig 1-19**. This works with metal tube, dowel or even flexible plastic tube.

Fig. 1-19

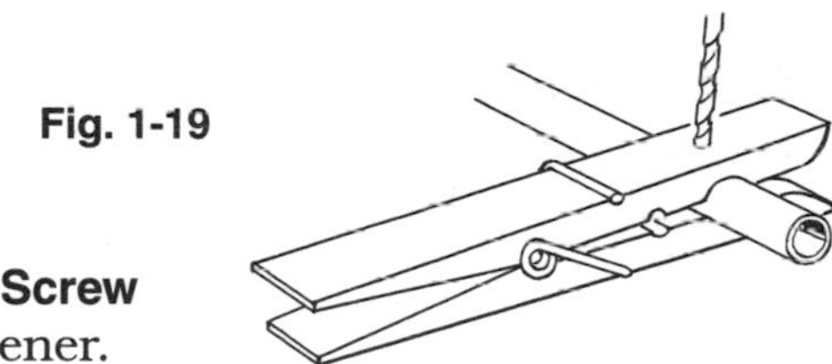

Taper Dowel or Plastic Screw

Use a pencil sharpener.

Tapped Holes

Apply **Devcon Plastic Steel** to Balsa or hardwood **before** tapping.

Roll Thin Balsa Sheet

You will be surprised at how much weight you can save by using a rolled 1/64" balsa sheet instead of a solid motor stick on those beginner's models or the neat No-Cal or profile scale model you are working on. Making such a tube is easier than explaining how **Fig 1-20.**

1. Soak 4-6 lb. springy Balsa sheet for 2 or more hours in warm water with B-Brite or white vinegar.

2. Lay a sheet of bond paper flat on your table with scotch tape on one end.

3. Tape end of bond paper to correct size of forming dowel or tube.

4. Lay wet balsa sheet on paper and roll forming dowel and paper over it.

5. Glue seam after Balsa tube is dry and removed from form.

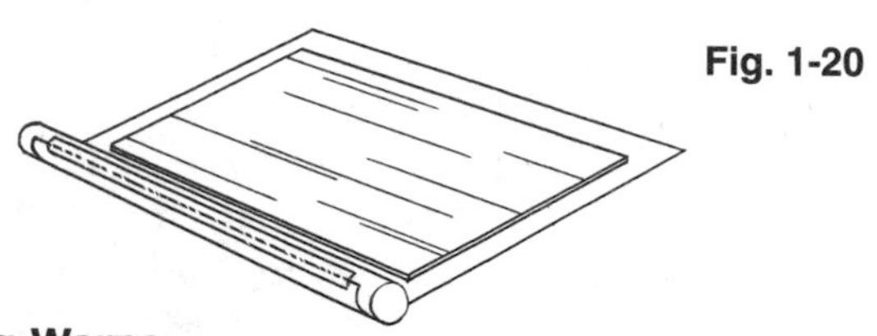

Fig. 1-20

Removing Warps

Buy a Gel heating pack in the drug store (used to relieve pain). Wet the warped part of the model thoroughly, even if it is covered and doped. I often pour boiling water right over a covered wing. Pin the part down flat or to a form of the correct shape. Heat the Gel pack in microwave and lay it over the warped area. Allow several hours to dry. Overnight is even better.

Marking on Dark Surfaces (John Brent)

Paint area with liquid paper (typewriter correction fluid), Mark with pencil, cut and remove white with thinner.

Spray the paint through a cocktail straw into a small cup. Touch up with a brush.

Making A Hatch Latch

The ability to drill & tap for 2-56 screws will allow you to fasten all kinds of hatch covers and other items. For a latch that is almost hidden and very light, simply bend a wire loop that is a tight slide fit in a piece of plastic fuel tube. Attach the loop to the hatch and glue the tubing to the fuselage as shown. Push the latch into the tube. It will hold through vibration and mild crashes.

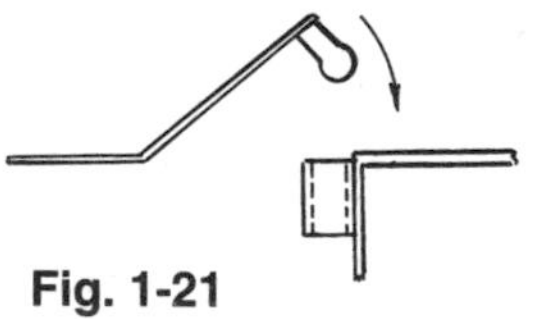

Fig. 1-21

Trim Tabs

Find a local manufacturer of pressure sensitive labels made from thin aluminum sheet or plastic film. Aluminum sheet comes in thicknesses ranging from .002" through .005" and is usually very soft and bendable. Since labels are made in a huge variety of colors as well as clear plastic, the scrap from printed sheets will give you a whole library of tabs to match your model. Just fold the material in half before removing the paper backing, remove the backing and slip 1/8 inch of the tab over the trailing edge of the wing, rudder or stab. This type of tab will retain its bend until you change it.

Sheet Covering on Curved Surfaces

To cover the curved top of a fuselage in the nose area or around an open cockpit, don't try for a one piece good fit. Start a separate piece of balsa sheet from the longeron on each side and leave a small gap in the center at the top. Now, carefully cut a wedge shaped piece to fill the gap. Glue in and sand.

Traveling Protection for Models

Visit a local engraver and ask for a few feet of the Polyethylene sleeving he uses to protect his products. The stuff comes in widths from about 3" to 8" and is strong enough to prevent rips & dents. For larger models, the plastic suit bag used for traveling can easily hold 2 wings.

You will find a thousand more hints and ideas at every flying session. Just get out to the field and meet the other flyers.

2

"COMPOUND INTEREST"

We free flighters often assume that we cut our wood with a razor blade while the R/C flyers use chain saws. Obviously, we're prejudiced but there is some truth in the idea that FF is much more concerned with weight than is R/C. Free Flight duration depends mostly on glide where weight is a very important factor. This chapter will explain how weight *directly* affects flight time, model wear and crash damage, and will outline several ways to decrease weight with no loss in strength.

Possibly the most important single factor controlling climb and glide duration is **total weight**. The average builder, however, is possibly not aware of how critical some very small changes in weight can be if applied to the right area of the model. I know I never worried about a few paltry grams. I assumed they could make little difference. Let's just explore how much difference three grams (less than 1/9 oz.) can make in the flight pattern of a 30-36 inch span model.

In most designs, the **tail moment**, (the distance from the wing Center of Lift, to the stabilizer C of L) is about three times the **nose moment**. For simplicity, assume the tail moment is measured from a point 1/3 of the way back from the LE of the wing to 1/3 from the LE of the stab. Therefore, if you can save 3 grams in the construction and covering of the tail feathers, you may have also saved 9 grams of nose weight **without changing the c.g**. If this is a rubber model and the rubber weight is 40-50% of the model weight, you can reduce your rubber weight by another 5 or 6 grams. This can be a saving of **18 grams** on a 60 gram model or a savings of **30%**.

A general rule in FF models is that a 25% decrease in all up weight (AUW) can result in a 40% increase in climb height. Obviously, higher climb means more duration. This is certainly "compound interest" at its best.

Now, if we can save weight without sacrificing strength, we will have added a whole new dimension to our modeling.

A lighter model will cause less wear and damage to landing gear and fuselage structure on rough landings and *certainly* a lot less crash damage. Lighter models fly slower and this makes flight trim adjustments easier to spot, simpler to make and less critical. Although saving small amounts of weight is more effective on small models, the principle is sound and useful on all sizes. I'm sure the performance of my 45 minute Goldberg Electra was enhanced by its 5 ounce lighter weight.

If this has convinced you or excited your interest, I'll explain some simple, low tech ways to reduce weight and increase strength.

In order to *reduce* weight we first need to learn to *measure* it accurately. A simple postal scale or the "Pelouze" type won't do the job at all. We are dealing here with a single factor that can double your flight time and maybe also *double* the life of your model. That's got to be worth a few bucks.

Probably the easiest way to get into accurate weighing is the **Micro-Air** Scale **(RPMA pg 98)**. Costing less than $5.00, it assembles in an hour and is accurate to a fraction of a gram. Next are simple beam balances from $25 to $75 sold by **Edmund Scientific** and others. Finally, the **Acculab Digital Scales** from Aerodyne, at $110 to $250 are my favorites. The more I use my Model 333, the better I like it. The 10 ounce capacity and 0.1 gram accuracy does the job for any but critical, very light indoor models.

Once you find a good spot to set up your scale - **leave it there.** Get into the habit of weighing *all* wood sheets *before* cutting them into strips. Weigh all components (wheels, props, nose blocks, motors, batteries, hooks, rubber, etc.). You will be amazed to find that your prop weighs almost as much as your rubber motor and your wheels weigh more than your stab and rudder combined! Once you begin to understand the weight values of all your flight components, you can make better decisions in construction that will greatly improve performance.

Wood selection is a good place to start. Balsa and other woods are graded by two factors, **density** and **grain**. Density is simply the weight of a cubic foot of balsa expressed as **Pounds per cubic foot**, but it's usually expressed only as **pounds**, as in "7-pound or 9-pound balsa". This will become our basic measuring tool with which to grade sheet or strip.

We will also be looking for **Hardness** and **Springiness** to help us decide where each strip should be used.

Fig 2-1 **Balsa Density Chart For 3x36 Inch Sheets**

	D	E	N	S	I	T	Y	lbs. Cubic	per Foot
Sheet Thickness	**4**	**5**	**6**	**7**	**8**	**9**	**10**	**11**	**12**
1/32	.125 3.50	.156 4.37	.187 5.24	.218 6.10	.250 7.00	.281 7.43	.312 7.87	.344 8.74	.375 10.5
1/16	.250 7.00	.312 2.73	.375 10.5	.437 12.2	.500 14.0	.562 15.7	.625 17.5	.687 19.2	.750 21.0
3/32	.372 10.4	.465 13.0	.558 15.6	.651 18.2	.744 20.7	.837 23.4	.930 26.0	1.02 28.6	1.12 31.4
1/8	.500 14.0	.625 17.5	.750 21.0	.875 24.5	1.00 28.0	1.12 31.4	1.25 35.0	1.38 38.6	1.50 42.0

Note: 1 pound = 453 grams and 1 ounce = 28.35 grams

Density, in pounds per cubic foot, shows in the second row (**bold numbers 4 through 12**) Numbers shown as fractions.125/3.50 and 1.50/42.0 are the weights of sheet in ounces/grams, ie. a 3x36" sheet 1/16" thick weighing .375 ounces or 10.5 grams has a density of 6-pounds per cubic foot.

Weigh and mark a new sheet of balsa then compare the size and weight (in grams or oz.) to the chart **Fig 2-1**. This will give you the density of the sheet. Note that all sheets called "1/16" will not be exactly .0625" thick. Make some allowance for those sheets that are thicker or thinner. Most won't be off by more than 10%, so increase or decrease weight by the percentage difference in thickness and apply to the chart. Use **Figures 2-2** and **2-3** to decide where to use the sheets or strips of each density group. **Figure 2-3** deals with a wood quality that is a bit difficult to measure. I call it the" **Spring Factor"** which describes how "whippy" or "springy" each strip will be when cut from the sheet. (**RPMA pg 12**) showed a single strip being tested . My new method will allow you to test an entire sheet before stripping and will help predict the behavior of each strip.

Fig 2-2 Density and Spring Factor Applications

4 - 6 Lb.
SOFT : Stab ribs, rudder cross pieces, sheet tails, HL glider wings, fuselage planking, wheel pants, scale details, all indoor duration models, most peanuts or small scale models. **MEDIUM:** Fuselage uprights, wing ribs, nose planking, gussets, wing planking, tail outlines, trailing edges. **HARD:** Wing tips, wheels.
7 - 10 Lb.
SOFT: High stress gussets, warp prevention strips, cross grain inserts on sheet parts, laminated wing tips, laminated tail outlines, fuselage stringers. **MEDIUM:** Nose blocks, landing gear bracing, props. **HARD:** Fuselage longerons, wing spars, wing leading edges.
10 - 12 Lb.
SOFT: Probably not available **MEDIUM:** Prop hubs, firewalls, nose formers, tail supports. **HARD:** Cabane struts, landing gear fairings, HL glider fuselages

This "Spring Factor" is very important in adding strength where needed. For instance, an 8-pound sheet would provide very good 3/32" or 1/8" longerons for a 30-36 inch span model as long as the strips were *hard and springy.*

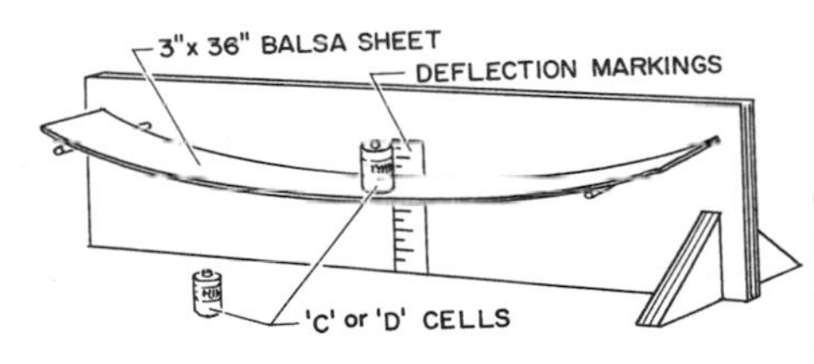

Fig. 2-4

The sheet testing method requires only a bit of construction with readily available materials and once done can be used forever. You will need a 12 x 36" piece of 3/4" plywood (an old bookshelf will do), 2 dowels 1/4" diameter by 6" long, one regular C- cell and 3 D -cell flashlight batteries . The batteries can be new or used since you only use them as standard weights. Construct the device as shown in **Fig 2-4** . I used some scrap ply on the bottom (back and front) to hold the board upright. Mark the vertical center line in 1/4 inch increments going down from the test sheet level. Now simply lay a sheet of balsa over the support arms at the 18 or 24 inch distance shown in **Figure 2-3**, Add the appropriate weight from the chart and check the <u>deflection</u> <u>of the center</u> against the chart. *Always* try to strip similar acting strips (fuselage longerons, wing spars) from the same area on the sheet.

Fig 2-3 **Hardness Deflection Chart**

WOOD SIZE	BEAM DIST.	SOFT	MEDIUM	HARD
1/32 x 36	18 in.	2-3/4 to 3 (1C)	2 (1C)	1-1/2 (1C)
1/16 x 36	24 in.	3-1/2 (1D)	1-1/2 (1D)	1 (1D)
3/32 x 36	24 in.	1-1/2 (2D)	1 (2D)	1/2 to 3/4 (2D)
1/8 x 36	24 in.	1-1/2 (3D)	3/4 (3D)	1/4 (3D)

Distance : Center to Center of Dowels Supporting the Sheet
Dimensions in Blocks : Deflection in Inches of the Sheet Below the Horizontal
Numbers in Parenthesis : 1, 2, or 3 Dry Cell Batteries <u>Either C or D Cell size.</u>

Note that the deflections shown in **Fig 2-3** are only approximate. Sheets can vary from batch to batch and even within the same batch. Balsa is a natural substance which is far from homogeneous. Use the charted deflections as general indications .

Many model books and wood catalogues (Sig has a very good explanation in theirs) discuss grain as a way of deciding which sheets to use for which purposes. Although this is a useful guide I prefer an actual spring test for three reasons. First, various grains are not always available "(C" grain is very hard to find). Second, spring and hardness will vary widely in each grain type and third, you will need a large inventory of balsa sheets to have enough choices. Therefore, I grade first by density, then spring, and finally a simple fingernail test for hardness.

It's also possible and practical to vary your wood densities from nose to tail and wing center to tip. Drop from 7# to 5# for tip ribs and fuselage uprights near the tail. Every little bit helps.

Once you have chosen the correct balsa sheet or strip for each application on your model, some study of the *engineering* of the construction is very worthwhile. Whether a kit , plan or your own design, the specific construction features have a vast effect on weight and strength. For instance, many old time designs called for heavy main spars in wings with sheet tips as much as 1/4 inch wide or more. Multi-spar wings, sheet stabilizer tips and full height fuselage formers add lots of weight with only a small advantage in strength. Many plans call for carved balsa block wing tips , cabin tops and nose formers. These can often be eliminated or changed to much lighter elements. **(RPMA pg. 119)** and the **SCALE** Chapter show suggestions for lightening structures.

First consider the areas of your model that will be under the most stress. The wing dihedral joints, fuselage nose, landing gear mounting, tail mounting and wing saddle require the most strength and durability but this can be done without adding a lot of weight.

Assembly and use of gussets to save weight and add strength to selected areas is discussed in **CONSTRUCTION** and **SCALE** .

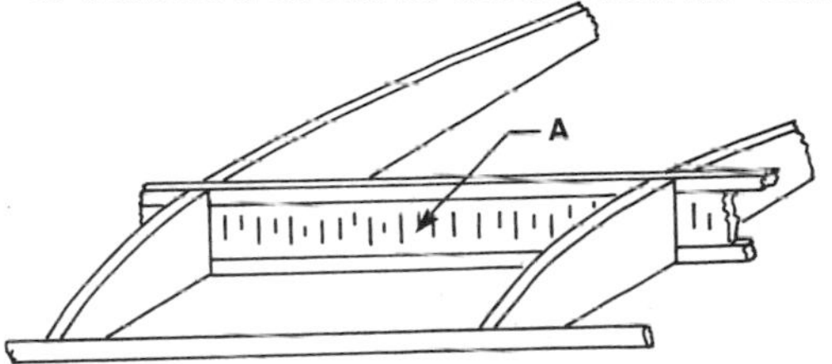

Fig 2-5

Webbing between wing spars will also allow you to reduce spar size. Be careful that the webbing grain is *vertical* to the rib **Fig 2-5 [A]**. I find small gussets in the tail help eliminate warping. *Careful* use of weight reduction holes in ribs can save a lot of weight Keep several different sizes of brass tubing in stock. Sharpen the tube ends with taper towards the *inside* , rotate the tube while pressing it against the rib, then sand the hole. Cut a couple of ribs leaving 3/32" minimum around each hole and 3/8" between holes. Then bend and twist the rib in your hands to test for strength. If the rib cracks too easily, reduce hole size.

Tyvek® and **Nylon®** are very good low tech bracing materials. **(RPMA pg. 52)** shows how to split and apply Tyvek®. The material is easily obtainable in building supply stores as "vapor barrier" and in office supply stores as "Overnight Mail Envelopes". Nylon comes from your wife's old panty hose or stockings. I use either one to brace many joints by simply saturating it with glue then molding it to the surface on both sides of the joint. All the stress locations mentioned above are good candidates for fiber bracing. This adds hardly more weight than a second coat of glue.

A good balsa stripper is a *very* important tool. All the above about weight and strength is pretty useless if you can't cut uniform strips. All your longerons *must* be *exactly* the same or your fuselage may get that "banana" shape after covering. The same goes for wing spars. It's not difficult to come up with a wing that is 20% heavier on one side with different spar and ribweights.

The **Jim Jones Adjustable Balsa Stripper** (ABS) at under $20.00 is about the best around. I have used mine for at least 10 years and saved much more than its cost by making all my own balsa strips. Just consider the economics shown below:

Cost of a sheet of 1/16 x 3 x 36" balsa	$ 0.90
Cost of a strip 1/16 square	.12
Minimum yield of good strips from above sheet	35 strips
Cost of 35 strips @ $0.12 each	$4.20
Cost saving on one sheet	**$3.30**

As you can see, it doesn't take long to pay for a balsa stripper. As a bonus, all your strips will be the same size within less than .010 inch which is only 2/3 of 1/64!

Once you have cut the proper strips for wing spar, fuselage and longerons, try an interesting experiment. Balance your 36 inch strip at the center on your fingertip. One end will probably be a bit heavier than the other. If a wing spar, place the heavier end towards the wing center. If a fuselage longeron - heavier end towards the nose. Simple techniques like this will have weight and strength working for you throughout the structure.

Sliced ribs and molded tips are another way to reduce weight while increasing strength. These are described in **TOOLS & CONSTRUCTION.**

I'm sure the above techniques, and some you will think up yourself, will provide stronger, better flying, longer lasting models and lots more fun.

As you build and design, develop a feel for the areas of maximum stress in each model. Some stresses come from flying - bending loads, and some from landing - crash loads. Just try to visualize the model in several different attitudes, say a climbing turn or a nose first crash. Picture which way the various parts will distort in each attitude and try to strengthen the areas that will bend or tear the most. Once you have a good idea of where strength is needed, there are a few simple, low tech ways to improve on the bare wood.

Cyanoacrylate "instant" glue not only dries quickly but when used sparingly will penetrate and harden the fibers of balsa sheet, strip or block in high stress areas. Use the thinnest formula *without* the accelerator. Just "wick" the glue around the area and allow to dry. This technique is useful for:

•Noseblocks and nose areas, Landing gear mounts, Stab platforms
•Nose block bearing hole, Wing Center section and dihedral joints
•Rear rubber peg mounting, DT mounting, Prop hub, Wheel hub
•Motor mounting screw holes Trim adjusting screw holes, nose & tail
•Wing tips, Wing or stab rubber holding areas.

In addition to instant glue hardening, ply made from Tyvek and balsa or Tyvek®, 1/64" plywood and balsa is much stronger than a single sheet of 1/16" balsa, or even 1/32" ply. Make nose blocks and stab mounts of balsa and 1/64" ply for high strength and springiness with almost no weight penalty. Laminate Tyvek® to balsa for thin prop blades that "flex" under high torque and won't shatter if the plane spins in. Wheels of balsa/Tyvek® will last for years.

Carbon fiber, now available in sheets, strands and cloth in many thicknesses is immensely strong yet light. It can be used to strengthen leading edges, ribs, spars and fuselage sections. It can be cut with razor or scissors and applies easily with instant glue or epoxy. Its dense black color can be a disadvantage but any serious modeler should begin to practice using this and other new materials.

As with any new system you will soon imagine many applications of your own and will delight in the increased performance and durability of your models.

3

ALL ABOUT ELECTRIC POWER

Electric power has arrived and is here to stay. Although still heavier than gas, rubber or CO_2, electric runs smoother, is clean and easy to start and will probably replace many other sources.

I think the biggest drawback to wider use of electric motors is that many modelers are put off by what they feel is complicated technology. Volts, amps, charging time, fuses and soldering seem to represent whole new and difficult subjects to master. Actually, when you compare electric power to other sources, it doesn't come off badly at all.

Most of us started with rubber power which requires rubber lube, winders, torque meters, winding tubes and stooges for every flight. We have to make sure folding props or free-wheelers are operating properly and we can only "approximate" motor run or torque which varies with every winding. Rubber motors require break-in and we can use up 2 or 3 in a day of heavy flying. Motor length, number of strands and strip width are part of a complex power equation that also includes prop diameter, pitch and blade shape.

CO_2 requires a large charging tank to make sure all charges are reasonably equal. Air temperature and humidity effect power and a tiny crack in one of the thin brass tubes requires very careful soldering. While motor speed is infinitely adjustable, outdoor flight at temperatures under 70 degrees F is marginal.

Glow engine or diesel power still represents the best power to weight ratio. A tiny .020 engine will easily lift a 200-square inch model in a screaming climb and run for 2 minutes on a full tank. However, besides the noise factor that can lose a fine field virtually overnight, engines present their own set of problems, for instance, you need a starter battery, fuel in a *safe* container, tubing, engine timer, fuel dropper or filler bulb and lots of rags to wipe the messy stuff off everything before you go home. Flipping a prop for 15 minutes before starting happens often and they won't run long if you don't keep them clean at the field and clean them thoroughly at home.

With just a little patience at learning the basics about electric power, you can show up at the field with a charger box and a model. Plug the model into the box for an automatically timed charge, flip the switch and away she goes. Almost no noise, no pollution, no mess to clean up and a steady motor run with a much smaller torque burst than rubber power. You can mount the motor in the nose or even in the fuselage at the c.g.. Run wiring as long as you need from motor to battery so the model balances properly with no bulky CO_2 tanks to bury.

Now you can build some of the models you have always dreamed about. Multi engines, pushers, WW1 fighters with short noses, push-pull WW.II fighters and old time replica gassies are easier projects. Even indoor electric RC has become practical.

Some basic understanding of the elements of electric power can be a great help to the beginner, but for those who prefer to skip the technology, it's quite possible to "jump-right-in". You can buy a motor, battery and charger system, stick it in an old gas or rubber model and go right to the field. There are also many electric "toys" available that will astound you with their flying ability. Good engineering, plenty of power and long motor runs will get these foam toys up there long enough to disappear.

In the next few pages I will present the technology of electric power simply, so the rawest beginner can assemble a circuit, break in a motor and calculate charging time. You can skip this section and go right to assembly, application and use but I suggest that a couple of hours studying these basics will result in better models, fewer field problems and much longer flights.

Basics of Electric Power

The easiest way to understand electric power is to picture it as a water system consisting of a **Tank** somewhere above ground level, **Piping** from the tank to a **Valve** or **Faucet**, a **Water-Wheel** turned by the flow and a **Reservoir** or **Pool** at ground level where the water comes to rest. **Fig 3-1**.

The relationship between these elements (Tank, Piping, Valve and Wheel), is similar enough to our Battery, Wiring, Resistor and Motor, that we can use it to learn about how these interact. Learning to calculate the various values will help us to predict the flight characteristics of a model.

Fig 3-1

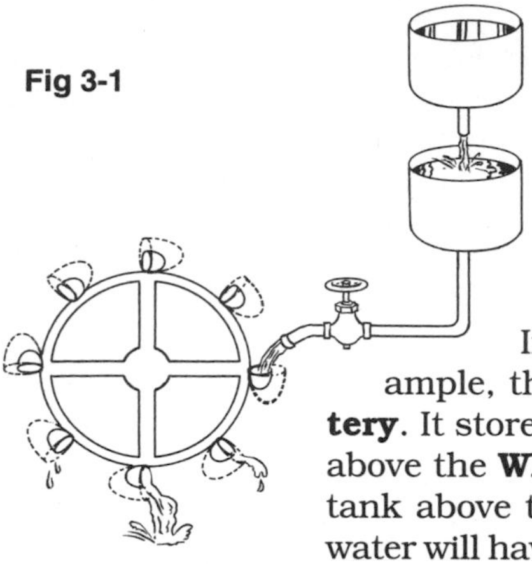

In our electric power system, example, the **Tank** is equivalent to a **Battery**. It stores water (energy) at some height above the **Wheel**. Obviously, the higher the tank above the wheel, the more energy the water will have as it descends, thus the faster the wheel will turn. In the language of electric power, this energy is called "Electromotive Force" or **Voltage**. Translated literally, this is the electric force that causes motion. So, the higher the voltage of your battery, the faster your motor will turn.

What would happen if we could pile another identical water tank on top of the first one? Wouldn't this double our height energy **(Voltage)** and make the wheel **(Motor)** turn faster? Certainly it would. This is what happens when we connect several cells together in *series* to form a battery. Series connection means connecting the Positive (+) terminal of each cell to the Negative (-) terminal of the next cell. Fig 3-2. Each **Cell** is an energy tank that we can fill or **Charge** with electrical energy, and together they form a **Battery**. The potential energy (height above the wheel), that a battery can store is measured in **Volts**. For our purposes, all cells are assumed to provide 1.2 volts nominally. Thus a 3- cell battery pack (always connected in series) will provide 3.6 volts and a 5-cell battery pack will provide 6.0 volts. Later in this chapter when you see **3x50 mAh** or **4x110 mAh** this is shorthand for **3 or 4 cells at 50 or 110 milliampere hour rating**.

With the basic "Water Wheel" analogy in mind, we can then isolate each element of the system and carefully study its properties and its relationship to other elements.

Fig 3-2

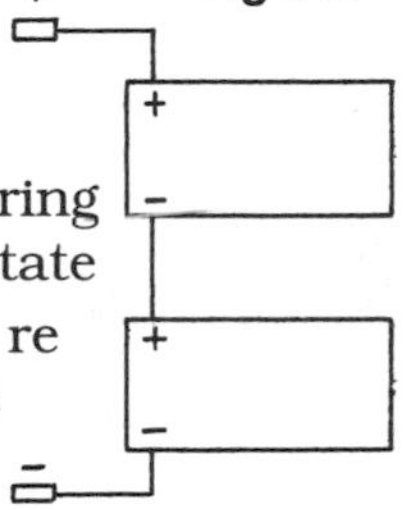

About The Battery

The battery provides us with a means of storing electrical energy, carrying it around in a safe state and delivering it to a motor system *exactly* when re required. Our **Ni-Cd** batteries contain Nickel and Cadmium and can be recharged many times...

In order to work with different sized batteries, we need some means of classifying the amount of energy we can store in each. We already know that **Voltage** measures the potential energy (height above the wheel), and that each cell adds 1.2 Volts to the total. Now, we need to know how long that voltage will continue to power our motor, or how long the water will flow from the tank.

Picture two tanks the same height above the wheel (Voltage) but tank B is twice the size of tank A **Fig 3-3**. If both tanks have the same size flow pipe, tank A will obviously empty in half the time of tank B. We might say that tank B has *twice* the capacity of tank A. This flow of **Current** is the movement of electrons through a wire, just like water droplets through a pipe and is measured in **Amperes**. Now you can jump right to the charging chart or study the following for a few minutes to get a better understanding of your battery - motor system.

Fig 3-3

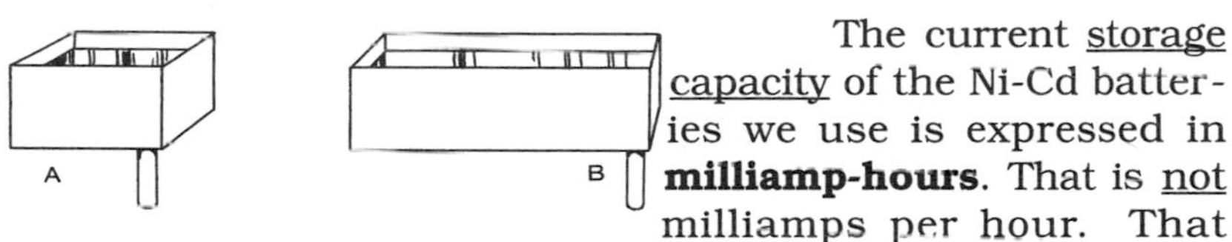

The current storage capacity of the Ni-Cd batteries we use is expressed in **milliamp-hours**. That is not milliamps per hour. That means that a 50 milliamp hour battery will deliver 50 milliamps for an hour and *then it will be empty*. This figure is regardless of how many cells make up the battery. If you add more cells, the battery will still deliver 50 milliamps for an hour but it will do so at a higher voltage, making your motor (wheel) turn faster ! It is important to understand the above. Each motor has wire windings that, like a water pipe, have more resistance to flow the longer they are. Thus you may need a larger battery (more cells) to push current through the windings of a larger motor or to make a smaller motor run faster because the higher **Voltage** will push the current harder.

If you wanted to charge such a 50 **milliamp hour** battery, it seems reasonable that you would have to spend an hour putting 50 milliamps into it. This is true, but we really don't want to spend an hour on each charge if we want to get in more than a couple of flights a day. Therefore, Ni-Cd batteries are capable of **fast charging** which means you can (if you have a high enough voltage charger) push current into the battery at a higher rate. The first thing you need is a charging battery or source that has more voltage than the battery you are charging. After all, you can't expect that current to flow up hill any more than water would. Most small flight Ni-Cds can be charged at 1 or 1.5 **amps** without harm. Larger flight batteries for RC electrics can be charged at up to 5 amps.

Now, all we have to figure out is how long it will take to charge up a typical flight battery at a 1 amp charge rate.

50 milliamps is 50/1000 amps or 50 one-thousands of an ampere or .050 amps. One amp is 20 times that amount (20 X .050 = 1). Therefore it seems reasonable that if we charge at 20 times the battery rating we can charge it in 1/20 of its discharge time or 3 minutes (60 minutes/20 = 3 minutes).

You can calculate any charge time the same way if you know the milliamp hour rating of your flight battery and the charge current you want to use. **This is regardless of the number of cells in your battery.** A quick formula to remember is:

Battery Charging Formula

milliamp rating X 60 = Charge time in minutes at one amp
1000 milliamps

Obviously, if you charge at 1.5 amps, then divide the answer by 1.5 which equals 2 minutes as shown. You can charge at any amp level from 1-2 amps this way.

Some Common Charging Rates and Times

Fig 3-4

Battery Capacity (mah)	1 amp Chg.Rate	1.5 amp Chg.Rate
50	3 min.	2.0 min.
75	4.5	3.0
110	6.6	4.4
250	15.0	10.0
50	2.5 amps	12.0 min.
900	3.5 amps	15.4 min.
1500	5.0 amps	18.0 mi

The last three rates shown are for much larger batteries usually used on RC models. Many modern chargers for these larger cells will automatically charge a battery to its peak by sensing temperature or voltage change as the battery reaches maximum charge. The charger will then switch to a trickle mode that will hold the battery at peak until used. **Never peak charge 50 mAh cells**. Their performance will deteriorate rapidly. **Remember**, your charger must have at least *one* more cell (1.2 volts) more than the battery you are charging. This is important if you are using dry cells. Also, as dry cells become depleted, their voltage drops a bit thus requiring a longer charge. This is why you should consider a

12-volt rechargeable (gel cell) type charger or one that delivers 12 volts from your car battery.

You may find that your charger does not have a variable resistance which allows you to set an exact current rate. Then, as long as your current is below 2 amps, just use your calculator to divide the current shown into the amp-minute product to get the proper time. If your amp-minute product is 6.6 (as with a 110 mAh battery) and you show a charge current of 1.2 amps, then divide 6.6 by 1.2 to get a 5.5 minute charge time. If you have no way to indicate current or time (as with a dry cell pack or lantern battery) then you will *not* be able to get uniform charges which can significantly affect your flight time and adjustments. Certainly you can start with four "D" dry cells (wired in series) and graduate to a charger when you get some experience.

Chargers

Chargers vary from three or four dry cells in a holder (about $3.00) through a gel cell 12-volt package with timer and ammeter ($40.00). Then there are AC-DC chargers that work off either house current or a car battery and automatically charge to the exact peak voltage your battery can handle, then switch to a trickle charge until you are ready, ($85-120).

Radio Shack sells a holder for four "D" cells in series that can start you off. A cheap timer stuck on the case and a couple of alligator clips will complete the assembly. **Fig 3-5** shows a similar setup with three cells, a switch and a co-axial plug that fits most charge systems. Alkaline dry cells, D size,will deliver about 1 amp and you will get 40-50 charges from a set.

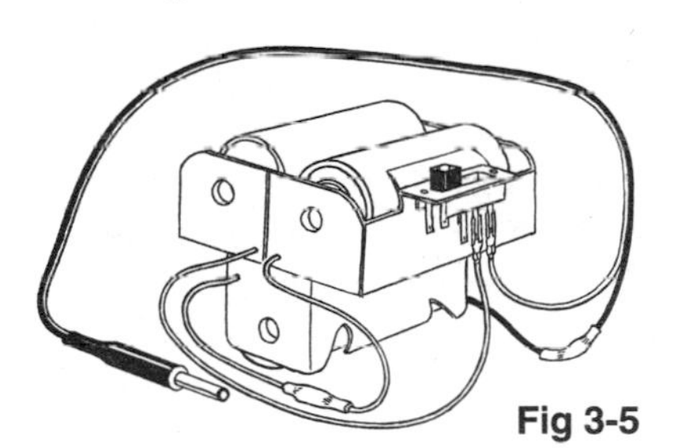

Fig 3-5

HiLine makes a neat, pocket sized unit that has its own timer, uses rechargeable Ni-Cds and is designed to deliver 1 amp for 2 and 3 cell packs. **VL** makes a unit that includes an ammeter, timer and three different sockets so you can vary the charge current according to the size of your battery.**EMPS** has a wiring diagram for a charger with all Radio Shack parts. EMPS also has a charger (Mark V) with automatic, audible cutoff and a 3-300 second timer that charges 1-5 cells @ 1 amp.

Fig 3-6 lists various chargers with price and usage comparison.

Chargers

Fig 3-6

HiLine MEC03 4 Alkaline D cells in holder **$ 3.95**
MEC05 5 Sanyo 2 ah rechargeable batteries with plug-in wall charger. Charges at 1 amp. **58.95**
MEC10 Car battery or 12 volt Gel charger.Cell (not included). Charges 2, 3, 4, 6 cells @ 1- 2 amps **84.95**

EMPS El Cheapo - plan
4 D cells with resistors to charge 2, 3 or 4 cells @ 0.7 to 1.2amps. You monitor timing. **FREE**
TC-LVI - plan
Controlled, variable current (.5-1.0 amp), kit with timer & low voltage indicator **6.00**
Mark V Automatic with AC adapter & NiCads **68.00**

VL FC-402 Universal Fast Charger. Includes 0-15 minute timer, 4 amp Ammeter and 3 different built in resistors for 3 charge rates. Runs off car lighter or 12 volt Gel Cell (not included) **39.95**

TOWER HOBBIES: Astro Flight 115D 115 Volt AC/DC Variable Rate Charger: Timer, Ammeter and Variable Rate to set current. Works off car battery or home 110 Volt source. Can be converted to charge 2-4 smaller cells by adding resistors in series with the output cable. **Do not** attempt this unless you are experienced in electrical work. Approx. **90.00**

Here's where our electrical system turns away a bit from the water tank analogy. Although you can fill a tank at either side, our batteries can only be filled or emptied in one direction. Electrons are stubborn little particles that will only move in a single direction. For convenience, we have settled on a system of + and - or **positive** and **negative** to define this flow. Every battery has a (+) **positive** and (-) **negative** pole.

Most batteries are marked right on the case but for those that aren't, or for the ones you may later make up for yourselves, we need a means of identifying the correct pole *before* charging. When buying your first motor/battery system, ask the vendor to mark the positive pole so you won't need extra equipment right away.

To identify the correct polarity of a battery we need a device that will tell us which way the electrons are moving. The same device can also be used to tell us whether our battery is fully charged or not. The device is called a **voltmeter** and there are two types in general use. The first is called an **Expanded Scale Voltmeter**, or **ESV**. This has a moving needle and a wide scale that covers only the 1/2 to 2-volt range in which we are interested. Tower sells one for about $20.00. A more accurate one that can be used in many other applications is the Micronta Model 22-188 **Digital Voltmeter** at Radio Shack for about $35.00.

Most voltmeters have two leads which can plug into either of the Positive (+) sockets, (one for AC and the other for DC), and one Common (-), or Negative socket, on the side or face of the case. **Fig 3-7**. The Positive lead is usually red and this color arrangement should be carried through all your wiring. You can easily buy both red and black colored insulation on your wire and using the colors properly can save you from a disaster.

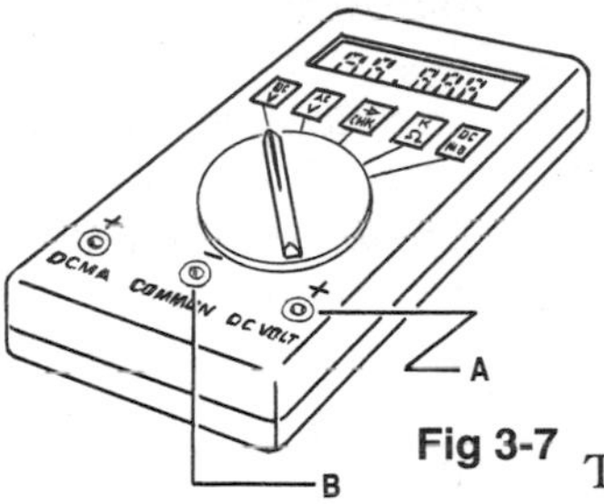

Fig 3-7

To test a battery for polarity, simply switch your Voltmeter to **DC Voltage**, turn it on and attach the leads to your battery terminals. The meter will immediately indicate polarity. The digital unit will show a plus or minus before the voltage reading and the ESV needle will move to the left (-), or the right (+) of center. If your voltmeter reads *positive* you have the battery terminals attached correctly. *Before* removing the meter, mark the positive terminal with some *indelible* marker, preferably with a prominent red cross. Now you can charge your battery with confidence. In charging, the polarity of your charger should be similarly marked. **Connect the positive lead of the charger to the positive terminal of the battery.**

As with any electrical system, certain safety factors should be kept *firmly* in mind at all times. Batteries store energy that can be discharged as *heat* instead of power if we get careless. Obviously, heat can start fires or even cause an explosion if the battery is near enough to highly combustible matter like fuel. If your battery is already installed in the model, careful charging is even more important. Many of us still remember the modeler (who shall remain nameless) who suddenly found his pants on fire because he had a pocket charger whose terminals were shorted out by his keys. Fortunately, others noticed and managed to de-trouser him quite rapidly in midfield.

The best indication of trouble is when your battery becomes hot enough to be uncomfortable to hold in your hand. If this happens, **stop charging immediately**.

Any battery that will be permanently installed in a model should be checked *before* and *after* installation so there will be no unpleasant surprises at the field. Just charge the battery outside the model and let it drive the motor until it runs all the way down. Then, install it in the model taking care that the wires are *insulated* all the way down to the terminals so there is no way they can short inside the fuselage. Mount the battery firmly, both to insure that its weight won't shift and affect balance and also that the wires are firmly held in place to avoid breaking or shorting.

Check the timer on your field charger every once in a while to be sure it isn't stuck. Also watch the ammeter needle. It can fluctuate a bit as charging goes on. If you are using a steady current charger like the HiLine or the EMPS, then **carefully** monitor charging time. Replace any frayed or cracked wire insulation. *Never* charge anywhere near flammable materials and leave ample cooling room around the battery. Most beginner's models will have the battery "out in the breeze" where it can be monitored and where natural air flow will cool it. If yours is mounted inside the fuselage or a nacelle, leave a path for air to enter, circulate and leave during flight.

As you begin to manipulate charging current and time, you may wonder why we don't charge at a higher rate, say 5 amps, to get back in the air faster. If we do that on too small a battery, we can easily overheat it and reduce life or damage a cell. Larger flight batteries such as 800- 1200 mah capacity may be charged at higher rates. The more sophisticated chargers carry a chart for maximum charging current relative to battery capacity.

When fast charging (as above) it is very important to **discharge your battery fully before recharging**. You can simply hook the battery up to a motor and prop, let it run down right on the model or, if this is not practical, buy a 1 or 2 watt bulb, wire it with two alligator clips and attach it to the battery until the glow begins to fade, **Fig 3-8**. The battery is now discharged.

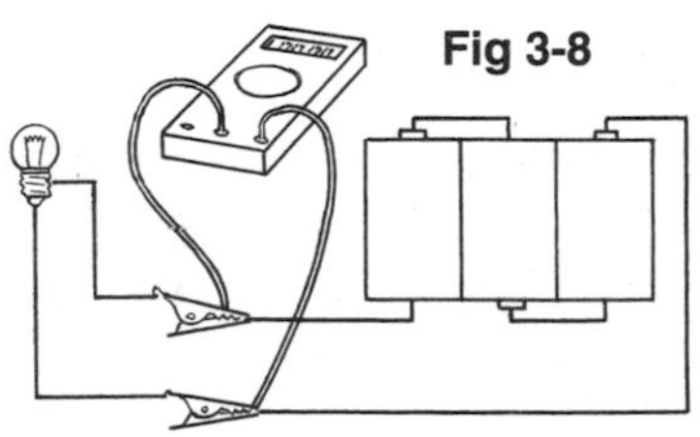

Fig 3-8

For best performance, all the cells in a battery should be electrically "balanced" so they will charge and discharge to the same voltage level. Ordinary packs don't come this way unless special ordered, but **SR Battery** packs *all* have this feature and therefore perform more consistently.

You also need to know that your battery will become quite warm while it is driving your motor. This is normal. Feel the battery just after a flight to get an idea of how hot it gets. This depends on battery location, cooling air flow and even motor and prop size.

Hooking up batteries, motors, switches and chargers will be covered later in this chapter. By now, you are probably comfortable with battery terminology and youcan manipulate charge times, battery capacity, voltage and current values and be ready to begin learning about motors.

Motors

The electric motor takes advantage of a well known law of physics. "When electric current passes through a coil of wire while the coil is *inside* a permanent magnet, the coil will rotate". It's just that simple **Fig 3-9.**

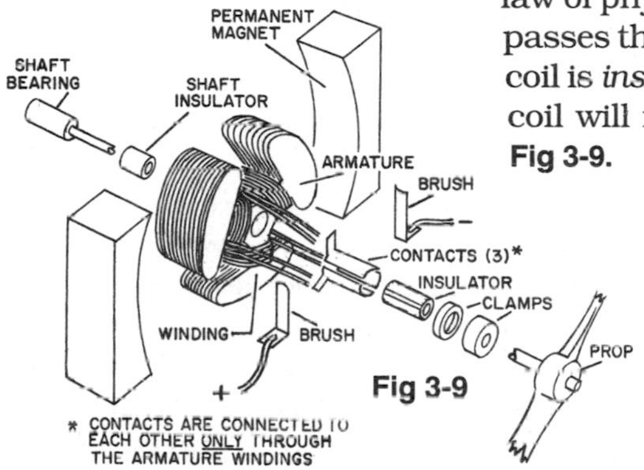

PERMANENT MAGNET
SHAFT BEARING
SHAFT INSULATOR
ARMATURE
BRUSH
CONTACTS (3)*
INSULATOR
CLAMPS
PROP
WINDING
BRUSH
+
–
* CONTACTS ARE CONNECTED TO EACH OTHER ONLY THROUGH THE ARMATURE WINDINGS

Fig 3-9

Electric motor power and quality are controlled by a wide variety of factors. Among them are the wire diameter and number of turns in the coil, the type and strength of the magnets, quality of bearings and the configuration and materials used in some things called "Brushes" or "Commutators". It's not really important to know all about these factors but some basic knowledge will help later in choosing motors and batteries.

It's easy to see that if the coil inside the magnet wants to rotate, then the electric current is going to have a hard time getting inside the moving wires. This little trick is accomplished with the help of contacts (brushes) that "rub" or "wipe" along a moving ring that is attached to the wire coil. **Fig 3-9**. The rotation will cause "grooving" as it wears so we want to run each motor **only in one direction.** Motors should be "broken in" to "groove" the brushes into a close fit with the contact ring.

Electric motors are broken-in by running them with as little shaft load as possible. No prop or flywheel should be attached during break in. Wire two "AA" size dry cells in series, hook them up to your motor and allow it to run for about an hour. For open motors like HiLine Micro 4 and Mini 6, I run them in a plastic container filled with water **Fig 3-10**. This helps carry away the carbon particles that come off the brushes. If you try this,use **only AA cells**.

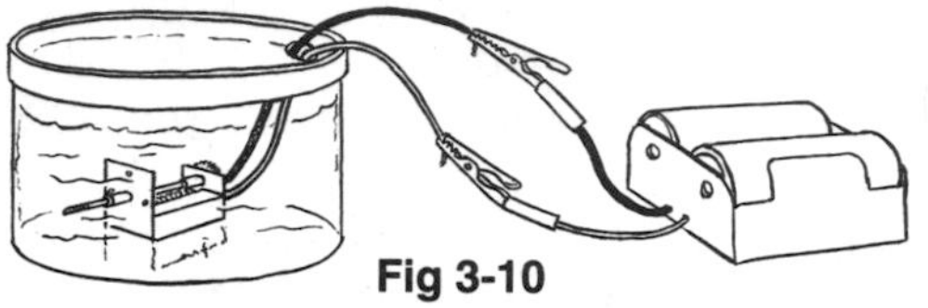

Fig 3-10

If you break- in under water, the millions of carbon particles that turn the water gray are also deposited in the motor. Let the motor dry out thoroughly then squirt some TV Tuner/Control Cleaner in at the shaft openings and the cooling vents. This stuff is available in any electronics shop. One brand is called **Archer, Cat. No. 64-2315**. This type of break- in will extend motor life and deliver an extra bit of power. "Can" type (enclosed) motors should be broken in *dry*.

It's a good idea to mark the direction of rotation and polarity right on the motor case. You may eventually have many small motors used in a variety of models and marking rotation direction will keep you from "reverse grooving" which will reduce motor power and life.

Like a water wheel with larger buckets **Fig 3-1**, a motor with larger diameter wire or more turns (longer wire) will take more amps (current/water drops) to fill the wire. Thus, that particular motor is said to "draw" more **current.** As you might expect, it also takes a higher **voltage** or more "push" (water tank at higher level) to drive the extra amps through the motor. Therefore, motors are rated in a combination of **volts** and **amps**, called **watts**. Watts are the voltage needed to drive the current through the motor TIMES the amps of current needed to fill the coil.

Our small motors are rated by the watts they draw in normal run mode. A HiLine Micro-4 draws about 4 watts, the Mini-6 about 6 watts. The Kenway direct drive motor draws about 2.5 watts.

Suppose you had a way to slow or stop your motor in mid-run by grasping the prop shaft ? The battery voltage would still be pushing the current through the coil driven by the motor energy. The coil might then start to act like a blocked garden hose that bulges under pressure. In the case of your electrical system, the wires won't bulge. Instead the energy will turn to heat which could burn off the insulation leading to motor damage, failure or fire.

Since your beginning models are free flight, you have no means of remotely turning off your motor in flight. Some geared motors are equipped with a free wheel device that allows the shaft to slip back out of contact, permitting the motor to run free **Fig 3-11**. This is not always effective in a crash. The model may hit the ground in such a way that the prop is stopped with the gears still engaged. This can damage the motor, which is another reason to test your model with a short (30 sec.) charge at first. Larger models with 25-50 watts and more power should be equipped with a fuse so that the power will be shut off if the prop is stopped and current starts to increase.

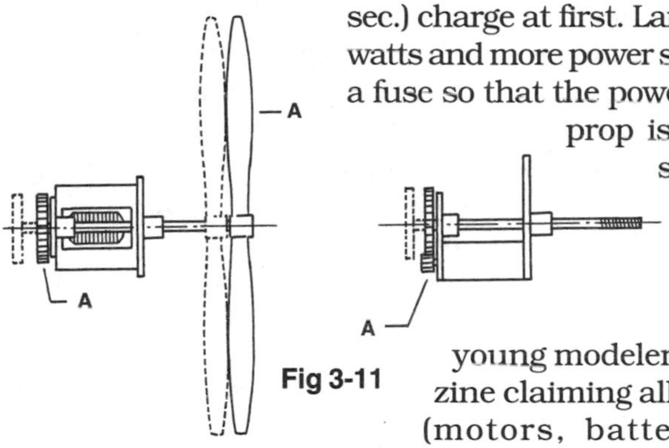

Fig 3-11

I have heard a story about the young modeler who wrote to a magazine claiming all his electrical devices, (motors, batteries, chargers and meters) ran on smoke. He reasoned that everything was fine until any one of these started to leak smoke. Then, he said, they seldom ran well afterwards. Obviously, once the smoke leaked out, the system was empty and couldn't be refilled!

The story may sound funny but you can be sure if you see smoke coming from your motor or battery, the system is in trouble. If *any* part of the system seems to get too hot to touch, either during charging or running, **shut down immediately**. Sometimes the problem is as simple as a shorted wire or plug. Possibly, you are using wire too small in diameter to carry the current you are drawing.

Airborne electrical systems get plenty of vibration and shock. A hard landing can easily crack or loosen a soldered connection. (This is true for CO_2 systems as well). It's good practice to attach wires mechanically to battery, switch or motor after soldering, **Fig 3-12**. This can be done with tape or thread (not wire or rubber band), or shrink tubing and will save you lots of trouble later on.

Just as with rubber power, different props will run at different speeds and cause the motor to draw more or less current. Adding a cell to your battery will speed up the motor but also add weight. Most motors have a recommend prop size and number of cells but props vary widely. Dick Miller's "What Works" chart, **Fig 3-13A** can

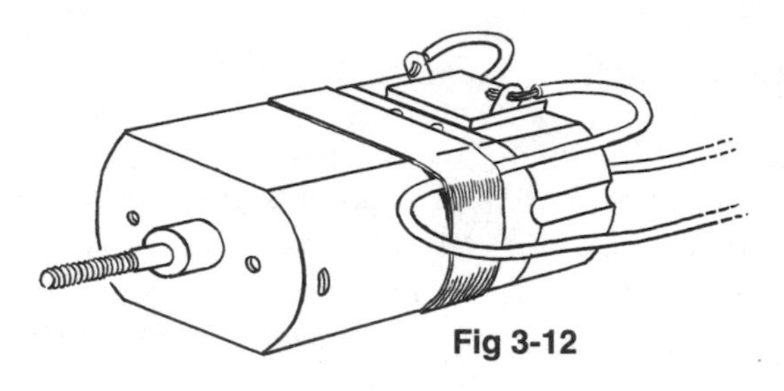
Fig 3-12

be a very fine guide for choosing motors, props and batteries. Printed with permission from Dick who is the owner of **EMPS,** the guys whohave "Got a motor for you". The chart shows a collection of successful electric projects contributed by various modelers. I have printed only a small part of Dick's "What Works" and some of his "Small Electric Motor Survey". The motor survey, **Fig 3-13B** comes from a very clever concept that Dick works out in his May 1997 article in Flying Models. He has tabulated a wide variety of motors, batteries and props to provide a **One Minute Motor Run** for various sizes and weights of models. Thus, you can use his table to choose the right power train for model from 20 to 1000 square inches of wing area and 1/2 ounce to 1-1/2 pounds of all-up weight. Complete updates of Dick's charts can be found in 5/97 and future **Flying Models** issues.

Many of the numbers in this book have "Units" attached, like 1.2 Volts or 6 Watts. These units **describe** what the numbers **measure** You can't work with just a number because you can't relate it to any result or any other number. To convert from one unit system to another, a very simple rule can be used. The rule states that **any fraction remains the same as long as numerator and denominator are multiplied by the same number.** For instance, 1/2 times 2/2 = 2/4 which is the same as 1/2. Thus to convert 50 milliamp hours to a usable fraction, we can multiply like so:

1 amp/1000 milliamps. This will let us cancel out milliamps:

$$\frac{50\ \text{\sout{milliamps}}\text{-hours}}{1} \times \frac{1\ \text{amp}}{1000\ \text{\sout{milliamps}}} = \frac{50\ \text{amp- hours}}{1000}$$

Strike throughs show how I have cancelled out the "milliamp" units. The same can be done by multiplying the new answer by $\frac{60\ \text{minutes}}{1\ \text{hour}}$, which leaves $\frac{50\text{X}60}{1000}$ = **3 amp-minutes**

In the above example I'm using the division sign (the horizontal line between the numerator and denominator) as if it is an equal sign. Thus saying $\frac{1\ \text{amp}}{1000\ \text{milliamps}}$ is the same as 1 amp =1000 milliamps

Fig 3-13A **What Works** (per Dick Miller)

MODEL	KIT/ PLAN	MOTOR	PROP	BATT. (mah)	WT (oz)	SPAN (in)	AREA (sq in)
Aeronca	Guillows K	Dual KR1	5	3 x 50	1.9	24	80
And.Pyln	HSPS-P	KR1-D	5.5	3 x 110	3.0	26	110
Answer	Lidberg P	HY-70	6	2 x 50	2.5	24	94
Baby	Klarick K	Mini-6	5.25 x 2	4 x 110	5.5	36	144
Ballanca	Scien K	MM-1	5.5 x 2	3 x 110	1.4	16	45
Bstnian	Peck K	KR-1	6.5	2 x 50	1.4	16	45
BklnDdgr	RN-K	Hy-70	6	3 x 110	4.7	32	150
B.Bmbsl	RN-K	MM-1	5.5	3 x 110	5.0	30	150
Csna BD	Guillows K	KR-1	6	3 x 50	1.6	18	45
D Demn	Pond P	Spd 300	6 x 3	3 x 110	12.3	48	327
Fchld 24	Herr K	MG-1	7	4 x 110	7.0	30	133
FA Moth	Peck K	ST-2	5.25 x 2	2 x 75	2.0	24	54
Foam Flr	Hillne-P	Micro 4	3.5	2 x 50	.90	14	45
F4F	Diels P	KR-1D	6	3 x 50	1.5	19	63
1/2A Zip	Pond-P	Cox FB	6	3 x 75	6.3	32	165
Half Pt	MB-P	MM 1	5.25 x 2	2 x 110	4,1	25	124
Intrceptr	Lidberg K	KR-1	6	2 x 50	1.4	22	70
Kerswap	Lidberg-P	Micro 4	3.5	2 x 110	1.9	22	69
P-38	Pond-P	2 MM-1	6	4 x 270	11.5	34	184
Ms Amer	MA-P	Peck 035	6 x 3	7 x 270	19.5	49	310
New Rlr	Lidberg K	Mini-6	5.5	3 x 50	2.1	30	162

K = Kit, P = Plan, KR = Kenway, Mini-6 & Micro 4 = HiLine
MM-1 & MG-1 = EMPS, HY = VL

AndPyln=Anderson Pylon, **Bstnian**=Bostonian,**B.Bmbsl**=Baby Bombshell, **Cessna BD**=Cessna Bird Dog, **D. Demn**=Diamond Demon,**FA Moth**= Flying Aces Moth, **Sundster**=Sunduster, **Trnth Tror**=Trenton Terror

Fig 3-13A **What Works (cont'd.)**

MODEL	KIT/ PLAN	MOTO-R	PROP	BATT. (mah)	WT (oz)	SPAN (in)	AREA (sq in)
OneNt16	Peck-K	KR-1	7	2 x 50	1.0	16	45
OneNt28	Peck-K	Micro4	3.5	2 x 50	2.6	28	120
OneNt28	Peck-K	Mini-6	6	3 x 50	2.4	28	120
OneNt28	Peck-K	MM-1	5.2 x 2	1 x 110	3.0	28	120
Playboy	RN-K	MM-1	5 x 2	3 x 110	5.0	36	180
Ranger	Pond-P	R-Shck	5 x 2	3 x 110	4.5	33	150
Simplex	MB-2/85P	mini-6	5.5	3 x 110	3.6	25	99
So Long	RN-K	MM-1	5.2 x 2	2 x 110	4.8	32	150
Sundster	Lidberg-P	micro4	3.5	2 x 50	1.5	19	50
Tntn Tror	Lidberg-P	Micro-4	3.5	2 x 110	1.9	22	72
Viking	Klarich-K	MG-1	7.25	3 x 110	8.5	48	285
Yogi	FM-P	MM-1	5.2 x 2	3 x 110	4.0	25	114
Zomby	MA-P	R Shck	5.2 x 2	4 x 75	4.3	31	150

Referring back to the previous "amp-minute" example, you can easily convert any unit designation to a more convenient system the same way. Suppose you want to see how fast your model is flying in **miles per hour**. Since you can't really set up a mile long course, just time the model in **seconds** over a course measured in **feet**. For instance, assume the speed you just measured was 20 seconds to cover 300 feet (football field length).

$$\frac{300\ \cancel{\text{ft}}}{20\ \cancel{\text{sec}}} \times \frac{1\ \text{mile}}{5280\ \cancel{\text{ft}}} \times \frac{60\ \cancel{\text{sec}}}{1\ \cancel{\text{min}}} \times \frac{60\ \cancel{\text{min}}}{1\ \text{hr}} = \frac{300 \text{x} 60 \text{x} 60\ \text{miles}}{20 \times 5280\ \text{hr}} = 10.227\ \text{mph}$$

In the above, I was able to cancel out feet. on top and bottom, sec. and min. on top & bottom to leave only miles and hour. This system can be manipulated to work with <u>any</u> unit quantities.

Fig 3-13B **One Minute Motor Run Chart** (per Dick Miller)

Motor	Prop	Amps	Thrust (oz)	Batt. (mah)	Tot Wt (oz)	Wing Area (sq in)
KR-1D	3.5 C	.6	.21	2 x 50	.86	20-40
		.9	.28	3 x 50	1.13	25-55
KR-1	5.5 S	.5	.25	2 x 50	1.00	20-50
Micro-4	3.5 C	2.0	.53	2 x 50	1.4	45-100
		3.0	.83	3 x 50	3.25	65-155
ST-2	3.5 C	1.2	.56	2 x 50	2.26	45-100
		2.0	.95	3 x 50	3.81	80-185
		2.8	1.34	4 x 50	5.36	110-260
Mini-6, HY 70 KP01	6 VL	2.0	.80	2 x 50	3.10	65-150
		2.5	1.5	3 x 50	5.25	110-250
		3.4	1.7	4 x 50	5.30	140-330
Dual Mini-6	6 P	2.1	1.0	2 x 50	4.0	80-190
		3.4	1.7	3 x 50	6.8	140-320
		4.8	2.5	4 x 110	10.0	200-480
MG-1	5.25K	2.1	.74	1 x 110	2.96	60-140
		4.8	2.1	2 x 110	8.32	170-400
		7.6	3.42	3 x 150	13.7	280-650
MG 1	7 S	2.1	1.4	2 x 50	5.6	120-270
		3.9	2.7	3 x 110	10.8	220-500
		5.5	3.8	4 x 110	14.2	290-680
IMP 30	6X3TD	6.4	1.73	2 x 110	6.91	140-330
		15.2	4.48	3 x 270	17.9	370-860
HY-42	7X4VL	3.7	1.76	2 x 75	7.05	140-340
		6.3	3.53	3 x 110	11.7	290-670
		8.80	5.26	4 x 150	21.0	430-1010

Props: C=Comet, K=Kyosho, P=Peck, S=Superior, TD=TD, VL=VL

Resistance

Every circuit of every kind, whether water, electricity, coal or air runs through it, has some **resistance** to the flow. Several factors can impede good electron flow and reduce power to your motor. The slowing of electrons is called **resistance** and often converts the loss in motive power to heat just like friction in a pipe.

Resistance is measured in **Ohms** and is caused by a combination of many different factors. The length of wire between battery and motor will use up some of your voltage. The diameter of the wire will help or impede flow. The number of strands of wire, the number and quality of your connections and even the internal resistance of your battery add resistance and reduce voltage.

Resistance, acting like a partially closed valve in a water system also reduces current flow. Some chargers have resistors built in to correct current flow. Some have a device called a "Variable Resistor" that can be adjusted to control current by simply turning a knob while watching the ammeter.

Resistance turns electrical energy into heat. This is how your toaster works. It has coils of very high resistance wire inside and when current passes through them, they turn red with heat. Of course, this is a condition we want to avoid as much as possible. The easiest way to improve the performance of your electrical system is to make **good solder joints and connections**. A poor connection is like a crimp in a garden hose. Alligator clips are fine for attaching test leads or charging cables but they are very poor as permanent connections in a motor system. I have seen some flyers use an alligator clip as an on-off switch to complete the circuit and start the motor. This is a simple, handy way to switch from charging to running but you may be throwing away 30-40% of your power as the motor and flight vibration reduce the efficiency of the already poorly connected clip. Many builders "hard wire" or solder all connections in the system but this can make battery changes and charging difficult. HiLine and others sell a combination charging and running switch that automatically opens the charge circuit while closing the motor circuit. This, and several types of efficient connectors are described later in this chapter.

Resistance is not always bad. It can be used to adjust motor speed, even in free flight models. This is done by wiring a **Variable Resistor** in series with your motor. A variable resistor is a coil of wire with a sliding connector at one end. Thus, you can add more or less wire to your circuit. Tiny variable resistors called Trimpots

(Bourns) are available through electronic distributors, Weighing less than a gram, they can reduce the speed of a 6 Watt motor by 40%. I used one to fly my indoor slow flight R/C. Just make sure the Trimpot is rated at least 50% more wattage than your motor and carefully bench test the whole system for heat rise before flying.

By now, you should be a bit more comfortable with the four basic areas of electrical measurement

- •**Watts (W)**, measures power and is equal to **Volts** times **Amps** (like engine horsepower). In fact, 746 watts= 1 horsepower
- •**Volts (E)**, measures the potential of electrical energy or the motive (pushing) force available to move the current.
- •**Amps (I)** measures the amount of current flowing or available in a battery.
- •**Ohms (R)**, measures the resistance to current flow.

Obviously, **E**, **I**, and **R** have some relationship to each other. If you add a certain amount of resistance, you can calculate how much the current will drop. These relationships are covered by a simple formula called "Ohm's Law", expressed as: **I=E/R**. However, I like to use the **Magic Circle, Fig 3-14**.

To use the circle, just cover the unknown quantity with your finger. The relationship of the other two quantities in the circle tells you what you have to do. For instance, if you want to solve for **E**, the **I** and **R** are shown next to each other which means you must multiply them, so **E=IR**. If you were solving for **R**, the circle shows **E** is over (divided by) **I**, so **R=E/I**.

Fig 3-14

The above came in handy when I wanted to use a 4-10 cell charger (used for 500 mAh batteries and larger) to charge 2 or 3 50 mAh cells. With no extra resistance, the big charger would load my tiny 50 mAh cells with 4-5 amps which would burn them out. Knowing that the big charger ran off my 12-volt car battery and that I wanted to charge at 1.5 amps maximum. I could calculate the resistance needed to get that result. The magic circle showed that R=E/I. Thus 12 volts divided by 1.5 amps = 8 ohms.

Resistors are available in a wide variety of values. 1,2,3,5,10 and 20 ohms are common. They are also rated by the wattage (total energy) (Volts x Amps) they have to handle. The higher the wattage, the larger and *heavier* the resistor, thus you want the lowest wattage resistor that will do your job.

To charge I would have to carry 12 volts (from the car battery) x 1.5 amps (desired for proper charge) (12x1.5=18) or 18 watts. I found a 10 ohm, 20 watt resistor at Radio Shack and soldered it to a pair of simple connectors so I could plug it into and out of the circuit as required.

Symbols and Circuits

Once you feel comfortable with the various factors affecting electric flight, we can move on to reading and using circuit diagrams. Just as in plumbing, carpentry or medicine, electrical work has its own language. The "nouns" are circuit elements and the wiring diagram acts as the "verbs" to tell us where the elements go and what they do. The elements you will use are universal so youcan work with a circuit diagram from any source. **Fig 3-14A** shows the most commonly used circuit symbols and conventions.

A = Variable Resistor **B** = Fuse
C = 3 Cell Battery, **D** = Positive
E = Negative, **F** = Male Connector
G = Female Connector
H = Normally Open Switch
I = Normally Closed Switch

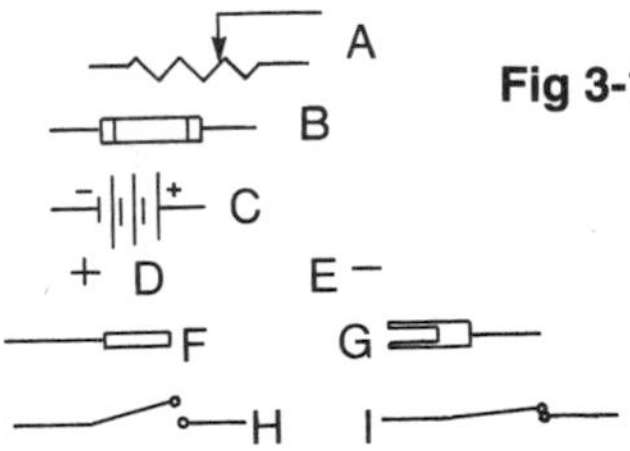

A
B
C
+ D
E −
F
G
H
I

Fig 3-14A

A typical 2-cell battery installation is shown in **Fig 3-15**. The motor on-off switch is usually shown in the off or open position. The co-axial charging plug is shown separately.

Fig 3-22B, page 60 shows the *circuit diagram* for a 3-cell system with a co-axial charging plug.

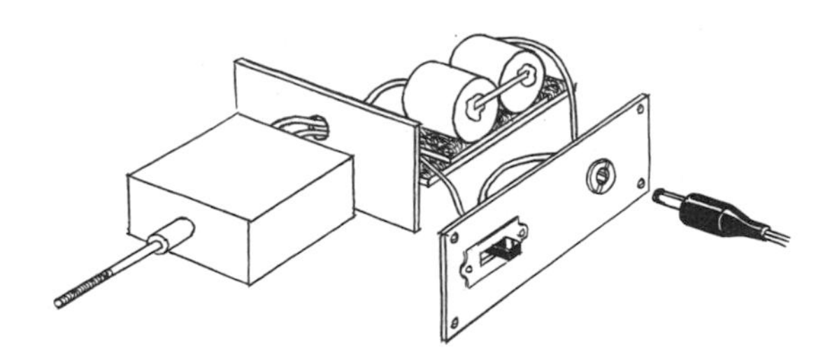

Fig 3-15

Soldering

Good connections, both mechanical and electrical are the heart of any electric system. Poor connections mean higher resistance which reduces power, and our tiny batteries don't have much to spare. A loose connection can create mysterious speed lapses that are impossible to trace inside a finished fuselage. Sometimes, a broken connection can short another wire, instantly turning the full battery power into heat. This could lead to fire and injury or the complete destruction of your model.

Learning some simple soldering steps can virtually eliminate loose wiring problems and ensure optimum, repeatable power patterns. The proper tools and about 15 minutes of practice will remove your soldering worries and produce almost professional results. Here's what you need: (Radio Shack stock #'s shown)

•Solder, Resin Core - Radio Shack-	# 64-001	$ 0.99
•30 Watt Pencil Soldering Iron	64-2055	10.00
•#20 Stranded, Insulated Wire	278-1225	1.50
•Wire Stripper Tool	64-2129	2.99

•Heat Shrink Tubing, Hair Dryer, Needle Nose Pliers.

Another handy device is some sort of "Third Hand" or holder to hold your work steady while you solder. Third hand tools are available from Micro Mark and others or you can easily make one from a piece of 2x4 pine, wire from a coat hanger and two alligator clips **Fig 3-16**

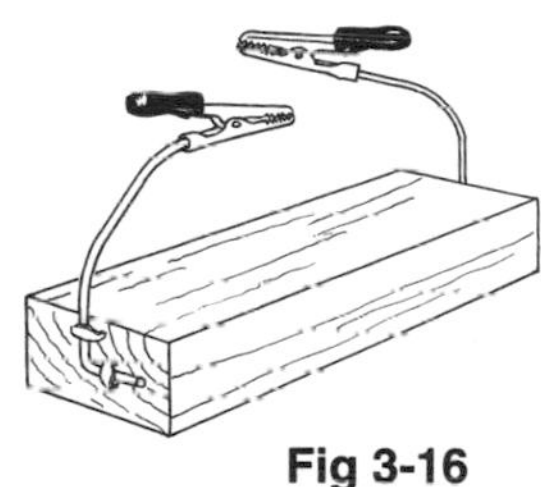

Fig 3-16

Good soldering starts with a clean tip on your iron. Sandpaper and a fine file will easily clean off solder and grime leaving a shiny surface. The tip of your iron can be "tinned" by allowing a small drop of solder to melt on to it. To join two wires, strip 3/4" of insulation off the end of each wire. Make sure you use the correct wire diameter slot in the stripper so you take off *only* insulation. On each end, twist the strands of uncovered wire tightly together so no loose strands are visible. Hold each wire in your fixture with the stripped end extended. Place the soldering iron tip against one side of the wire, while holding the tip of the solder against the other side **Fig 3-17**. The wire will heat quickly and cause the solder to

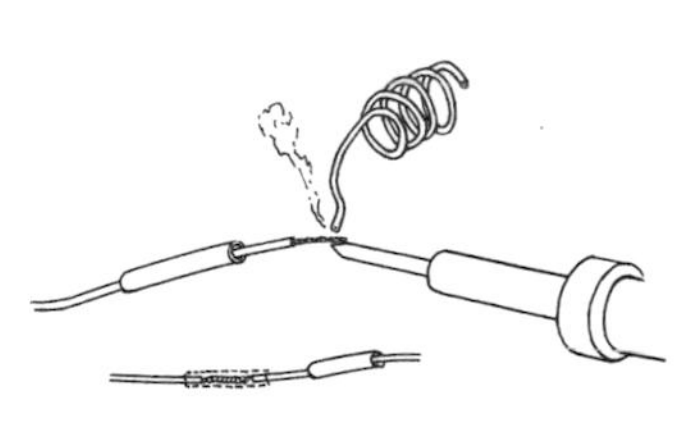

Fig 3-17

"run" along the wire and sink into the strands. Do not touch the tip of the iron directly to the solder.

Once each stripped end has been tinned as above, slide the appropriate size shrink tubing over the wire and as far back from the joint as possible. Twist both wire ends tightly together and heat *again* with the iron tip. The solder should "run" at the joint, covering both wire ends. You may want to add just a drop more solder while the joint is hot. After a few tries, you will quickly recognize when the solder runs. It turns glossy silver, something like mercury for a moment, then dulls as it cools.

After the joint has cooled, test it by tugging fairly hard to make sure the wires are firmly joined. Slide shrink tubing over the joint and heat with hair dryer or heat gun until it shrinks tightly over the wire. To wire a motor, tin the wire lead, slide on the shrink tubing, bend the lead through the motor lug and back on itself, solder, then fit the shrink tubing over the wire and lug.

Most builders prefer to "hard wire" or solder all the joints in a motor-battery circuit. This certainly provides good electrical integrity and shock resistance. However, it makes changing of batteries or relocation of motors difficult. Since I do a lot of experimenting with different combinations, I use plug-in connectors on most of my models.

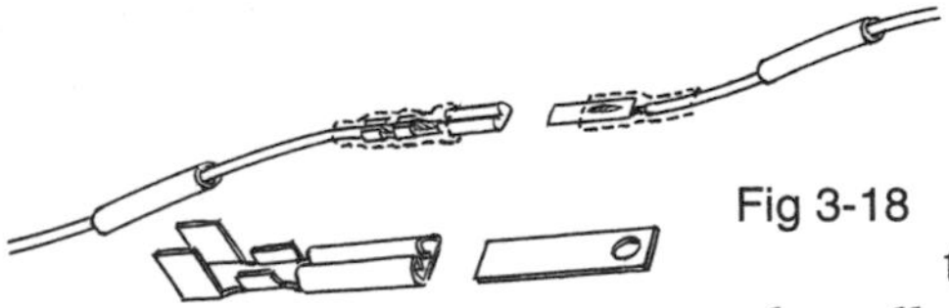

Fig 3-18

While standard **Sermos** connectors are far too heavy for our small systems, the tiny **Deans** units work well, as do some very nice individual male and female plugs sold by VL. **Fig 3-18**. The male comes without a hole so drill a 1/16 hole in one end, solder the connectors to your wire, then slide shrink tubing over the ends. Mine have lasted for hundreds of flights and show no signs of loosening or wear.

For those who like to "roll their own", **George Harris** has come up with a system that costs almost nothing. **Fig 3-19** shows connectors made from HO Atlas Brass Track. Just get a length of track (9" for $0.50), cut into 1/2 inch pieces, grind away the top with your

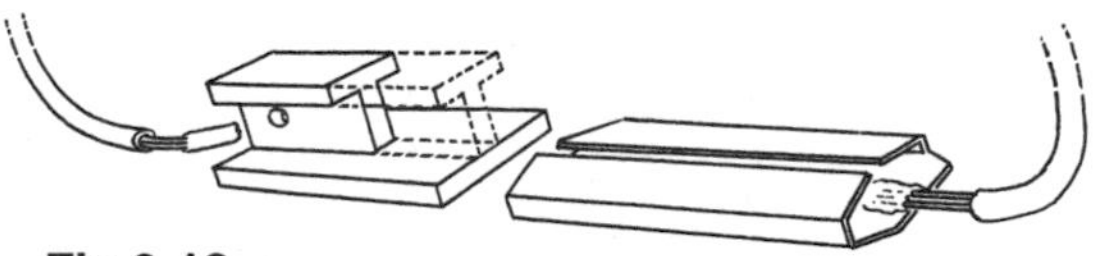

Fig 3-19

Dremel tool, solder to wire, and cover with shrink tubing. The female is a Brass Track Joiner (48 for $2.00), soldered and tubing covered.

You can even make a serviceable connector from two pieces of telescoping brass tube **Fig 3-20, (C & D)**. Solder each to wire, then flatten the smaller one slightly (at **E**) so it holds firmly in the larger tube . Slide some shrink tubing **(A)** over the wire-tube solder joint **(B)**.

Fig 3-20

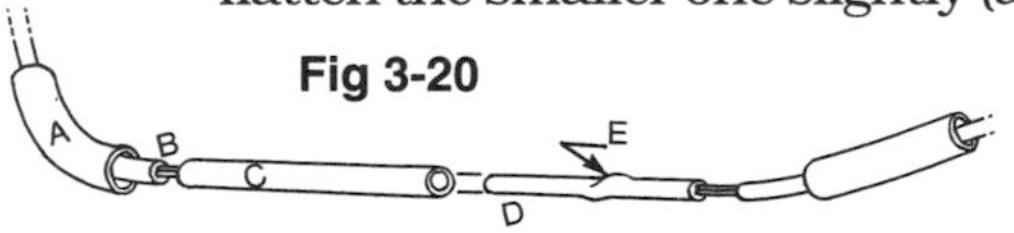

Most of my motors are directly soldered to switches or charge plugs but *all* my batteries are plug-in. Also, my charging and testing system is *carefully* wired male and female related to positive (+) and negative (-), terminals of the various components **Fig 3-21**, so that I *never* make a connection that will short a battery or charge it in reverse or reverse a motor rotation. The diagram is simple and, if you stick to it, you can make adjustments and changes in the field without worrying about polarity. In **Fig 3-21**, **A** is a battery, **B** is a motor and **C** is a charger. **Fig 3-14A** page 56, shows male and female connector symbols.

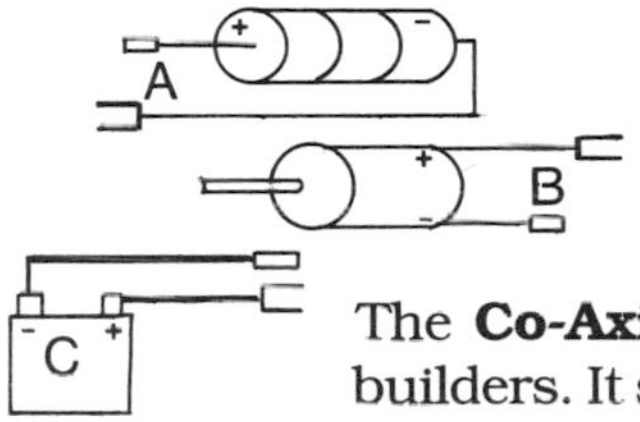

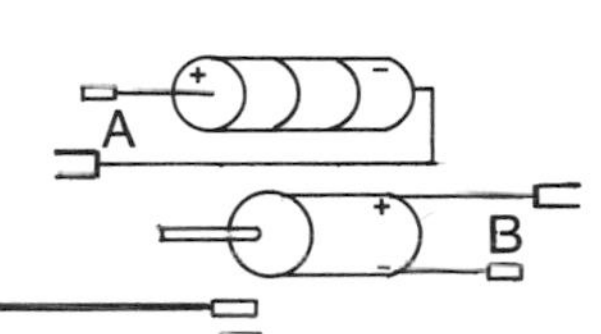

Fig 3-21

The **Co-Axial Charging Plug** may be new to some builders. It serves a useful function and is worth some explanation and careful study. This female receptacle allows you to charge your battery while the motor is disconnected, then when you remove the male plug, a spring moves back to disconnect the battery from the charger and connect it directly to the motor. **(Fig. 3-22 A,B,C** (next page)

- **Fig 3-22A** = Exploded view of a **Male Charge Plug** showing + and - wiring.
- **Fig 3-22B** = Schematic of Motor and Battery wired with **Female Charge Plug.** Note charge plug is seen from the **bottom** with regard to which wire goes to which terminal. All terminals are located from the spring (shown as # **1** visible inside the unit)

  2 = Neg. connected to Neg. of battery and motor
  3 = Pos. to Pos. of battery
  4 = Connector to Pos. of motor
  5 = Motor
  6 = Optional safety switch, normally open.
- Fig 3-22C= Male plug inserted in **(A)** female charge socket.

This pushes spring **(Y)** away from contact **(X)** and circuit to motor is *open* while battery circuit is *closed* and charging. When male plug is withdrawn, **(X)** and **(Y)** connect and battery current is delivered to the motor.

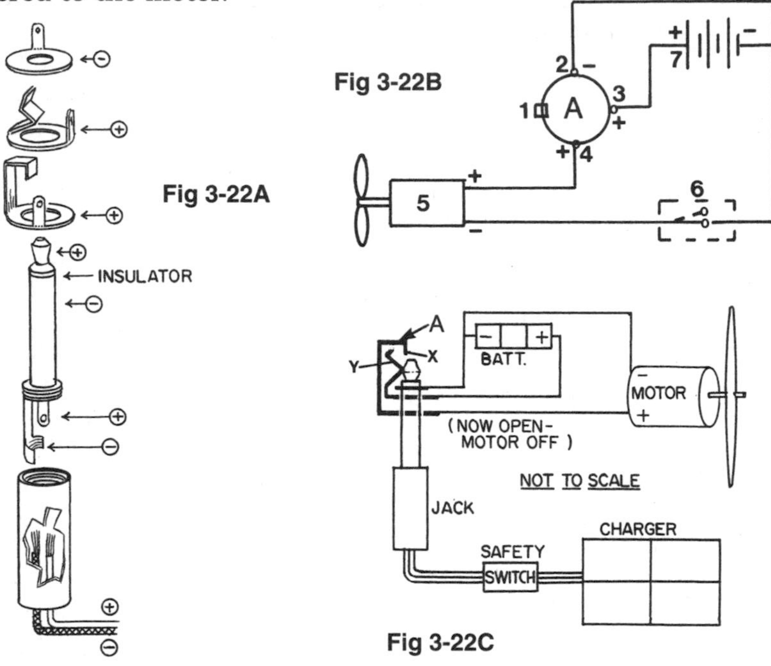

Fig 3-22A

Fig 3-22B

Fig 3-22C

This system can also be used as a switch. When the male charge plug (attached to your charger) is in the female receptacle, you are in charge mode. The instant you remove the male charge plug, your motor will start. You can eliminate a starting switch by simply attaching your male charge plug to the charger with removable connectors, then disconnect the plug from the charger, **leaving it in the female charge receptacle** while you walk to your launch site. Pull the plug and launch. Another friend uses a 3/32 dowel to replace the male plug while he walks to the launch point.

It's important to wire this type of plug correctly so your battery will get proper polarity charging and your motor will run in the right direction. Study the drawing carefully and test your first assembly by attaching leads from the male plug to alligator clips on your break-in battery. Then check polarity on the male end with your voltmeter as described earlier for batteries. After attaching wires to the female end, connect the two while still attached to your break-in battery and recheck polarity. A safety switch wired to your charger is always a good idea. This will allow you to make the connection between male and female charge plugs and then start the current flow.

On my indoor models, I simply wire the motor and batteries with VL connectors, disconnect to charge, then reconnect to start the motor. This saves charging plug, start switch and the weight of extra wire

Universal Motor Mount **Fig 3-24 A&B** shown below, made of 1/16 ply can fit 3 different ways. Just epoxy to the motor.

Fig 3-24A

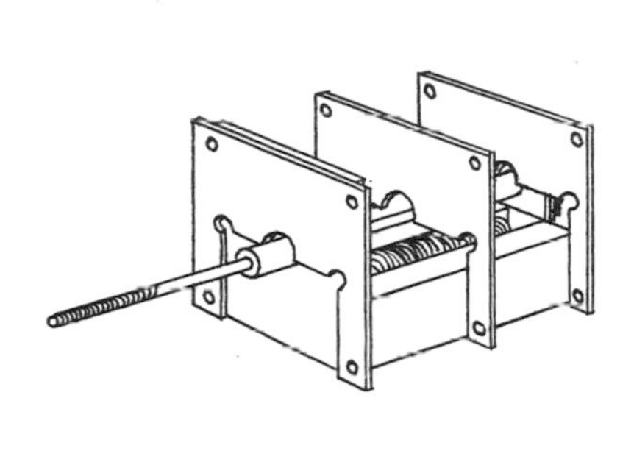

Fig 3-24B

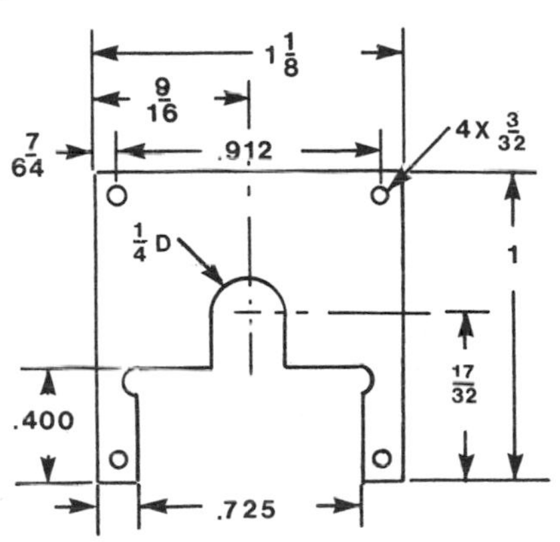

Motor Installations

With the wide variety of motors available, installation deserves some study and discussion. You won't need as much thrust adjustment with electric as you do with rubber or gas, therefore a more rigid system is practical. **Fig 3-23** shows **half size** three views of several different types of motors. Your local photocopier should be able to enlarge these and copy them on transparent plastic so you can lay them right over your plan to design the installation.

A new motor system from **K&P** arrived just before publication. The KP00 weighs only 4.7 grams and comes in geared or direct drive. The geared unit comes with a 3.375" diameter adjustable pitch prop which weighs 0.8 grams. Dick Miller says the unit will fly a 3 ounce model.

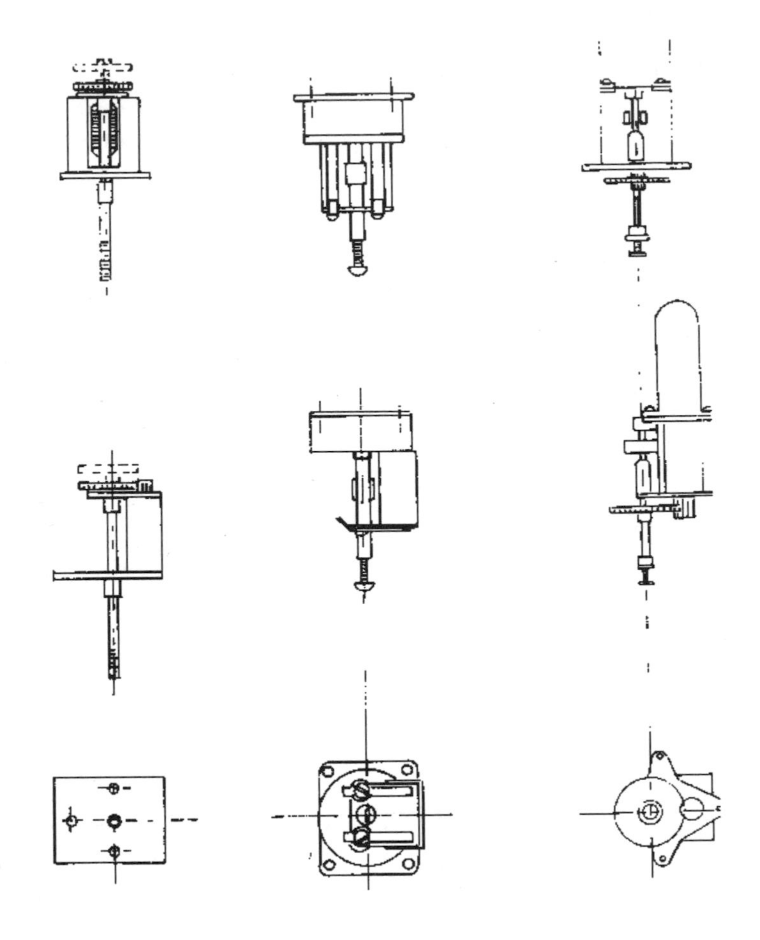

HiLine
HiLine Mini-6

VL HY-70

K&P KP01

Four different types of motor mountings are shown in **Fig 3-25 A-D**. One of the very big advantages of electric power is that the motor does not have to be mounted right at the nose. It can easily be remotely mounted to drive the prop through a flexible shaft or a rubber loop. The flexible shaft is simply a piece of RC pushrod (sold as **Gold-N-Rod** or **nylon push rod**) which is sized to take a 2-56 thread. The motor drive shaft is already threaded, so just screw it into the pushrod, add a lock nut behind the rod, then use a 2-56 screw to hold the prop. To set up a rubber band drive, drill & tap a Crocket or similar hook to fit the motor shaft, add a lock nut, then simply hook a rubber loop between the motor hook and your rubber power front end. This is probably the *simplest* way to convert an old model from rubber to electric.

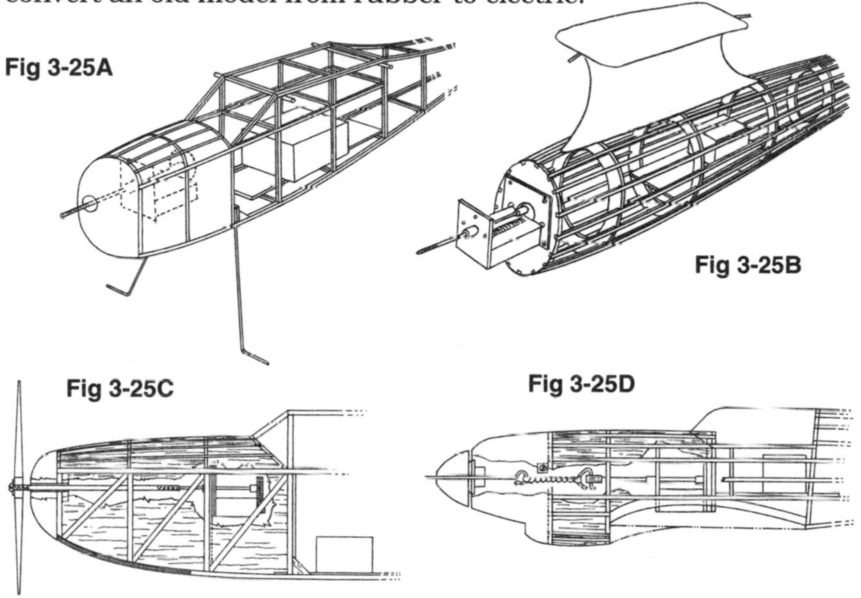

Fig 3-25A

Fig 3-25B

Fig 3-25C

Fig 3-25D

The advantages of remote motor installation are obvious. You can still use the tilted nose block system to adjust thrust without moving the motor. Nose first crashes will not damage the motor installation and, with the rubber motor drive, even if the free wheel system doesn't release the prop in a crash, the rubber will simply break *before* the motor is overloaded. In scale models, you can better control the c.g. and now you can *finally* build that P-39 Airacobra with the motor right between the pilot's legs. The rubber loop drive is a perfect system to use on a stick type model like the old time

"Ritz" or the Sig Cub, **Fig 3-25E** shows a simple conversion that allows you to actually switch back and forth between rubber and electric power.

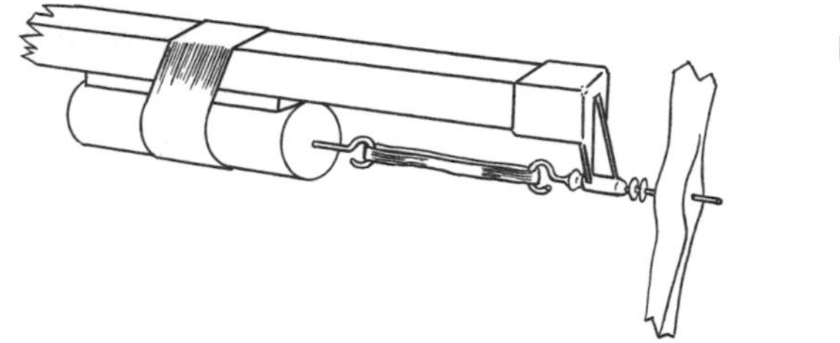

Fig 3-25E

If the shaft extension between motor and prop seems too long, just epoxy a bit of the *outside* pushrod tubing into a bulkhead to guide the shaft, or drill out a nose bushing used for rubber power **(Peck PA 006)** to take the shaft. This will keep the shaft from bending during a crash and will also reduce vibration.

I think the stick type model is the perfect vehicle for the beginner to learn how to handle electric power. With a rubber loop drive, the motor can be moved fore and aft right along with the battery to adjust the c.g. Charging and cooling are simple and props can be easily changed right along with thrust angle so flight trim experiments are easy. My own "Slow Voltage" is a stick pylon design that placed well as an indoor electric RC last year. Don't think the extra weight of motor and battery will ruin the flight of a 24-inch Sig Cub. I have seen two of them fly OOS on only a 2 minute charge with 3x50 mAh battery.

All my batteries have a strip of Velcro® epoxied to the side. A longer strip is epoxied to the fuselage allowing me to shift the battery a bit yet still fasten it firmly. Charge plugs and switches are *firmly* mounted on 1/16 ply with a bit of slack wire to allow for hard landings.

Series and Parallel Circuits

For the beginner, all components of an electric circuit are wired in **series**. This configuration is much like the old time "christmas tree light" string where one bad bulb or loose connection would black-out the whole line. Test each component *individually*, wire carefully, then *test again*. The most common reason for a balky motor is a loose connection.

If we go back to our tank and water wheel analogy, it's easy to see that batteries connected in series will *add* their voltage just like tanks piled on top of each other. However, the current flowing will be the same as a single cell because it still follows the same path through the wire. *Batteries are connected in parallel only in very sophisticated R/C endurance models or in multi engine systems.* Batteries in Parallel would deliver twice the current at the same voltage. **Fig 3-26** shows a **parallel** battery configuration.

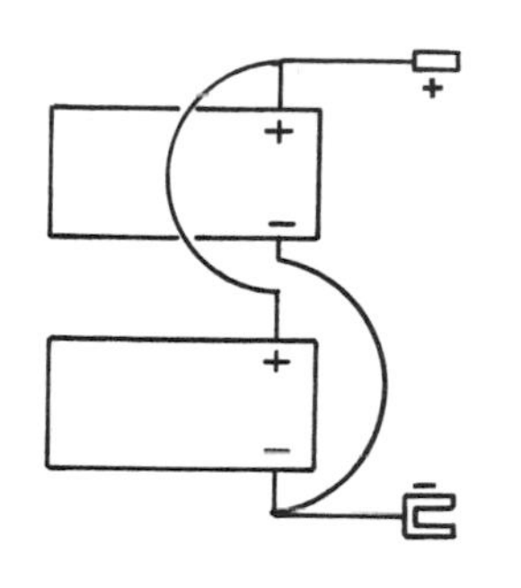

Compare this figure with **Fig 3-2, page 40** which shows batteries in series.

Fig 3-26

Multi - Motor Systems

Suppose we take two motors and mechanically mount them so they drive the same prop shaft through a gear train **Fig 3- 27.** HiLine makes a Dual Mini-6 which consists of two of their standard 6 watt motors geared to a single shaft. K&P makes a similar unit. These motors are rated at about 12 watts and will fly models of 200 square inch wing area and 5-7 ounce all up weight. I made a smaller unit using 2 Kenway motors on a single shaft.

This type of system is easier to wire, install and handle than a system of two *separate* motors driving separate props. We have two choices in wiring a "twin cylinder" system. We can wire the motors in **series** or in **parallel.** This requires some experience and understanding.

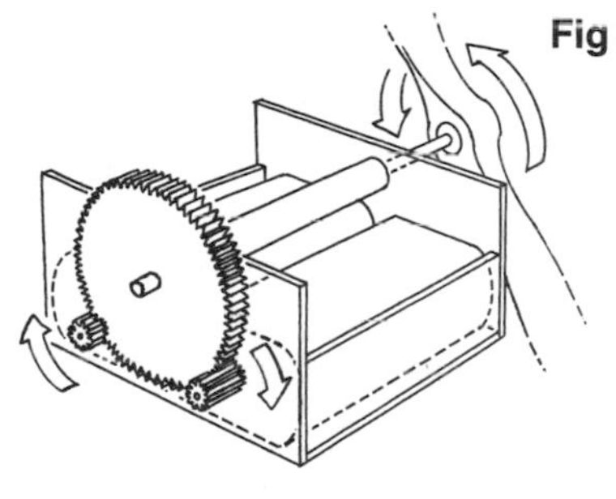

Fig 3-27

We know that batteries wired in **series** will *add* their voltages just like two water tanks, one on top of the other **Fig 3-1**. Batteries wired in **parallel** have the same voltage as a single battery **(A)** but will deliver twice the current **(B)** like two tanks next to each other pouring water down the same pipe. As shown in **Fig 3-28**,

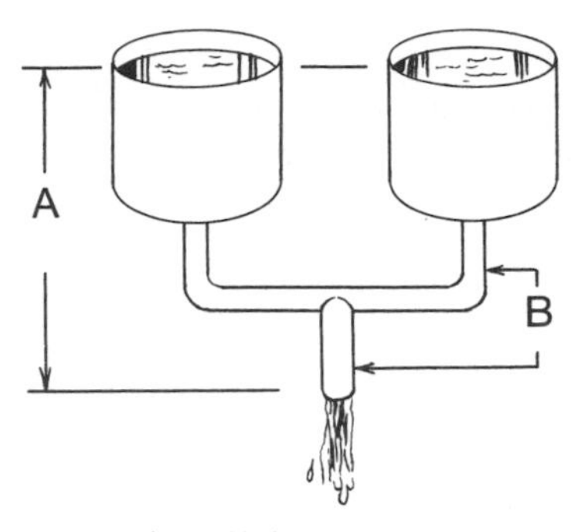

Fig 3-28

Let's consider motors wired in series or parallel. It's easy to see **Fig 3-29** that when the motors, (water wheels) are in series, the first wheel will use up some of the energy of the water as it is turned. The next wheel (being in the same stream) will have somewhat less energy (will turn more slowly), but will have the same amount of current flowing past it. The water can't go anywhere else but through our pipe so the same volume of water (the same amount of current) must pass each point in the circuit in the same time period. Therefore, in a **series circuit** we assume that the **current** remains the same throughout but the **voltage** drops as it passes through the **resistance** of each component. The water analogy is not perfect here since the first motor doesn't really rotate faster than the second one. Each has its speed reduced because of the voltage drop. If both motors have the same resistance then they will each run at the same, reduced speed.

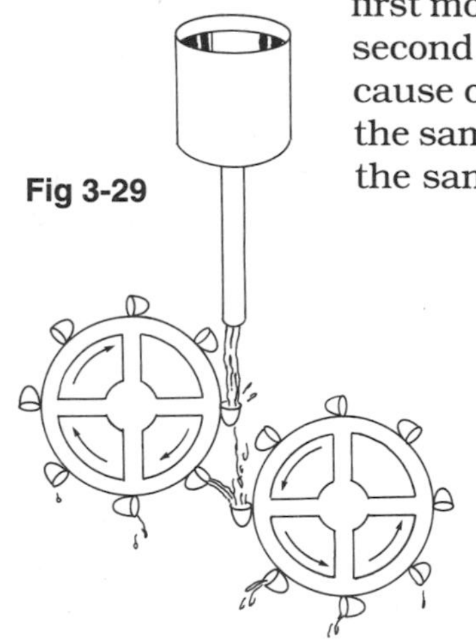

Fig 3-29

If we wire the motors in parallel, then each will operate at the same initial **voltage (A)**, but now the **current** will be divided between the two **Fig 3-30**. Thus, our series - parallel choice is between a longer run *or* more power. In series, we will lose some power (rpm) but get a longer run. For example, a twin Mini-6 motor arrangement with 4 cell, 110 mAh (4.8 volts) battery wired in series will use 2.4 volts for the first motor and 2.4 volts for the second, thus getting less power per motor than a single mini-6 running on 3 cell 110 mAh (3.6 volts).

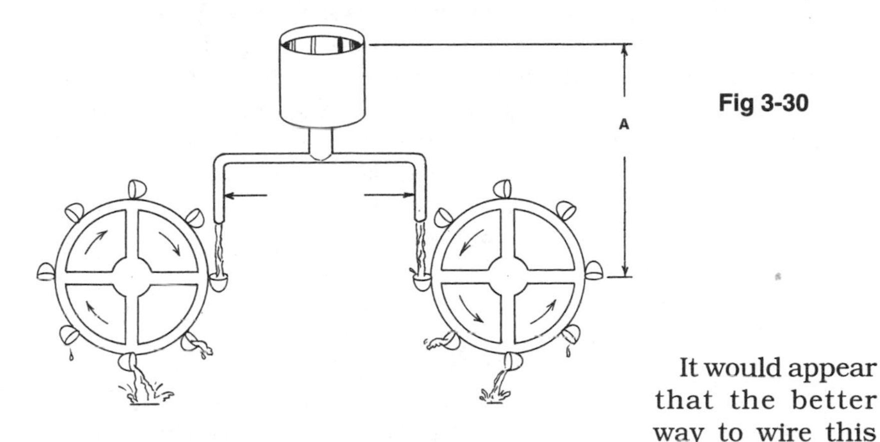

Fig 3-30

It would appear that the better way to wire this system would be in *parallel* where each motor would have 4.8 volts to use and the run would be shorter. This is based on the assumption that both motors have equal resistance and, therefore, split the voltage equally. If the motors were different, then the voltage would be split **in proportion** to their resistance.

In modeling, we use "trade-offs" all the time. For instance, let's consider a 10-gram rubber motor as used in **both** a P-30, which has a 120 square inch wing area and weighs 40 grams, and a Coupe which has a 220 sq. in. wing area and weighs 80 grams. The 10-gram motor for the P-30 is made up of four strands of 3/16 rubber about 22" long. It will run a 9-1/2" plastic prop for about 30 seconds on 800-900 turns. In the Coupe we need more power to fly the larger, heavier airplane so we double the motor over making eight strands about 11 inches long.

If we tried to run the same prop (9-1/2") to fly the bigger Coupe, we would only get a 20-sec. run from the doubled motor at 600 turns. Instead, though, we trade off rpm for torque by changing to a 16 " prop which will run slower and we can exceed a 30-second motor run. The same kind of thinking takes place in choosing electric motor systems.

A quick way to compare motor run length in a parallel circuit is to consider two Mini-6 motors powered by a 4cell,100 mAh battery. Remember from earlier in this chapter, 100 milliamps is equal to 0.1 amps (100/1000 = 0.1). The rating of 100 mAh tells us this battery will deliver 0.1 or 1/10 amp for an hour, or 1 amp for 1/10 hour (6 minutes) or 2 amps for 1/20 hour (3 minutes). Thus, if that battery was powering a **single** motor which drew 2 amps, that motor would run for **3 minutes**. If we run 2 motors from the same battery, **each** will draw 2 amps so now we have a 4-amp current draw which means our system will run only for 1-1/2 minutes. 100mAh = 0.1 amp for 1 hour, 1 amp for 1/10 hour= 2 amps for 1/20 hour= 4 amps for 1/40 hour. 1/40 hour = 60/40= 6/4= 3/2= 1-1/2= 1.5 minutes. Of course, this is only an approximate calculation which doesn't take into account the resistance from extra connections to two motors, possible unequal cell or motor resistance, or the friction of shafts and bearings. But it's close enough to give you a good idea of what's going on in your system.

This trade-off works best with our small motors (2-10 watts) and batteries (50-250 mAh). As we get into bigger systems, heat and resistance become more critical and battery values (for rpm and run time) must be calculated more carefully. However, these are mostly RC systems in much larger models where a bit more weight can be handled without adversely affecting performance.

To Fuse or Not To Fuse

A fuse is a self-acting "off" switch that operates when something causes too much current to run through a circuit. It is usually a piece of very fine wire encased in a glass tube. The wire material and diameter are engineered to melt and part (breaking the circuit) when heat (caused by current) reaches a certain level.

Fuses are useful because electric motor circuits have an interesting property we haven't discussed before. Motors of any size are like the worst spoiled brat you ever met. When, for any reason, they are prevented from rotating, they simply scream for attention (more current). If they still can't rotate, they will convert this current into heat which can burn out the motor coil, melt your wiring or cause a fire. When a fuse senses extra heat, it melts and opens the circuit, reducing current flow (and heat) to zero.

In our small systems, current is not usually a major problem. The very small direct drive motors, (Kenway KR-1, HiLine Micro-4) draw only 2-4 amps and use 2-or 3-cell 50 mAh batteries which aren't a very high risk. The larger, 6-10 watt motors (HiLine Mini-6, K&P, Kenway geared, MG-1, VL) usually have built-in free wheeling devices which disengage the prop when the model crashes, thus allowing the motor to run free. Also, the weight penalty for a fuse and wiring on such a small system can exceed the weight of the switch and charger plug. Some builders feel that fuses aren't necessary in smaller systems but the **heat danger** *still* exists.

For those who like to work with test data in designing models or choosing components, be aware that a motor running "free" with no prop will run faster **and** longer because it is not doing much work and thus, draws less current. When motor tests are run on stationary motors, they are usually "loaded" with some sort of friction clutch and various meters which simlulate a prop load. However, when actually flying, the motor is cooled better and the prop load varies somewhat as the model climbs or cruises.

Your bench test of a 6 watt motor with 3cell 50 mah battery on, say a 2-minute charge, may result in a 1-minute motor run. This run could easily become 1-1/2 minutes or more **in the air**, so work your charge times up **slowly** on any new F/F model.

The Power Module

If you are anything like me, somewhere in your home there is a place that looks a lot like the "airplane graveyards" of the late "40s where everything from P-5's to B-29s were laid to rest. Wings and tails that survived the "Death Spiral" on to concrete that destroys many rubber jobs, fuselages with wheels and nose blocks still attached after the wings folded and lots of other spare pieces that adorn a closet or a corner in the basement .

Also, if you are from the "Depression generation" every time you look at your spare parts bin you feel that lots of good flying stuff is somehow being wasted. Electric power is the way to resurrect that old 26-inch Aeronca on floats or that 28 inch Spitfire that looks like it lost the Battle of Britain. Instead of a 30-second motor run and a 15-second steep glide, you can now get a fully charged 90-second motor run and a 30-second glide. Evening flights of a dozen smooth, silent circles at 30 feet with a realistic landing 10 feet away, how does that sound for a geriatric Grumman ?

You can do all this with several different models using a **Power Module** Fig 3-31. I have a separate power module for each size motor so I can insert them into the appropriate model and be ready to fly in a couple of minutes. The power module carries your motor, battery and charging plug and allows for easy mounting at the front, rubber shock absorbing at the back and a movable battery for balance. It is intended for quick conversion of rubber powered models. The front bulkhead **[A]** is 1/16 ply and holds the motor *and* the charging plug just under the motor base. This bulkhead is tapped for 2-56 screws (or has blind nuts inserted). These screws go through the *separate* nose block **[B]**, from the front and the screw heads can be countersunk to clear the prop. The carrier strip **[C]** is glued to the motor base and has a strip of Velcro along its top. Each battery has a strip of Velcro® epoxied to the side so it can be moved along the carrier strip.

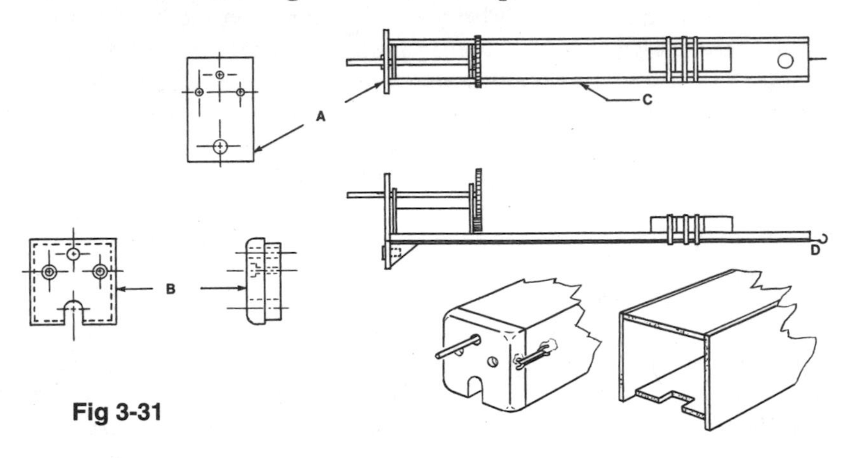

Fig 3-31

Rubber bands hold the battery firmly in the proper location. The rear hook **[D]**, holds a rubber band which goes over the rear rubber dowel to anchor the back end of the power module and still absorb landing shocks. The nose block should be a firm fit in the nose. If the nose opening is too small to accommodate the charge plug, just make a cutout in the noseblock and the bottom of the fuselage as shown.

Thrust adjustments are made by shimming the noseblock the same way you would with a rubber model. Now you can bring several rubber models to the field and fly them all with electric power! I have just tested Ed Wickland's new 6-inch diameter wooden props for the HiLine Mini-6, VL, K&P or any of the small 6-watt motors. They are *definitely* a lot better than the plastic 6-inch props we have been using. You might see a 20% improvement in flight time.

What To Buy? What to Build?

When I decided to fly an R/C electric powered glider I felt that with a license to fly full-sized aircraft and 45 years of building and designing freeflight models, an electric sailplane would be easy to handle. I therefore bought a hot little number called a UHU and proceeded to re-kit the thing on the second flight. Moral: Beginners need to start with simple models!!

Even if you have flown rubber, gas or CO_2 models of many types, try a simple stick model or convert an old *simple* rubber job for your first electric. An easily moved battery and motor, sliding wing and rubber mounted tail feathers will be a tremendous help in learning to handle this new power source. Also, for your first electric model, I don't recommend any of the small, direct drive motors. These turn over at high rpm with very small props thus producing a fairly fast flying model that is tougher to trim.

Probably the best beginners' unit would be a Kenway 4-watt or HiLine 6-watt geared unit with a 5-1/2-to-6 inch prop and 3cell 50 mAh battery. Drive the prop through a rubber band coupling and attach the whole system to a 24-28 in. span stick model. Attach the battery to the motor with VL connectors or Deans plug and eliminate the charge plug and start switch. Remove the battery to charge and simply plug it in to start. Charge withfour dry cells (D size) for 1 minute then build up to three minutes.

With this set-up you can mount the motor near the CG and balance with the battery. Thrust can be adjusted just like a rubber model without upsetting motor orientation and shaft damage is eliminated. Props can be easily changed and wing, rudder and stab adjustments are simple. Dethermalizers are easy to install and may be essential. I have seen several of these go OOS on test flights.

The Sig Cub and Dare Hummer at 24" span and the Ewing Scooter at 28" span, all fit this profile. For larger models (30-36 inch span) the EMPS MG-1 can be rigged the same way. I use a Crocket rubber hook drilled and tapped for 2-56 thread which simply mounts on the motor shaft and holds with a locknut. Now you can use the same motor as either remote, rubber loop coupled or with a prop directly mounted.

Use your first, simple electric models to experiment with charging times, speed reducers, battery size, props and flight adjustments. Slow the model enough to fly indoors and shoot for that 2-minute barrier. You will learn invaluable lessons that will greatly enhance your later flights.

After you have flown the stick model a few dozen times, remove the motor from the c.g, glue a platform on the nose and simply tape the motor there. You may find the climb improves, turns are tighter and flights longer <u>or</u> you may find the opposite is true and you now know as much about electric FF as I do.

The small, direct drive motors like the Kenway KR-1D and the HiLine Micro-4 are 2.5-4 watt motors that drive small props and require very light models. Wing spans around 14 inches, wing area 45-50 square inches and All Up Weights of 28-30 grams are acceptable range. This even allows for all-sheet balsa models. Several plans are available. (HiLine Foam Flyer, 14", HiLine Micron, 13", and the Ewing Hummer and Humdinger, 13-14").

The guys in Tony Naccarato's Black Sheep Indoor Squadron have been very successful with tiny motors on some very light indoor models, both the endurance type and profile scale. This requires careful, light building technique and is *not* for beginners.

Once you have progressed beyond the stick model, there are many plans and kits in the 4 watt range for the Micro-4 or the Kenway geared unit. HiLine's Micro-E and Al Lidberg's full line of 20-22 inch span nostalgia gas models like the New Ruler, the Kerswap and the Playboy Senior work well. Guillow's Javelin and Lancer also fit this profile. Try a 5 or 6-inch prop with these models to slow the flight and make adjustment easier. **Fig 3-32** shows Dominick Antonelli's "sorta scale" Sopwith flying boat with two Kenway geared motors in a push-pull configuration. This is the kind of fun you can have with electric power.

Fig 3-32

The electric motor is doing for scale models what Balsa wood did for all modeling so many years ago. Now, all kinds of scale projects become practical. The Guillow's line of scale kits, sometimes a bit heavy for long flights with rubber power are sturdy enough for electric conversion with almost no construction changes. My very good friend Tony Peters, a rubber scale builder of some repute, was delighted when his 18-inch span Guillow's Cessna Bird Dog (Kit 902) with a Kenway geared motor, a 6". prop and 3 cell 50 mAh battery almost went OOS on its first full charge test flight.

Guillow's also has Cessna 180 and Piper Super Cub kits at 20-inch span for the KR-1 geared motor. The Guillow's 300 and 400 series kits cover the Golden Age private planes like the Fairchild 24 and Aeronca. The 400 series are 24-27inch span kits of W.W.II Spitfire, Mustang, Messerschmitt. All fly well with HiLine mini-6 motor and 3 cell 50 mAh battery. For long flights just switch to a 3 cell 110 mAh battery. More specific information is covered in the **What Works** section and we thank Dick Miller for his research and efforts in collating this information.

In general, models up to 1.8 ounce and 90 square inches wing area will do fine with the KR-1 geared motor. The HiLine Mini-6, VL-70, and the KP01 will handle up to 4 ounces and 250 square inches area. For larger models from 200 to 350 sq. in. area (some of those old .020 replica kits), the EMPS MG-1, the VL HY-42, or the HiLine twin Mini-6 will work well. I have converted my 34" span Brooklyn Dodger and 32" Sniffer from .020 glo power to electric and am getting good, silent and clean flights from both. Try a 7 or 8" prop for best results. I have stopped a bit short of the upper limits that Dick indicates in his "One Minute Motor Run" chart. You can go to 4- or 5-cells with these motors and increase model weight and wing area as you get more experience with lighter, slower airplanes.

How to Make The Best Choice ?

Shall we take ohms against a sea of troubles? Watts in a name ? How is the winter of our discontent made glorious by this sum of torque? (maybe Old Will was a modeler too?) There's just no best choice. You aren't wrong to use a direct drive with a small prop and one less cell or a geared motor with a larger prop on the same model. A One Nite 28 will fly well with direct drive Micro-4 and 2 cell 50 mAh battery (3-1/2" prop) , a direct drive MM1, 1cell 110 and 5-1/4" prop or a KR1D. The very same model will also fly well with a geared HY-70, Mini-6 or KP01, 6" prop and 2 or 3cell 50 mAh, 2 or 3 cell 110 battery. SR Batteries' 3cell 150 weighs almost the same as a 3cell 110 yet delivers 30% longer run. Surely, there must be a best combination for steepest climb, longest flight, smoothest cruise, best glide or longest life. That's the beauty of electric flight. You can choose the flight parameters you want for each model and, with very little effort, arrange a power train to suit.

For multi-engine scale models, the EMPS MM-1, the Graupner Speed 300, Scientext ST-2, Peck 035 and the HiLine Imp 30 are all good direct drive choices. All these will deliver power somewhere between an .010 and .020 glo engine. **Guillow's** has a nice line of multi engine kits including a P-38 and a great DC-3 (see Scale - Chapter 6). **Scientext** also has some nice multi-engined flying boats.

Since modeling is at least 50% imagination, electric power certainly opens the gate to projects we would never have considered before. With an electric multi, all motors will run at close to the same speed and will all stop **together**. Motors can be made to run left or right rotation by simply switching the leads and small props with right and left pitch are available. How about a Vickers Gun Bus with the motor behind the pod between the booms ? VL's new, HY-50 series with concentric motor and gears can fit into smaller spaces for scale front ends. My old, rubber powered 30-inch Porterfield **Fig 3-33**, converted to HiLine Mini-6 with 3 cell 110 mAh battery and 6-inch prop regularly does 3-4 minutes of smooth, realistic flying. A tiny Kenway direct drive motor on an old Hand Launched Glider why not ? An electric Old Time Twin Pusher - WOW !!

Once you start building really good looking scale models, you will surely want good pictures. **Matt McCarthy** took both **Figs 3-33 & 3-35**. In **Fig 3-33**, Matt used a real hangar and shot at an up angle to make the model look in proportion. In **Fig 3-35**, proper lighting and contrast emphasize Leo's building talent.

Fig 3-33

Fig 3-34 shows my "Slow Voltage" sheet foam 30-inch span electric RC with HiLine and CETO. You can build one in 3 hours and fly RC indoors the next day.

Fig 3-34

Fig 3-35- Leo McCarthy's magnificent 48-inch span, 4 (Scientext) motor Boeing 314 Flying Boat. Electric power <u>really</u> can let you play with "the stuff of dreams".

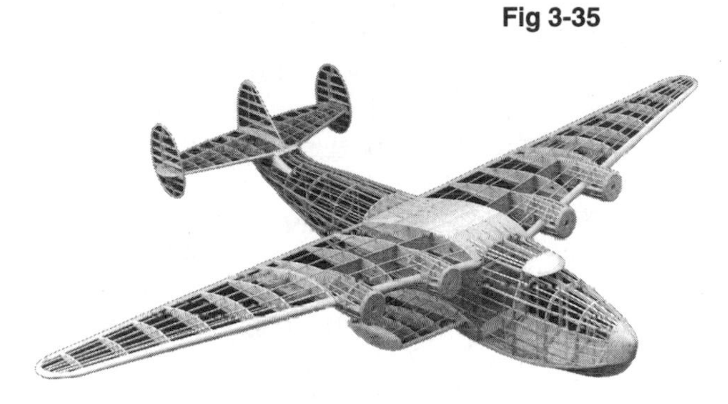

Fig 3-35

Get a Scout from Herr Engineering and add a **Power Module** with a 6-watt motor. Switch from rubber to electric power right at the field, then add a CETO or Hitec "Shredder" R/C unit for real schoolyard flying.

If you have an old Wakefield, Unlimited or large, old time rubber model, EMPS makes an MG-23. A motor kit with a <u>23:1</u> gear ratio. This can swing a big, 16 inch balsa rubber prop that can fly that old, beat up monster for several minutes.

Electric power for indoor free flight has become very popular using the small, direct drive motors furnished by Kenway and K&P, with two cell, 50 mAh batteries. Small, two to three inch diameter props made by Ed Wickland offer three to four minute flights. Many builders are converting super light (2-5 gram) indoor rubber power models to electric with amazing results.

For indoor R/C slow flight, try Hobby Lobby's Bleriot. Prebuilt with a 50 inch span, its 4 mph speed allows turns in a school gym.

I think once you start to experiment, you will look forward to decades of new building and flying experiences.

4

THE "EVOLUTION"

I'm told that Frank Zaic was asked by the father of a young modeler, "What should my son build after he has finished a Delta Dart ?" Frank is supposed to have replied, "Another Delta Dart." There's a lot of thought behind that answer. We all tend to build lots of different models and rarely even stay with one type long enough to *really* learn about construction and flight trimming. If you ask a group of contest winners how long they have flown their winning model, you will probably find that the model you saw is number 3 or 4 or even 5 of an *evolving* design.

In this chapter let's try to do the same thing. We'll start with a simple, 28-inch rubber sport model and watch it evolve into a more complex and better performing rubber powered contest-type model, then a free flight electric model and finally, a small, single channel electric R/C. The basic framework will remain but we will build on it and change flight trimming techniques to accommodate each new development. With an original investment of $9.95 plus about $6.00 extra for wood, glue and dope, we can add capabilities as we add investment and knowledge. Each step will be safe for the airplane and will lead naturally into the next one.

The basic kit, called the **One Nite 28**, is made by Peck and available through Peck, SIG and your local hobby shop. Designated **Kit PP014** it costs $9.95 and includes clear plans and instructions, plenty of good strip wood, fairly hard sheets (OK for a beginner whose model needs some extra strength) containing ribs, formers and gussets, a 9-1/2 inch plastic prop, nose button, wheel, tissue, wire and 10 grams of good, Tan 2 rubber.

With some glue and dope you have enough to build the **Mark 1** right away, but, you may want to look over the list of additional materials to stock up for later modifications (mods).

Bill of Materials

Basic Kit and ROG Competition Rubber Model

- One Nite 28 Kit
- 2 sheets 1/16 medium 6pound balsa, 8-10 sticks hard 3/32 balsa
- 2 sheets 1/32 medium 6 pound balsa, 8-10 sticks hard 1/16 x 18 balsa
- 1 sheet 1/64 ply, 2 balsa wheels 1-1/4 diameter, 36" .045 wire
- 1 sheet 1/32 ply, 1/4 pound Tan 2 rubber 3/16 or 1/8" wide
- 1 Superior Free Wheel, Replaceable Blade Hub with Pitch Gage
- 1 set Superior 12-inch prop blades (get a 10-, 11- and 13-inch set also if you can afford them)
- 2-56 tap drill and tap set plus 1 dozen 2-56 x 3/4 Nylon screws Crocket hooks and a *good* winder
- Silly Putty or other good D.T. System
- .045 I.D. Alum. Tubing

Free Flight Electric Model

- 1 Hiline Mini 6, MG-1, VL HY42-35, or KP01 electric motor system with charge plug and switch
- 3 cell 50 mAh battery for above
- 3 cell 110 mAh battery for above for those <u>really</u> <u>long</u> flights
- 6-or 12-volt battery charger (see Electric chapter) Solder, soldering iron (10-watt) and hook-up wire

Micro RC Model

- Cox Fail Safe single channel system with motor and 4cell 110 mAh battery (This system has a BEC,Battery Eliminator Circuit that allows you to use the motor battery to power the radio too).

Alternate Systems

- CETO single channel <u>very light</u> RC system used with same HiLine, VLor MG motor as in FF electric. The CETO system works very well with CO_2 power using a Brown B100 or Gasparin motor.

Both of the above systems are <u>not</u> proportional. They simply swing the rudder to full position, then back. The Cox Fail Safe has the advantage of returning the rudder to neutral even if you hold the signal button down so it helps to avoid a dangerous spin that starts with a turn signal causing a steep bank that can't be recovered. Cox also offers instructions to modify its system to hold the rudder in right or left position. The Cox system is considerably heavier than the CETO. With the CETO system, the rudder is always left until you signal, then it swings right. For straight flight you have to "pulse" the rudder which takes a bit of practice.

If you have some experience with R/C, you might try the "Shredder" or one of the other super-light proportional systems with rudder and motor control. Remember, this is not intended as an acrobatic RC model but as a pair of training wheels to get you confident enough to fly an expensive radio system and give you lots of fun while doing it.

Construction

In order to later support the weight of a pylon, extra rubber or an electric system, we are going to make some mods to the structure before starting the basic kit. These mods are simple and you should clearly mark them on the plan before starting.

We'll enlarge the fuselage to inside dimensions of 1" wide x 1-1/4" high. This is a good dimension for almost any rubber model. You will find that most are very close to this size and making them all uniform will hardly be noticeable but will allow you to use a standard nose block for many models. (I wish I had thought of that 14 years ago when we started our One Design Contest. I now have 14 different nose blocks that vary by only small fractions from each other).

Tape the plan to your building board but don't cover it with Saran yet. Number the upright stations **1** through **11** starting at the nose and ending just in front of **F5**. Now, draw a line parallel to and 1-1/4 inches below the inside of the top longeron. Run the line from station 1 to 11. From that point, run the line to the inside of the original bottom longeron at the tail post. Cover the plan with Saran and pin a straight edge down to locate the top longeron. This straight line is very important because it locates and controls the angles of wing, stab and thrust alignment. **Fig 4-1** shows the front of the assembled fuselage.

Use four 3/32" spruce strips for your longerons. This will add lots of strength for a very small weight penalty. Lay down the top longeron against the straight edge first. Now cut 22 uprights 1-1/4" long from 3/32 balsa strip. The Chopper is a good tool for this or make your own jig **Fig 4-1A**. It's very important to have all these uprights exactly the same size or your fuselage may distort as the glue dries and shrinks. After you cut the uprights, adjust your fixture and cut 24 cross pieces, 1 inch long.

Glue uprights to the top longeron at stations 2-11 with a *double set* at station 4. Cut a special upright at station 1 and continue to cut and glue uprights from station 11 to the tail post to fit btween the top longeron and the top of your new, bottom longeron location. Now you can lay in the bottom longeron to fit *tightly* against all the uprights. Replace any uprights that aren't a perfect fit. This is no place to save time.

Fig 4-1

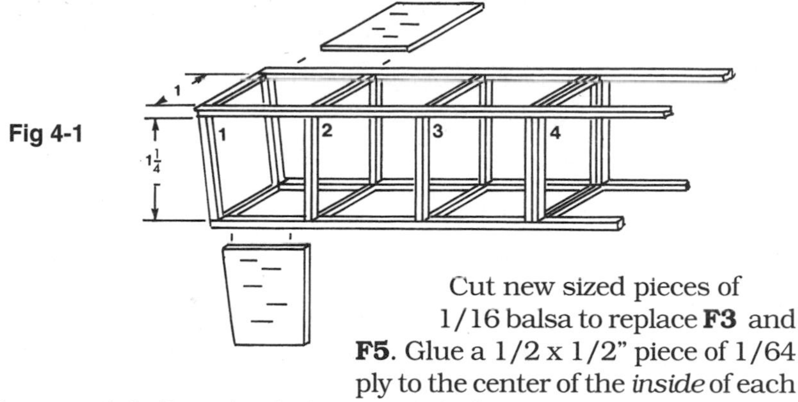

Cut new sized pieces of 1/16 balsa to replace **F3** and **F5**. Glue a 1/2 x 1/2" piece of 1/64 ply to the center of the *inside* of each of these and drill a 1/8" hole in each before assembling. Fit sheet balsa (grain longitudinal) between uprights 1-2, 3-4, 4-5, 5-6 and 8-9. These will strengthen your fuselage for later additions and will help with the inevitable crashes while flight trimming.

Once the first side is dry, remove the pins but leave it on your board. Lay another piece of Saran over it and replace the pins into the same holes. Remember you have just built the right side of your fuselage because the 1/16" sheet inserts are flush against the board which is the outside of the right side.

Fig 4-1A

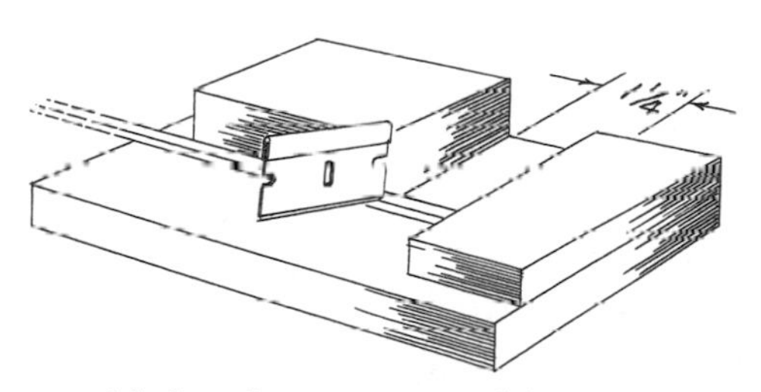

Proceed with the left side of the fuselage as above *except* place your 1/16 inserts so they will be flush against what will be the *outside* of the left side. All this right and left side is not terribly important to the structure or the flight but will give you a smoother, neater covering job.

From scrap balsa or pine cut a couple of blocks 1 x 1 inch by 3 inches long. These will serve as spacer blocks to keep the fuselage sides exactly 1 inch apart and parallel. When the sides are dry, remove the left (top) side and lay in the spacers between stations 1 and 11. Using a right triangle, *carefully* pin the left side of the fuselage *over* the spacers so it is *exactly* parallel to the right side at all stations **Fig. 4-2**. Use blocks of scrap to hold the sides in position. Glue in 24 cross pieces from stations 1-11 (place 2 cross pieces at station 4) and allow to dry thoroughly. Once dry, remove the spacer blocks and insert 1/16" sheet pieces from stations 1-6 and 8-9 as above.

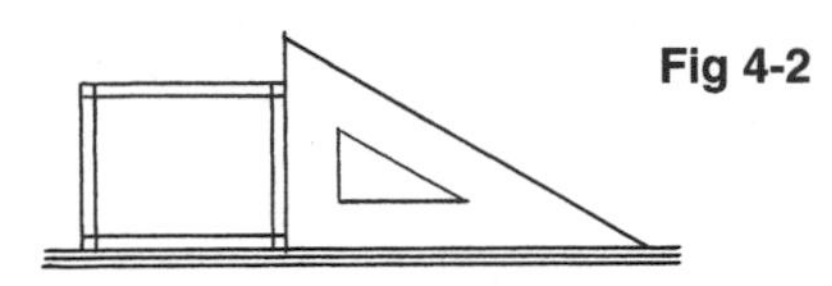

Fig 4-2

When the entire fuselage is dry, remove it from the board and insert small (3/16x 3/16) gussets in 20 places **Fig. 4-6** at stations **6**, **9** and **11**. You can only see 10 gussets in the figure. Also see **Fig 6-1**, chapter 6. These will create a rigid, rectangular block in the fuselage that will insure square locations of wing, stab and motors. Now you can cut a tapered balsa block to fit between the tailposts so they are separated by 1/8 inch **Fig 4-7**. The block should be 1/2 inch long and a good fit between the longerons at the rear. When you pull the sides together at the rear, make sure the taper is uniform and not twisted towards one side. When the tail block is dry, cut and glue crosspieces to fill all the other stations.

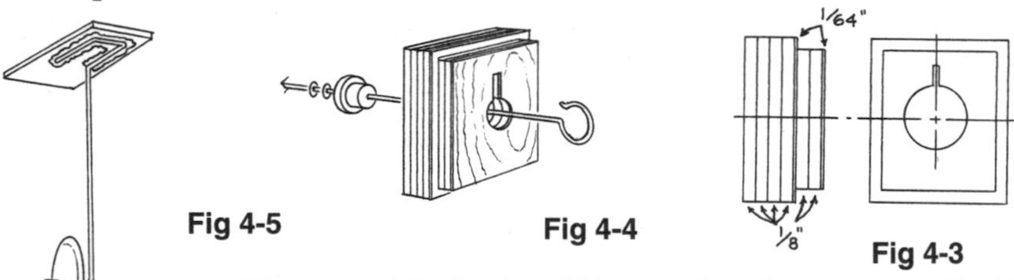

Fig 4-5 Fig 4-4 Fig 4-3

The nose block should be made of six pieces of 1/8" sheet (cross grained) and two pieces of 1/64" ply as in **Fig 4- 3**. Drill a 1/4 hole in the *exact* center for the nose bearing and file a key slot to facilitate prop changes **Fig 4-4**. Cut or laminate a piece of 1/4 x 1/4 x 1 inch hard balsa or spruce. Drill and tap for 2-56 screws, drop in some CyA glue and re-tap, **Fig. 4-8**. Glue this adjustment block inside the nose, to the 1/16" sheet top piece between crosspieces 1 and 2 and back 3/8" from the nose **Fig. 4-6**. This will become your infinitely adjustable thrust system.

Don't be put off by this new process of drilling and tapping. No special skill or tools are needed. A pin vise will hold the drill while you twist it through and the pin vise will also hold the tap while you run a couple of turns, back off one turn, then twist in a couple of more turns.

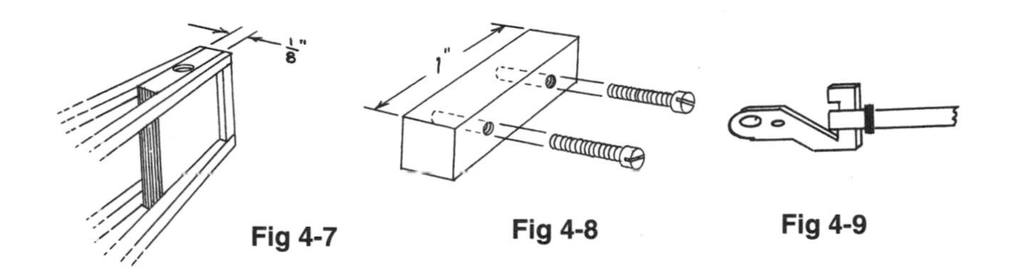

Fig 4-7 Fig 4-8 Fig 4-9

Make sure your nose block is a snug fit in the fuselage front. A Crocket Hook **Fig 4-9** will keep your rubber from climbing off the hook in flight. Shim the nose block with 1/64" ply if necessary. With the wire supplied, bend a single wheel landing gear **Fig. 4-5** and epoxy it to a 1x 2 x 1/16" piece of hard balsa so you can attach it with a rubber band and remove it when desired. The prop is assembled with the nose button and washers, with a hook small enough to pass through the key slot. Check all joints, sand with 220, then 400 grit and set aside for covering.

Stabilizer

The stab is built per plan except for doubling the center sticks with a 3/32" space between them to hold the fin and adding 1/16" sheet where shown **Fig 4-10**. This will help hold the DT wires. Epoxy .030 DT wires in place (**RPMA pg. 55-56**) Note that this type of DT wire acts as a hook for the front stab rubber band and also a locating stop to hold the stab at an angle of 40 degrees.

Fin and Rudder

Cut a new rudder from *light*, 4-5 pound, 3/32" thick balsa with the grain *vertical*. Cut off 3/4" of the rear for a movable rudder. Cut some lightening holes in the fin. Cut the fin with a 3/32" deep tab at the bottom to fit into the stab **Fig 4-11**. After covering both parts, skin some ordinary household electric hook-up wire and remove a few strands 3/4" long. SIG also sells thin copper wire for this. Insert the strands (evenly spaced) 3/8" into the fin and hold with CyA glue. Put a drop of epoxy on the exposed end and insert them into the rudder with a bit of *waxed* 1/64 inch ply as a spacer. When dry, remove the spacer. You now have an adjustable rudder that will hold position while you flight test. You can easily cut the wire flush and insert flexible hinges when you convert to R/C.

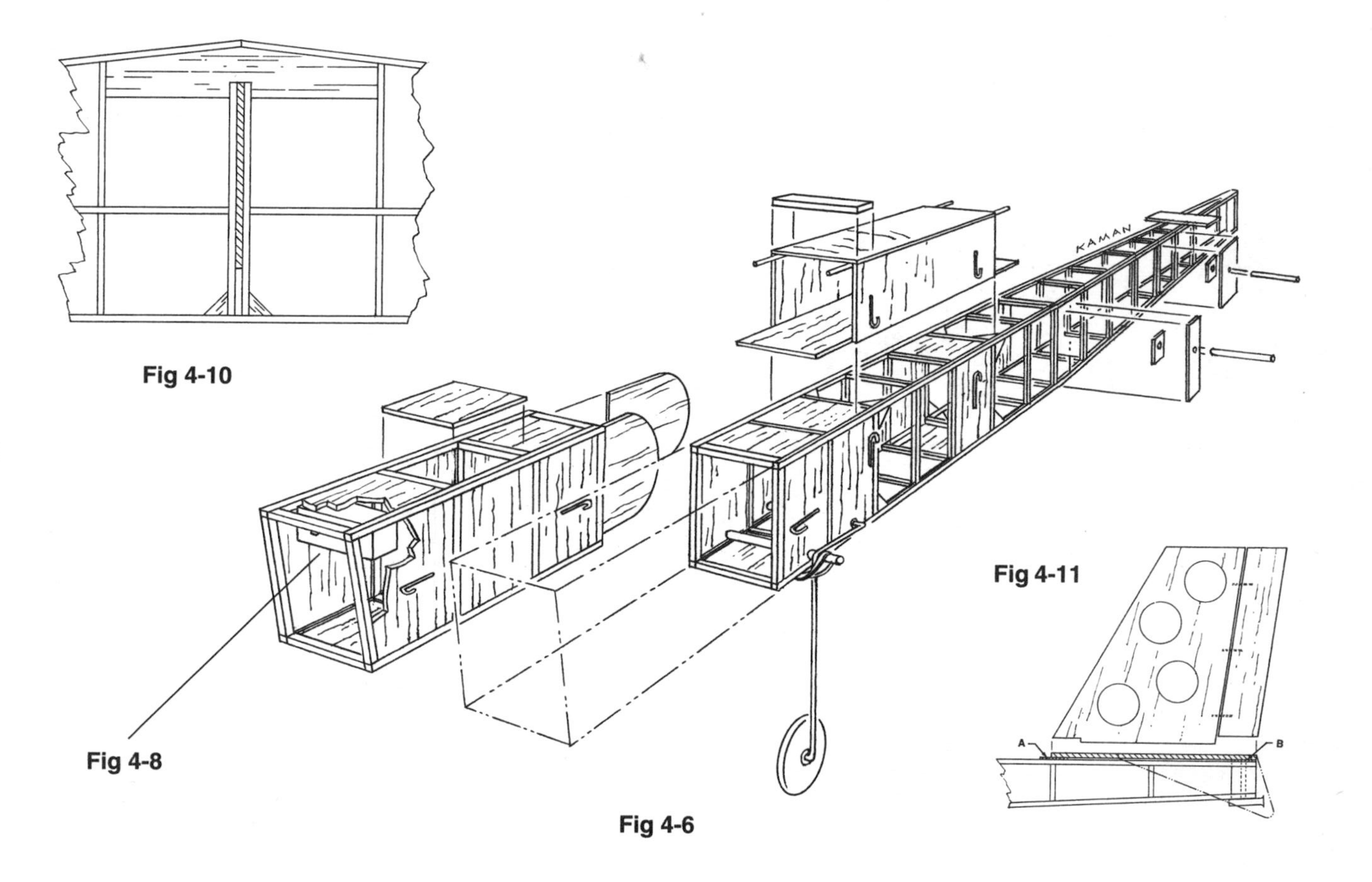
KAMAN
A
B
Fig 4-10
Fig 4-8
Fig 4-6
Fig 4-11

Wing

Just as we modified the fuselage to carry extra loads, we'll do the same for the wing. Some of these mods will be useful on almost any model you build in the future. They will add much strength with little weight penalty.

1. Very *carefully* cut out a W2 rib *exactly* on the line. Glue it to a piece of thick cardboard, 1/16" plywood, or hard, 1/8" balsa. Again, *carefully cut or saw* the outline. Alternatively, you can photocopy the rib, then glue the copy to ply or hard balsa. Don't worry if you spoil the first one. There are more on the printed sheet. Cut or saw the 3/32" sq. spar slots in top and bottom of your master rib at **A** in **Fig 4-12A**. If Balsa was used, harden the edge with CyA.

2. Use the master to cut and slot 14 W2 ribs from 7-8 lb. 1/16" balsa. This wing will not use any W1 ribs. Cut a few extra to allow for breakage. Select <u>two</u> W2 ribs for the center instead of the single rib shown. Cut an extra bottom spar notch 3/32" wide and 3/16" high in these two ribs, behind the regular spar notch at **B** in **Fig. 4-12**.

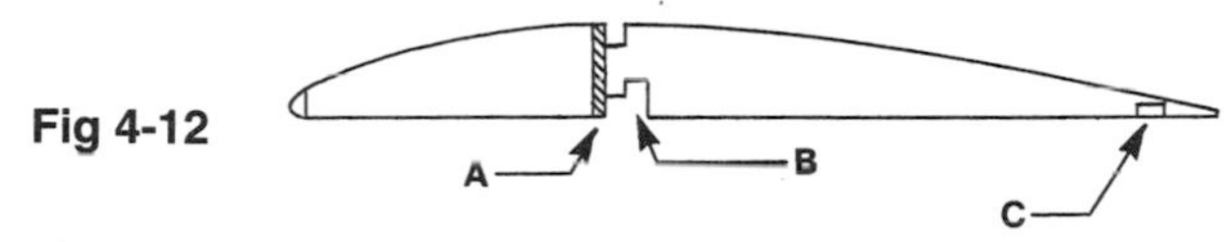

Fig 4-12

3. Cut and notch all other ribs **(W3-W6)** from the printed sheet. Use 3/32" spruce for leading edge and bottom spar. Top spar and trailing edge can be medium Balsa.

4. Before pinning down the wing plan, slip two 3/32x1x3" shims under the corner of the T.E. at both tips **(RPMA pg. 49-50)**. This provides "washout" at the tips (wing tips higher at the TE than the LE). Washout is very important in flight trimming and should appear on almost any model you build <u>including</u> RC. Washout causes the wing tip to fly at a lower angle of attack than the center of the wing. Thus, as the angle of climb increases, the center of the wing (flying at a few degrees <u>higher</u> angle) stalls <u>before</u> the tip preventing the model from falling off on one wing into a spin. Now pin down the plan and cover with Saran.

Many modelers prefer to taper the T. E. and round the L. E. after assembly. Sanding while attached to the structure may give a smoother finish. Some prefer to do this before the strips are assembled. You will have to find your favorite way. The T E *does not* have to be tapered to a knife edge. A thickness of 1/32" to 1/16" will be almost as aerodynamically efficient and will be a lot stronger. The L E should have an entering radius of around 1/32 inch.

A good sanding job will help here. Tony Peters rounds the edge of a sheet, then strips it off as a leading edge **Fig 4-13**.

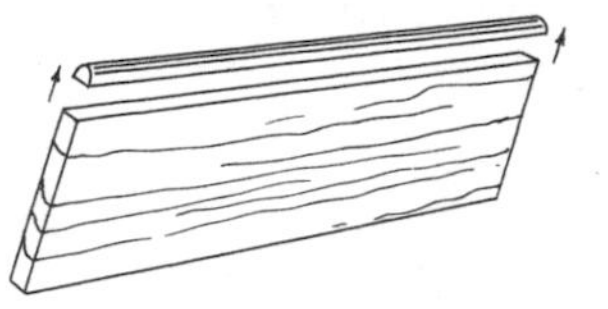

Fig 4-13

5. Make the bottom spar from 3/32" square spruce. Use a straight edge to pin it to the plan. *Perfect* alignment here will make flight trimming a lot easier. Test fit all ribs by placing them over the bottom spar and checking L E and T E fit. Replace any that are short. Trying to fill a gap with glue not only makes a weak joint, it leads to warps. Glue shrinks as it dries and imparts strains to any structure that has gaps. When all the ribs fit well, glue to the bottom spar and L.E. *Remember* that the tip ribs (**W6**) will be lifted 3/32" at their rear point by your shims. Also, slant the *tops* of these W6 ribs 15 degrees towards the outside of the wing. When gluing in the specially notched W2 ribs at the center, do not glue them together. You will be separating these ribs to insert an extra wing panel later on. Now, glue in the T.E., allowing for the slight washout twist at the rear corner.

6. After the assembly is dry, cut short strips from 1/16 X 1/8" light scrap and glue in between all ribs at the T.E. This will lock the ribs at their thin, weak end and stiffen the whole wing **Figs 4-14** and **4-12C**. On future models where the T.E. is 3/8 - 1/2" wide, you can simply extend the ribs and notch the TE.

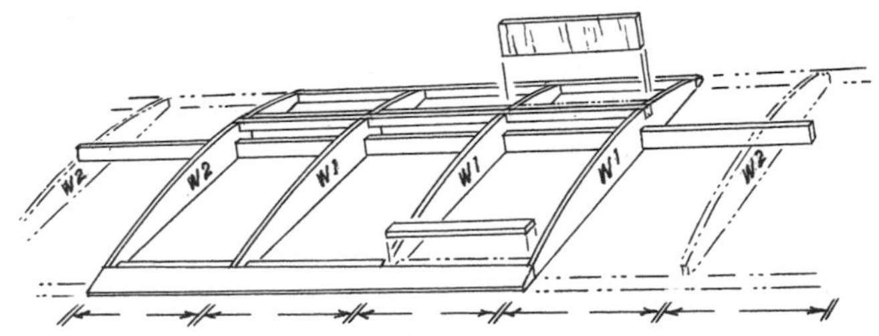

Fig 4-14

7. When the wing is dry, lightly sand to smooth the transition from rib to L E and T E. Cut the L E and T E at the dihedral joint and sand in the proper dihedral angle. Set up two dihedral blocks 2-1/2 inches high, with a 3/32 shim added to the rear of each to maintain washout (**RPMA pg. 50**). You may want to add an extra rib at each dihedral joint for strength. Glue in the dihedral and allow to dry overnight.

8. When the wing is completely dry, add gussets at the corners and the dihedral breaks. At this point, I also cover the dihedral joints and tip corners with a strip of Tyvek ®, or nylon, with glue worked into the weave. This adds strength to a high stress area.

9. Cut the top spar from hard balsa and assemble.

10. Now we add a mod that you will find useful on many future models. It's called a "shear web" and is built between the top and bottom spars from the center out to the **W4** rib. Cut medium 1/16 and 1/32 and glue to the front of the spars. Grain on the shear webs must be **vertical** !! **Fig 4-14**. This provides resistance to bending under load. Use 1/16 webs out to the dihedral breaks and 1/32" from there. This also shows as "**A**" in **Fig 4-12**.

Bend and epoxy DT stop wire to the stab **(RPMA pg 55-56)**, Add a 1/4" high piece of scrap 1/16" to each side of the fuselage between uprights 5 and 6 to hold a piece of .045 ID tubing across the bottom. Sand the entire structure with 220, then 400 grit, dope and cover with your favorite system from the **COVERING** chapter. It may be interesting and instructive to try Litespan on the fuselage,mylar & tissue or airspan on the wing and tissue on the tail.

When covering is complete, assemble the rudder and stab, glue on the stab tip rudders, add wire hooks to the top of the wing at the center and two hooks to the fuselage sides for the nose block retaining rubber band. File a horizontal slot in the front of the nose block for the retaining rubber and add the 1/2 x 1-1/2 x 1/32" ply stab platform **Fig 4-11 (A)**. Make sure to compensate for the added 1/32" height at this point by shimming the rear of the fuselage with balsa **Fig 4 -11 (B)**, to match. Otherwise you will start with positive stab incidence which can lead to disaster. You can also add the wing tiplets **Fig 4-15** with tops slanted 15 degrees to the outside. These will reduce the bank in turns and increase the glide.

Fig 4-15

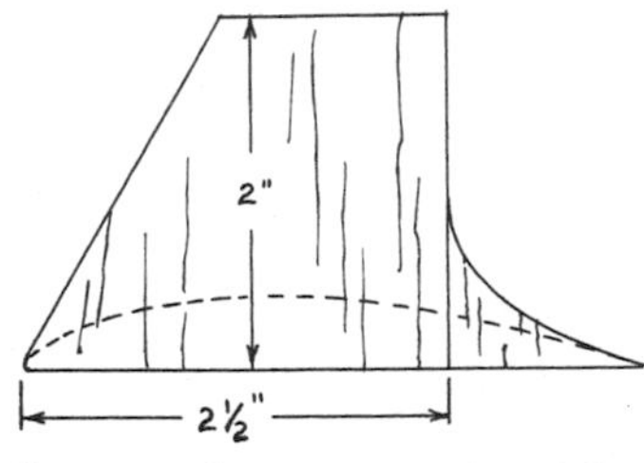

This is the time to check all surfaces for warps. Steam out mild warps by bending the opposite way while in the steam stream. For big warps, pour boiling water right over the area. Don't worry, the water will sink right through the covering and wet the wood. Then, pin the part in a jig and allow to dry overnight. The tissue will shrink right back.

Drill and tap the tail block for a 2-56 screw and add a DT snuffer tube extending out 1/4 inch to the rear. Epoxy a 1-inch piece of .032 wire to the bottom rear of the fuselage as a DT wire **Fig 4-16**. Insert the 1/8" alum. rear rubber tube in **F5** and insert a rubber motor made up of four strands of 3/16" rubber about 15-16 inches long. Note that **Fig 4-6** shows two alternate locations for the rear rubber peg. Start your flight tests with the shorter rubber motor. Hook up the prop, wind the motor just enough to remove the slack. Pin the prop in place and balance the model at the front spar by moving the wing back and forth. Don't move the wing L.E. more than **6-3/4** inches from the nose. If more distance is needed, add weight to the nose. Don't ever be afraid of added nose weight. It's a lot better to have a slightly heavier model than to have a badly balanced one. You might also want to balance the plastic prop by scraping the heavy blade.

Once the model is balanced, add your 1/8" square incidence block under the L.E. as shown on the plan. Unpin the prop, crank in 100 turns or so and proceed with basic flight trimming.

Mark I Flight Trim

When fully trimmed, the model should climb fairly steeply in a right circle about 60 feet in diameter, then level off to cruise and finally, transition to a flat right circle glide. Since all the factors that control flight pattern are interactive, you must work with the whole group together like the notes in a chord. For instance, right rudder will cause a right turn and will also lower the nose during climb because the bank that goes along with the turn reduces lift. The same nice, gentle right rudder turn in glide can become a deadly descending spiral under power because the rudder is much more effective at higher speeds.

The above is not as scary or complicated as it sounds. It's merely a warning to consider each trim option as only one instrument in a whole orchestra. I don't prefer "cook book" trim instructions like, "If the model climbs too steeply, add down thrust". That will certainly work for the climb but maybe the wing is set at too high an angle of incidence or the stab at too much negative. Either of those will also result in a stalling climb as will too rearward a c.g. and these latter will also show up in a glide.

Before starting your trim procedure, wind the motor to 100 turns or so, then allow the prop to wind down while holding the model in your hand. Watch for vibration from a bent prop shaft, a loose nose block or an unbalanced prop. Check all the parts held on by rubber bands to see if anything shakes loose or even wobbles. Now take a close look at the DT wire on the stab. Is the rubber band causing the rear of the stab to bend down? This will cause a steep dive under power and the problem will disappear when the DT rubber burns through. That's the kind of check-up your model needs before you can trust even the simplest flight trim

All FF trim, like Gaul, is divided in three parts- climb, cruise and glide. It is in the transition from one to the other that trouble can start. That's why I prefer to trim using just a bit of power instead of a hand glide. With 100 turns or so, hand launch your model from shoulder height aimed at a point on the ground about 50 feet away. The model should glide gently towards that spot with a slight right turn. Don't worry about the turn at this point. Just look for a smooth descending pattern. If the model dives steeply, recheck balance. If that's OK, add some more negative incidence to the stab by advancing the tail post screw. Don't use more than the 1/8" square wing incidence block and 1/8" negative in the stab. If you still have a dive, start moving the wing forward 1/8" at a time but don't move the c.g. more than 1/4". to the rear of the main wing spar. By this time, unless you have built your model with steel beams you should be getting a decent powered glide. If you still have a steep descent, add some more turns to see if a bit more power can help. If the model stalls, reduce the stab negative incidence and move the c.g. forward.

Do not increase down thrust at this point. You have enough built in to the fuselage nose to handle low to moderate power. Now is the time to insert and light your DT fuse. (It's entirely possible to lose a model in a thermal that starts 6 feet off the ground).

Once a decent descent is established, wind in 200 turns and start to create the right turn. Bend the rudder to the right a bit at a time with a maximum deflection of 3/16". If, as you add power, the model flies straight or turns left, it is trying to tell you a new player has entered the game. This guy is called **torque** and is a really nasty fellow who will take over control as you add power. Just when you think you are ready for a full power climb, he will create a suicide dive to the left, usually over the nearest piece of concrete. Torque is an invisible *reaction* force that causes the model to twist to the left as the prop turns to the right. The more prop power, the more reactive torque. Of course you can reduce torque by reducing power but we want to use all the energy we have in the rubber, so this won't help. The most common way to reduce torque effect is to add some **Right Thrust** at the nose block. Just advance your nose block adjusting screw 1/2 turn at a time as you increase to 250-300 turns. Try to establish a right turning climb as described above. Obviously, some combination of rudder displacement and right thrust is needed to get you a smooth right turn in *both* climb and cruise. With high powered contest models, the inboard section of the left wing is often twisted downward at the rear as if it were an aileron. This has the effect of adding lift at that area thus counteracting torque and helping to create a right turn glide. See how much fun this stuff can be?

If rudder deflection and right thrust of 3/32" still doesn't help, you may have to add a tab to the inboard section of the left wing at the dihedral break. A quick field tab can be made from Scotch tape doubled over a couple of short pieces of ultra fine bell wire and stuck on the TE **Fig 4-16 A**. Don't deflect the tab more than 3/16 inch or it will create more drag than lift and will double your trouble. If the model turns too steeply to the right under high power, reduce right thrust. Sometimes a tab under the right inboard wing panel is necessary to turn a right descending spiral into a right climb.

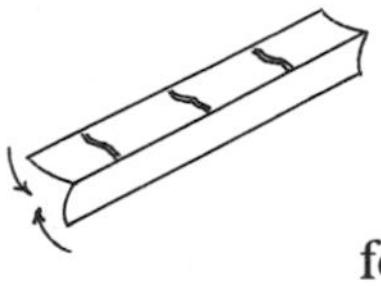

Fig 4-16A

Assuming all the above works to some degree, your model should climb to 100-150 feet on 400-450 turns and, hopefully transition to a relatively flat glide. Here's where the fine tuning comes in. Since the glide time should be about twice the climb time, you may have to back off or advance on some of the power adjustments to get a good glide. Make only *very* small changes at this point.

An interesting glide adjustment discussed in (**RPMA pg 112**) is **Stabilizer Tilt.** This is a flying surface adjustment that is effective only in the glide. Tilting the stab up on the right side will swing the tail of the plane to the left and create a right turn with very little bank. In other words, the plane will always turn towards the *high side* of the stab tilt. This is a very useful adjustment for outdoor models and carries little danger. A 1/16" to 3/32" shim under the right side of the stab platform will do the job nicely.

Now you can test your batch of rubber, establish a constant, (see **Rubber** chapter) calculate the maximum turns, light your DT fuse, face into the wind and get ready to chase.

Once you have your model flying well, start experimenting with *small* changes in trim adjustment while timing the flights on a calm morning or evening. The stop watch is your final tool for evaluating trim changes. While a skyrocket, steep climb may look very exciting, your model may get quite a bit higher and fly longer with a shallower climb where the wing is doing the work instead of the prop.

Now you are ready for a full, 10-gram motor. Four strands of 3/16" rubber, or six strands of 1/8 about 20-21" long will do for a start. Move the rear peg to the **F3** position, braid the motor, (**RPMA pg 92**), to reduce slack and work up from 500 to 800 or 850 turns for a 2 minute flight you will never forget.

Another interesting experiment is to balance right thrust and left turn stab tilt (raise the left side of the stab) to create a right - left pattern where the model climbs right then glides left. This sometimes creates a smoother transition from cruise to glide but usually requires a larger field. You might save this for Mark II.

Mark II Competition Model

Here's where we add some small changes to allow your model to handle a larger prop and more rubber. These mods are simple and won't permanently change your model so you can always return to Mark I for small fields.

The major change is the addition of a **Pylon** that will help to handle a higher power burst and a steeper climb. The entire pylon is made of 1/16" hard balsa with a couple of bamboo skewers to hold the rubber bands and four, .030" wire hooks for mounting **Fig 4-6**. The pylon is 1inch high (outside dimension), exactly as wide as the fuselage and its length matches the wing chord. The bottom plank should extend 3/4 inch front and rear for more stability. The 1/8 wing incidence block should be fastened on top of the pylon. Make sure grain is as shown **Fig 4-6** for best strength. Mount with rubber bands under the fuselage.

The prop should be a **Superior** 12-inch diameter free wheeler mounted on the **Superior** Free Wheel Hub. I recommend this combination because the hub contains a fail safe free wheel latch as well as set screws that allow for blade replacement or pitch change. Order the 3/64" shaft size for this model. This is very important as a learning tool as well as a quick repair device (chapter 15 Propellers). Order a Pitch Gage along with the hub and blades and you can test and change prop pitch <u>in the field</u>. Start with 15inch pitch

If you can afford it, now is the time to begin to collect a whole set of **Superior** Prop Blades from 10 inches to 16 inches in diameter. For this model, you may want to test 11, 12 and 13 inch diameters to compare performance. The prop blades come ready to sand and a few *careful* minutes with a sanding block will give you a nice airfoil shape. I like to cover my prop blades with silk for strength and appearance. A detailed description of silk covering on props is in Chapter 5, **"Covering Techniques"**

The downthrust built into the nose should be OK for this mod. If, while flight trimming, you want to *reduce* the down thrust, simply glue in a piece of hard 1/16" to the bottom of the nose. Once you have the right nose angle, fair in the thrust adjustment block to make a neat assembly.

This model is fully capable of exciting ROG takeoffs with a better landing gear configuration. Bend two separate pieces of 3/64 (.045) music wire **Fig 4-17A**. Slip a piece of dowel 1-1/2 " long through the fuselage along the bottom between formers 4 and 5. Slip the end of the wire through the alum. tubing (already installed in the original assembly), and over the dowel and hold with a rubber band. One and one quarter or 1-inch balsa wheels will work just fine. You can make the LG in one continuous piece as shown, **(Fig 4-17 B)**. The two piece gear allows for easier replacement and transportation and will be helpful on larger models as you progress.

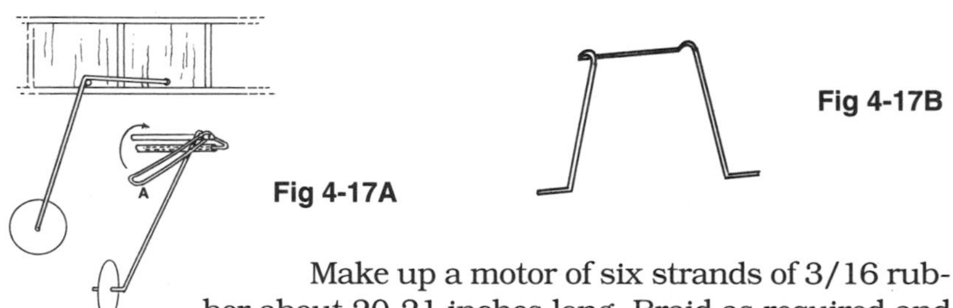

Fig 4-17A

Fig 4-17B

Make up a motor of six strands of 3/16 rubber about 20-21 inches long. Braid as required and begin flight testing as before. To balance under the main wing spar, you will probably have to move the wing (on the pylon) forward from the Mod I site due to the extra weight of the larger prop, hub and LG. You will still need a wing incidence block but you may be able to reduce it from 1/8 to 3/32 during fine-tuning. All the instructions from Mod I are still applicable but, remember, you are dealing with at least 50% more power and a larger, more fragile prop. "Old Man Torque" can get really vicious now. Increase winds slowly, (50 at a time) until you have a really stable pattern. Correct the slightest stall tendency with more downthrust, added right turn, or a more forward c.g.. **Make only one adjustment at a time**.

If you haven't started one yet, now is the time for a flight adjustment log. Open a notebook page for each model and record weight of components, prop pitch and diameter, rubber size, turns, flight trim adjustments and results. Also note the general wind conditions. This may sound like a nit picking enterprise but just wait until you get to the field and can't remember where the wing sits or which incidence block you used. Also, this type of exercise will be immeasurable help in learning the *art* of flight trimming and figuring out which interconnected adjustment to try next.

Once you have established a stable climb, cruise and glide, it's time to play with your power train. The total available power from any source, including rubber, can be calculated and theoretically predict the climb altitude available from that source. This is arcane stuff and not needed here to make the point that the important factor is **the efficiency with which your model converts the power to thrust**. This depends on the friction in the system and the <u>most efficient prop diameter, pitch and blade shape for each specific model</u>. You can actually test for this efficiency with a calm morning, a counter on your winder or, even better, a Torque Meter and a stop watch.

Work with 80% of Maximum Torque or Winds, set the model up for best climb attitude and try 13- 14- 15 and 16-inch pitch on the 12-inch diameter prop. Time each flight and watch for a significant difference in climb with a particular pitch. Some models, (like my Jabberwock) will show an immediate change that's easy to spot. With others there may be very little difference. Now try the same experiment with smaller and larger props. Stop when you have a pretty good idea of the top of the curve. Now go to an 8-strand (20-gram) motor and watch for improvements. You may find, for instance , that the heavier motor requires a lower pitch prop. My Sparky flies best on 25 grams of rubber while the glide suffers at 30 grams with no improvement in the climb.

Even if you just fly for fun, the type of experiment described here will at least let you know if the model you spent so much time and care building is performing somewhere near its best level. Also, this type of training is invaluable for fine tuning *any* model including R/C. To really improve performance, once you have decided on best prop diameter and pitch, buy a **Superior** "Z"- Bar folding prop. Put a stop screw on the rear of your nose block and watch the glide improve when the prop folds. Remember, you may have to adjust c.g. again with this new mod.

As I said in the beginning, all trim adjustments are interacting. Thus you may find a better climb with a 12 x 13" prop with thec.g. at the wing spar but the glide may improve with the CG 1/4 inch to the rear which now requires a higher prop pitch. Since this model is so adjustable and so rugged, you can get a lot of these experiments out of your system with a minimum of crashes and frustration. There is no "Uniform Flight Trim Code" or set of standards. Each airplane requires a unique set of flight trim adjustments for optimum performance of that particular airplane. Certainly, there's a general procedure that will work most of the time. You can remember it by a piece of my "verse" or make up your own. It goes like this:

Why Be In Far Germany To Trap Some Whales

Warps, Balance, Incidence (Wing & Stab), Flat Glide, Thrust, Turn, Stop Watch

(More about this in the **Flight Trim** Chapter)

My point is that the *order* in which you make adjustments is quite important and the final adjustments can only be made by monitoring the flight with a stop watch. You may be surprised to find that a skyrocket, steep climb doesn't necessarily result in the longest flight or even the highest altitude.

Electric Free Flight

This is a particularly easy model to convert from rubber to electric power. Only a slight shortening of the nose is required. Pylon, wing, landing gear and tail feathers remain intact. Just cut off the first **four** inches of the nose at **Station 4** where you have already doubled the uprights and cross pieces. You can even make the change reversible by gluing two hard 1/16" cheek pieces inside the removable nose and a set of hooks to the outside of nose and fuselage to hold rubber bands **Fig 4-6.**

In the **Electric** chapter, I describe a "Power Module" that can be inserted and removed from any conversion model. This is a good way to electrify the One Nite 28. Just cut a 1/8" hard balsa nose block that fits inside the nose (1 x 1-1/4) and a "face" piece (1-3/16 x 1-7/16"). Glue these together and drill through both for the two 2-56 holding screws that attach to the motor front plate **Fig 3-31**. Remember to drill a 1/4" hole through both blocks for the charging jack. Now you can insert the Power Module, hold it in with the side hooks and a rubber band and attach the rear hook to the **F5** rear rubber peg with a small rubber band. You can still make thrust adjustments by shimming the motor front plate.

If you want to mount a motor directly into the One Nite 28, refer to the electric chapter for several mounting methods. Don't try to mount the motor on the c.g. with a remote drive on this model. You will just complicate the trimming procedure.

Start with a 3 x 50 mAh battery moved along the mounting strip to balance the model at the wing spar as before. The L E of the wing should be about 3 inches from the nose. I used a HiLine Mini - 6 motor on my model but a VL HY-70 or KP01 will do as well. I prefer the geared motors with a larger prop to the direct drives for this type of model. The MG-1 is a bit too heavy and powerful for this job. The Scientext direct drive motors are lighter but rev higher with a smaller prop. Although there are very few choices in props for these small electric motors, you still need to test a bit to find the best prop for your particular model. Dick Miller's "**What Works**" chart in the electric chapter will help.

Flight trim for electric is a bit easier than for rubber. There's almost no initial burst of power to contend with and the climb angle can be quite a bit lower with a more steady rpm for most of the run. With a motor run of a minute or more you can get plenty of altitude with a shallow climb. The electric motor produces a lot less torque than rubber so the left spiral problem is greatly reduced. The concentration of weight in motor and battery also helps a bit, compared with the sometimes changeable in- flight problem of bunched-up rubber at front or rear.

Start with a 30-second charge and proceed with flight trim as discussed before. Gradually increase charge to 3 minutes at 1 amp for a 3 x 50 mAh battery. If the model turns left, add a bit (1/32 - 1/16") of right thrust. I think you will find trimming simpler and flights more uniform but perhaps a bit less exciting than those "leap-off the-ground" rubber flights. Once you are confident of a stable flight pattern and have found a large enough field, test a 3 x 110 mah battery. This can give you a motor run of two minutes with a full charge so make sure you have a DT, ID and a calm morning. With even a 5 mph breeze, a model can travel almost 900 feet in a 2-minute flight !! With a decent glide you can easily make 1/4 mile.

This is also a good time to test some small trim changes which will help you when you switch to RC. Move the c.g. 1/4" to the front or rear. Compensate by increasing or decreasing wing or stab incidence (the difference between wing & stab incidence is called **Decalage**). Open the turn to 100 feet. Observe all these changes and note their effects in your log. Some day you may win a 2-meter glider contest just because you "tweaked" your model for a windy day.

Micro RC

This is the one you have been waiting for. If this conversion works out well, you can take another look at all those old rubber and gas models, even the left over parts from previous crashes. You know you never threw out the pieces. Micro R/C has come so far in the last 2 years and development is continuing at a fever pitch. There are already several choices for RC systems that will fly a model of 100 - 150 square inches of wing area. For this exercise, I chose two of the most easily available and usable. My purpose is to illustrate a general category and teach you to use it with facility rather than to develop a top performing model.

To convert your electric FF model to micro R/C you need a new pylon, a motor mount , a simple change in the rudder and a whole new wing section. Since the R/C system will *double* the weight of the model, you need to add some wing area to handle that. Build a new pylon **Fig 4-18**.

Using the **Cox Fail Safe** unit as a guide, cut appropriate openings in the side for the switch panel on the Fail Safe unit, or the switch and battery charge receptacle on the CETO. Leave the front and rear open. In both cases, the servo mounts separately behind the pylon. The easiest way to hold the servo is to insert a piece of 1/16 sheet between top cross pieces **10** and **11**, cut a slot to fit the servo and glue it right in. The connecting wire from the receiver will still allow you to move the wing a bit. The servo must be solidly mounted because a hard landing that can cause it to shift even 1/8 inch can deflect the pushrod and move the rudder.

Mount the motor on a piece of 1/16 ply which is glued to a piece of 1/8" balsa 1 X 1-1/4" to fit inside the nose. Just hold the motor with a rubber band through the side hooks and plug it into the Rx with the wires right outside on top of the fuselage. The 4 cell 110 mAh battery can be unplugged to charge and fitted right inside the front of the pylon and held with a rubber band or a bit of tape.

This is a good time to go over every glue joint and flying surface platform. If you have been flying the model for a while under rubber or electric power, there is sure to be some loosening and softening of the structure. Cut away tissue from suspicious spots and reglue joints. Add gussets where you feel weakness. Check carefully for warps and steam or soak them out.

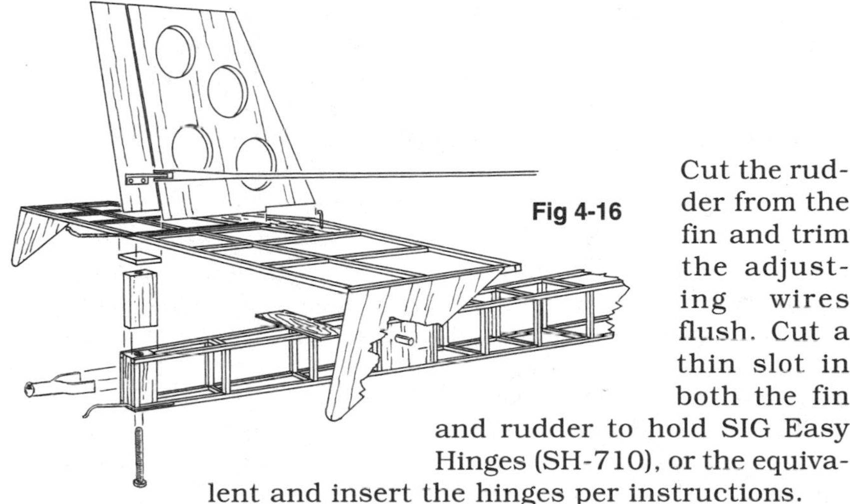

Fig 4-16

Cut the rudder from the fin and trim the adjusting wires flush. Cut a thin slot in both the fin and rudder to hold SIG Easy Hinges (SH-710), or the equivalent and insert the hinges per instructions.

You will also need a snap connector (clevis) with2-56 threaded rod (Sig GD-331) and a small control horn (SIG SH-220). For the servo, I prefer a swivel connector that allows for rod length adjustment rather than a clevis or a "Z"- bend. You will want to adjust the push rod length for smooth motion once you set the final location of the wing and servo. GD-360 by Goldberg and DU-121 by Dubro are fine. **Figs 4-16, 4-18**. The control horn can be on the right or left of the rudder. Just make <u>sure</u> that your servo and Tx are set up so a <u>right</u> turn signal moves the rudder to the <u>right</u> side. Switch the control horn to the side that works best.

Fig 4-18

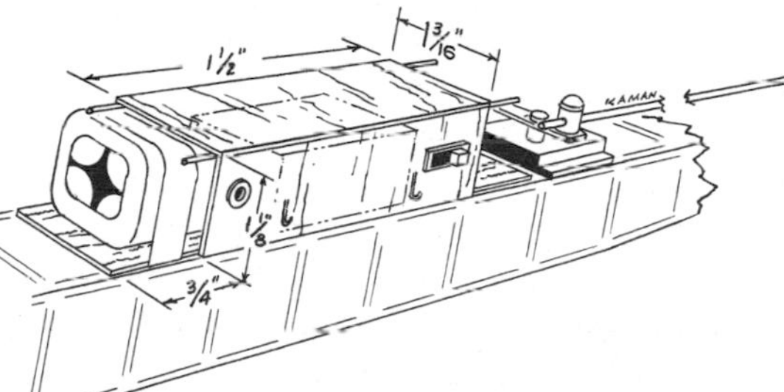

Get out your wing plan and those extra W2 ribs you cut. Cut an extra main (lower) spar slot 1/32 wide x 3/16" high <u>behind</u> the regular slot. Laminate 2 pieces of <u>hard</u> 3/32 square strip x 8-3/4 inches long to make one spar, 3/32 x 3/16 x 8-3/4". Pin this spar to the plan so it covers all three W1's, the W2 just to the left and extends slightly over the W2's on right and left **Fig 4-14**. Pin down a 3/32" square spar in front of the laminated spar and pin your four special W2 ribs at the three locations shown for W1 and the left W2. Assemble the L E, T E, and top spar, and add the 1/16 shear web with grain vertical between the 3/32 spars. Trim all spars **except the laminated 3/32 x 3/16" spar** flush to the outside of the last rib.

You have now constructed a very rigid but light wing insert that can be assembled to your wing with little effort and perfect alignment. Take your original wing and carefully separate it into two parts where you have built in the extra center rib. Remove the covering from only the rear portion of the bottom between the last two ribs, the bottom spar and the T E. Clean out the extra 3/32 x 3/16 spar slot you cut and slide the special spar in until it touches the second rib. Slide it out and sand or razor trim until the spar just touches the second rib while the side ribs of your new section mate nicely with the two end ribs (the ones that used to be in the center). When a good fit is achieved, set up a new jig to hold the wing in dihedral and washout position and glue all three parts together **(Fig- 4-19)**. Cover as required, shrink and dope, then put right back in the holding fixture. You may want to double cover the top center section where the now heavier rubber bands will chafe.

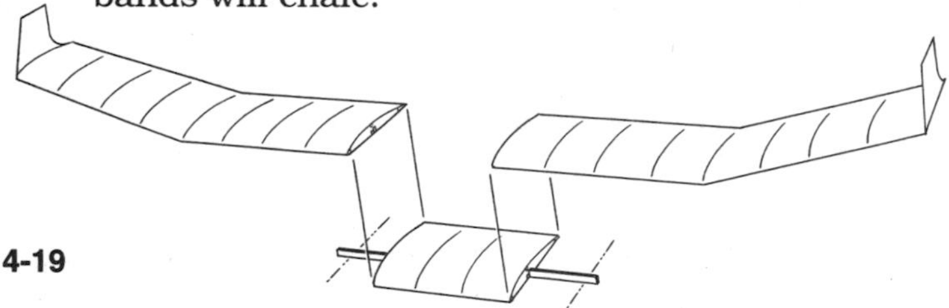

Fig 4-19

Your model with R/C system is now twice as heavy as before, will fly twice as fast and will crash four times as hard ! From here on in, slow, careful and "over long grass" are the watchwords.

The most common crash of beginner's R/C airplanes, particularly those without aileron or motor control, starts with a large rudder deflection which quickly becomes a steep bank from which the model cannot recover. Sometimes the pilot may turn the plane too close to the ground which can actually "leap-up" and smash against the airplane (I have seen this phenomenon attack my own airplanes). To help avoid this problem, set rudder control for the smallest possible deflection.

The center of the rudder horn should be mounted 1/2 inch rear-ward from the hinge. The clevis should be in the outermost hole of the horn. You may have to open the servo horn hole to accommodate the pin of the swivel connector. Test the whole system carefully in your shop before even going to the field. You are now in the area of machine magic where the slightest mistake or loss of focus will be seized upon by "Murphy's Law" and expanded into a disaster at "twice-the-speed-of-light." A loose clevis, a frayed wire, a poor glue joint, even two parts allowed to rub together when moving - any one of these is a big enough opening to let the "Gremlins" in.

Have someone hold the model while you run the motor and exercise the controls. Gently shake the whole model while moving everything you can. Try the trim knob to make sure the rudder is centered with the knob. Now do it all over again with the model held upside down.

The idea of these exercises is to get your model "4 or 5 mis-takes high" before youstart turning. At the field, find a some tall grass and run some hand launch tests without power. Make sure the wind is no more than 5 mph and launch (into the wind) with enough power to glide smoothly about 30 feet straight ahead. Make several glides with the model balanced. I needed the whole 1/8 wing incidence block for mine. Keep working the glide and mak-ing small adjustments in wing location and incidence until you are satisfied the model will descend fairly safely.

You have no control over power level or duration except to limit the charge. Start with a 1-minute charge at 1 amp and go for a straight ahead launch with no turn signal until the model is at least 50 feet high. If the climb out is satisfactory, crank in a bit of right trim using the trim knob. Be alert because the model may bank with the first hint of turn. If you have decided to use winglets, they will help flatten the bank. As soon as you sense a turn, return the trim knob to neutral. Notice that the nose tends to drop as soon as the model begins to bank. .

Walk along with the model at this point instead of trying to bring it back to you. Try some simple "S" turns using the trim knob and, if these are successful, hit the right button and watch the reaction. Turning with the Fail Safe system takes a bit of practice. To main-tain a turn, you have to "pulse" the button to make it return to the deflected position. Too fast a pulse and nothing will happen. Some-thing like 1 pulse every 2 seconds will do fine. If you see the model starting a bank, hit the opposite button immediately.

Once the motor stops, establish a very gentle right turn with the trim knob and allow the model to glide to a landing. Don't attempt to steer it home. It is still as heavy as it was when the motor was running but now has no help from thrust, the crash can happen even faster and with just as much damage. After a few trim flights, increase the charge and try for a thermal. Remember, this model is not designed to turn close to the ground.

With the CETO unit you have a much lighter model that will fly slower and land lighter. The unit is always set in a left turn and will hold a right deflection as long as you hold down the button. Again, you can set for the smallest rudder deflection by mounting the push rod 1/2 inch out from the rudder surface. Make sure the basic left turn is very shallow and start with a 1 minute charge as above. For more information on CETO mods, write to John Worth for his newsletter.

For those who are still die hard rubber fans, the pylon contained CETO unit is your chance for **rubber powered R/C**. Just put the 3-inch nose piece back on the fuselage, use a 12 inch prop with 15-20 grams (6-8 strands of 3/16) of rubber and steer it with the CETO unit. The extra 12 grams of R/C weight will reduce the glide a bit but you will still have thermalling ability with the larger wing.

Other R/C systems should be treated with the same respect as described above. Even if you install a 4-channel Rx, you should start with rudder and motor control only. I hope this chapter helps to get you started on simple, pleasant RC flying which will be a lot easier on your old ankles and knees.

John Worth publishes the very best newsletter on Micro R/C. He also sells some special products like the CETO system and tiny, light actuators, switches and motors. See the **Kits and Suppliers** for the **Cloud 9 RC Newsletter**.

If you want to graduate from smaller, simpler electric R/C models, the SR Batteries X440 is the finest example I have seen of a medium-sized, great performing electric sailplane. I think it is the first true link between Free Flight and R/C. At only 64.5 inch span and 22 ounce weight you are flying at a very efficient wing loading of only 7.5 ounces per square foot (more than 30% lower than most electric sailplanes). With 4-5 climbs to "edge- of -sight" altitude on a single charge, you can look forward to 30 minute flights!

I think once you start to experiment, you will look forward to decades of new building and flying experiences.

5

COVERING TECHNIQUES

After working hard on your structure, sanding it glass smooth and tacking wings and tail on just to stare at it for a while, you certainly don't want to spoil that "Bird In Space" with a sloppy covering job. Fortunately, space age technology, new materials and techniques have arrived to make your job easier and better looking. Even the traditional "Tissue and Dope" method has been improved with brand new adhesives and tools.

Like sewing or cooking, model covering is a bit more of an art than a science. You will need to explore several methods and materials and practice with each before you develop your own technique. It seems each modeler has a preference and each method has some advantages. However, the quality of any covering job depends on the quality of the surface it is covering.

Preparation

Your best tool here is lots of sandpaper in at least four grades, several sanding blocks and some patience. Start with a clean structure. Cut away any glue globs and carefully "eyeball" the structure to spot any bumps where wing rib meets leading or trailing edge, uprights meet longerons and tips meet front or rear of stab and rudder. Don't be reluctant to unglue or break up bad spots and rebuild. You will be amply rewarded with not only a better finish but a stronger, better flying machine. Stock sandpaper sheets in 180, 220, 400 and 600 grit. Acquire 4 or 5 types of sanding blocks and wands and a "T"- Bar or long 2 x 4" block is a must. Try small jeweler's files for tight spaces.

As I mentioned in **Chapter 1 Construction**, **listen** while you are sanding. You will clearly hear hard spots and glue globs as the block passes over them. Also, you can lift a dented area by wetting it lightly (saliva is swell) and heating with a sealing iron, (very low heat) until it raises up ready for sanding. A couple of drops of vinegar on the dent will raise it too. There are many balsa fillers available but I have found ordinary spackling paste found in any hardware store to be just as and it sands easily.

Some of you may decide this is a good time to re-cover an old framework . You can try out a new technique and dress up that old Korda in the attic. Before you start struggling with razor blades, dope thinner and sandpaper to remove 20 years of tissue and patches, get some **Red Devil Liquid #99** Paint & Varnish Remover, also available in hardware stores.

Brush the stuff, full strength on your framework wherever covering has adhered. It will penetrate right through a doped surface and soften the tissue bond. Use a 1/4 inch brush and work an area of about 3 or 4 inches at a time. Brush the liquid on, wait 45 seconds and tease up an edge. Then brush right under the edge as you peel. Too much will weaken your glue joints so work carefully and you can remove almost any porous covering in whole sheets. My Sparky has been recovered twice, once after three months lost in the woods and it still does better then two minutes in still air.

Once you have removed all covering, sand the whole surface again. If you are going to use a glue stick, dope and thinner or white glue to cover with, you may want to seal the wood surface with **Balsaloc**. This is a very fine product that weighs almost nothing and gives you a well prepared surface before covering. For just sealing purposes, use the green striped can that is a thinner formula and not as strong an adhesive. This can also be final sanded with **600** grit paper.

Now for some don'ts. ***Never* sand without a block**. Many a model has been spoiled with "just a touch up sanding". Once you sand in a valley or leave a hard spot because the paper wasn't backed up, you are in the world of "chair leg shortening" which can become a lifetime occupation. Make sure your block spans an area of at least several inches and sand with strokes not pressure. Counting your sanding passes is a surprisingly accurate way to sand uniform surfaces on both sides of a fuselage or a right and left wing. You may decide to run 20 passes up and down on a fuselage side, first with 180 grit, then 220. Then repeat on the other side. Wings should be sanded **chordwise** with a long block or "T" Bar. Sanding a wing spanwise can result in a "wavy " airfoil from root to tip which affects flight as well as appearance.

Tissue

Two methods of attaching tissue are described in detail in **RPMA**. The simplest is to mix white glue with water, 50-50, and apply to the outline of your structure. While still wet, lay the tissue over the structure and stretch lightly while smoothing down and rubbing in with a finger tip. Tissue gets very soft and tears easily when wet so this method requires some care and doesn't allow much stretching. Once dry, you can water shrink and dope. Because of the water in the glue, tissue is harder to apply and thin structures may warp.

The other method uses 50-50 dope-thinner mix (either nitrate or butyrate) on all the areas where tissue should stick. Two thin coats will do. Then, tissue is laid over the structure and pulled tight while thinner is flooded through the tissue by brushing a small section at a time, as the tissue is stretched. This method allows for repositioning or removal by softening the dope with thinner. Then, the tissue is water shrunk and doped. I use three coats of dope on fuselages and two coats on the rest of the model.

A word about water shrinking tissue. Most modelers believe that the thinnest possible mist of water or water and alcohol should be used to shrink covering. I however, feel that gluing a structure while it is pinned to a board can impart warps in many areas as the glue dries. Certainly, all your wood-to-wood fits aren't perfectly mated thus some ribs are pressing the L E and T E apart while some, only a few thousandths shorter are held tight by pins. As the glue dries and shrinks, these wood parts are squeezed and twisted even more. When you shrink your tissue with a thin spray, you leave these strains in the structure. Instead, I slop on a heavy spray and immediately pin the part into a scrap balsa jig that holds it flat **Fig 5-1**, or at the proper dihedral and washout angle while it dries slowly overnight. Several of my models have been lost in the woods and weathered for months and returned without warps.

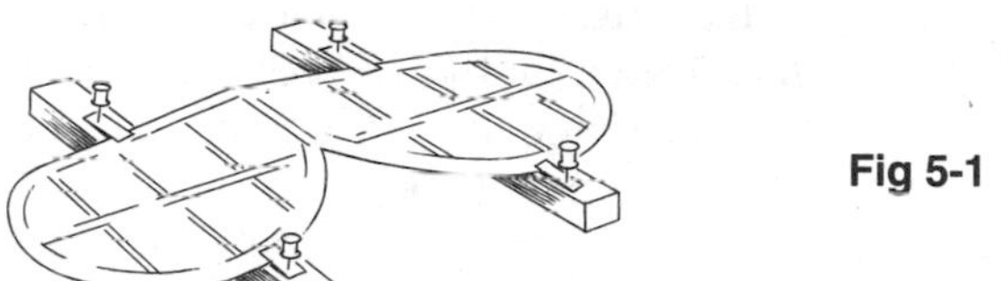

Fig 5-1

Many scale modelers who want to do the marking work on tissue before they apply it to the structure, or simply don't want to shrink it on a fragile structure, will first tape the tissue on to a frame **Fig 5-2** and pre-shrink it.

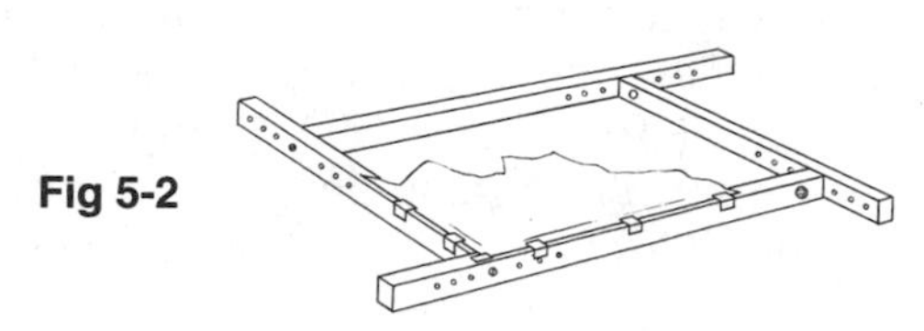

Fig 5-2

Now, a **new method**-using glue sticks- has been discovered for tissue covering. They are available in almost any stationery store and most will do a good job.

Uhu makes one that goes on purple and dries clear so you can tell if you have covered all the area you need. Just apply the glue stick with a smooth motion(to the perimeter of the area to be covered) and lay the tissue on the surface. Smooth it down while stretching lightly and press it down with a finger tip. You can lift to reposition and add a bit more glue to stubborn areas. Once dry you can water shrink and dope as before. This has the advantage of no bad vapors like dope and no weakening of the tissue as with white glue and water.

Another neat covering tip that can be very useful in both scale and sport models is the ability to mate two different colors of tissue before attaching them to your model. Tony Peters uses this process to create camouflage patterns. Just overlap two sheets of tissue slightly, then cut a straight or curved line through both layers. Now lay a fine bead of glue along the cut edge and overlap by 1/8 inch and allow to dry. Tape the tissue down to dry so it doesn't wrinkle at the joint. Now you can cover as if it was a single sheet, **Fig 5-3.**

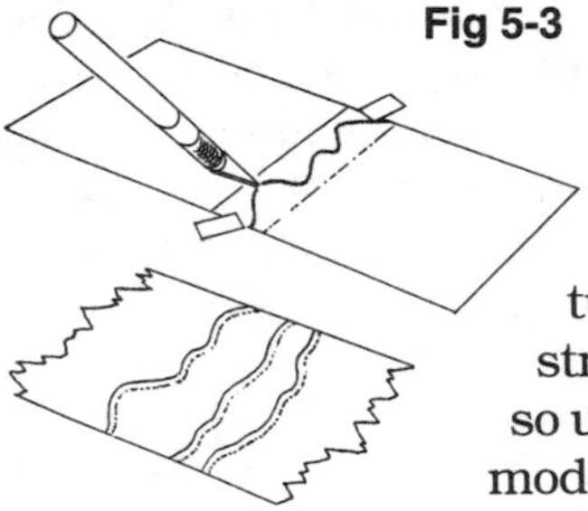

Fig 5-3

There are also several ways to use heat to attach covering. I do not recommend any heat applications for thin structures 1/16 or smaller. Even 3/32 and 1/8 structures can be easily deformed with heat so use heat activated adhesives only on larger models. Once dry, white glue can be heat activated but remember that you are sinking water into your structure when you apply it.

Tissue comes in several different weights so be careful of using package wrap which may weigh twice as much and absorb twice the dope. The best tissue I have found used to be sold by Champion Models and was called "Esaki Tissue". It has a definite grain and handles very well wet or dry. The best Esaki has a dull and a gloss side and weighs about 1.2 grams per square foot. It's available from Peck, SIG, Campbell and others. This stuff doesn't come from a big company like Dennison. I understand it's made in small lots of and can vary quite a bit, so weigh each batch you use. For those who want to save every gram, Campbell sells a tissue called "Gampi" which is the lightest and smoothest grain you can get.

Doping

All tissue, silkspan, silk and a few other materials need to be doped to seal them airtight and prevent shrinkage or wrinkling with humidity changes. Only the lightest indoor models can get away without at least a thin coat of dope. Dope is available in two types, **nitrate** and **butyrate**. Usually, the nitrate type is best because it is non-tautening and won't tend to warp your framework. Butyrate is fuel proof so it **must** be applied over the Nitrate if you are flying any kind of gas-powered model.

The very best way to apply dope is with a spray gun but that gets a bit expensive and requires a spray area or a spray booth. **Do not** spray dope from a spray can in any kind of closed room. You are courting serious respiratory and combustion problems. Also, I feel the dope-thinner mixture in a spray can is too thick for light models. Airbrush and pressure spraying are fine techniques for the more experienced modeler.

Mix dope 50-50 with thinner and apply with a brush. The foam brushes sold in hardware stores do a good job except that they last for only one application. To cover large areas, I like the "**Tissue Drag**" method **Fig 5-5** Tape or glue a sheet of toilet tissue to a small wood block. Then saturate the tissue with dope and "drag" it over the surface. With just a bit of practice, you will be able to cover a wing quickly and with a very uniform coating.

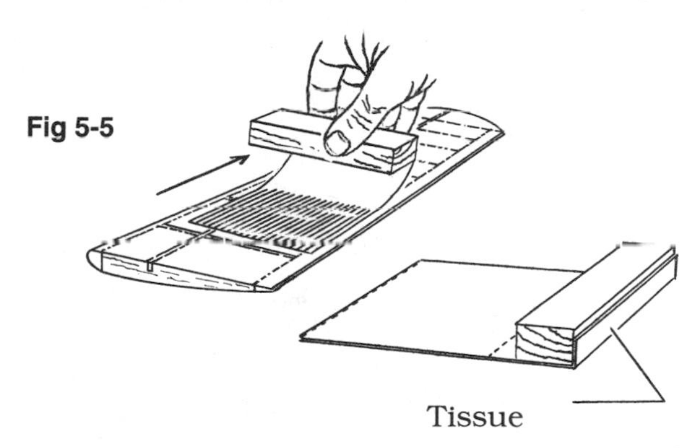

On larger models (36 inch. span and up) you may want to use heavy tissue or silkspan put on damp. The dope and thinner method works fine here and you can strtetch the heavier stuff without tearing it. Balsaloc or Balsarite can also be used to seal the structure and adhere the covering with heat. Just paint it on with a 1/4 inch brush, allow to dry, then apply covering. Some practice is necessary because you may have trouble at first getting the wrinkles out before the covering is stuck on. The techniques used for plastic, heat- activated films like Monokote will work here.

Mylar

Many of you are familiar with heat-sealed coverings like MonoKote, Ultracote and Towercote. These are usually mylar with an opaque or transparent color impregnated in the adhesive. They are applied with a heating iron and shrunk with an iron or heat gun. These coverings are **much too heavy** to use on small models below 36 inch span. The mylar is thick and completely covered with adhesive. The weight chart **Fig 5-8** gives you comparisons.

Not only will you pay a weight penalty but you may also find your wing looks like a two-foot red potato chip. That stuff is strong enough to easily twist any light structure. Even if you manage to do a decent job , you will probably sacrifice some glide due to the slick finish which almost eliminates turbulation.

Don't despair though, you don't have to live with tissue and dope forever. I once lived in a small apartment and I can certainly sympathize with coughing and complaining wives and children. With 1/4 and 1/2 mil Mylar available in both clear and metallized (chrome) finish, you can now apply this much thinner and lighter covering by painting a special adhesive on just the framework. You will actually achieve a weight advantage over tissue and dope. Of course, this is no good for a scale finish but looks great on any sport or endurance model.

1/4 mil means 1/4 of a thousandth of an inch or .00025 and is very light yet tough enough to handle. Just paint Balsaloc or Balsarite on the framework wherever the mylar touches it. Don't just paint the outside edges because you will then be pulling too large an area when shrinking and may produce warps or permanent wrinkles. Also, patching a small area will be very difficult. One coat of full-strength is usually enough, although wing tips and undercambered ribs may need a bit more.

Before putting on the mylar, punch a few pinholes through the ribs so air can move from one bay to another. This will help eliminate "ballooning" that can be troublesome.

Before attempting to cover any structure, test the mylar- adhesive bond on a piece of scrap. You want the lowest temperature that will tack the mylar. Now begin attaching the mylar by "tacking" it in a sequence similar to **Fig 5-4** while pulling out the wrinkles as you go. This is very similar to MonoKote work so you guys who are moving from R/C to FF have done this before. Once the mylar has been tacked, complete the job with a "wiping" motion of the iron along the edges. Edges can be sealed by painting another layer of Balsaloc on the edge and overlapping the covering. Wing tips can often be covered in one piece by stretching the mylar around the tip while heating it with the iron. This distorts the mylar enough to conform without wrinkles but takes a bit of practice.

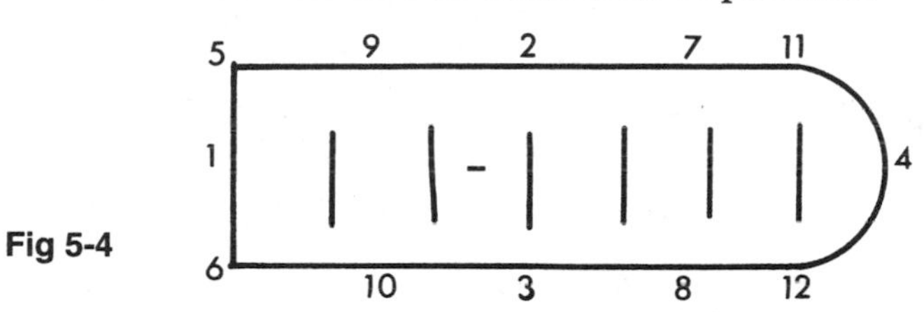

Fig 5-4

Another method, pioneered by Al Rametta, is similar to the way indoor modelers cover their fragile frameworks with .00016 mylar. Construct a frame from 1/4 square Balsa, Pine or Spruce at least 1 inch larger than the wing planform. Attach the mylar to the frame and shrink out all the wrinkles. Then apply Balsaloc to the wing outline, press it against the Mylar <u>inside the frame</u> and attach with a hot iron. This will greatly reduce the wing twisting when the Mylar is heat shrunk.

By all means expect some failures. This stuff can be heated and repositioned but you may be better off just discarding a bad piece and starting over asyou get some experience.

If you use chrome mylar, be **sure** to have the chrome on the **inside**. Just test by scraping with a razor or putting a drop of dope thinner on the film. You can also color the stuff with magic marker or even dye it by cooking in RIT and water at a simmer for 30 minutes or so. Just fold up the Mylar into about a 6-inch square, immerse it in the dye - water mix, stir and keep immersed until you get the shade you want. This however, is tricky and, hardly worth the effort compared to some other methods.

Once the mylar has been attached and edges sealed, it shrinks with very little heat. . A hair dryer is ample or even your heating iron passed over but not touching the surface. It's a good idea to pin down structures that might be deformed at this step. Fortunately, washout can be created or unintended warps removed by heat shrinking while twisting the structure. This type of covering is airtight without dope and won't sag or warp withhumidity changes.

Mylar - Tissue

Here's a new technique borrowed from my British friends. Attach 1/4 or 1/2 mil mylar either with heat or canopy adhesive as described in the **Mylar** section.

Once sealed all around, heat shrink the mylar with low heat. You can seal or fold over the edges with more Balsaloc and a "wiping" action around the edge with your iron, **Fig 5-6**

Fig 5-6

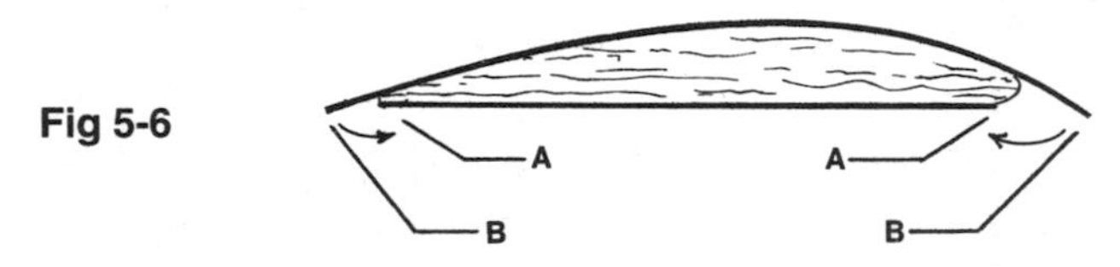

Now comes the interesting part. Put a layer of thinned dope (50-50) on top of the Mylar. Now lay on your favorite color of **damp** tissue and flood thinner through the tissue on to the Mylar while you pull the tissue tight. Brushing will not work well here. You can use a lightly loaded foam brush, say 2 inches wide, or try the flooded toilet tissue method. When dry you may see a terrible, cloudy, whitish finish on the tissue. This is due to wet dope. Don't despair. Another coat of dope or a quick wipe with thinner will cure this. Last, a thin coat of dope over all and you will have a puncture resistant, warp-free air tight surface that not only looks like plain tissue, it may even be lighter because most of the first coat of dope on top of the non-porous Mylar evaporated

If you want to get some brilliant colors, just use chrome mylar under the tissue. If you do this you need to make sure the chrome surface is towards the wood because dope will strip off the metallizing.

This technique can be used with light tissue, silkspan, and even silk, to get a very permanent surface without losing that "sun shining through the covering" effect many modelers like so much.

Plastic Wrap

There are some other plastic wraps that make very nice covering and can add a special luster to your finish. For very light models like indoor electrics, Reynolds Wrap has come out with some stuff called **"Crystal Wrap"**. It is a thin, Saran-like material (I suspect it is a type of polyethylene) and it comes in glorious colors. Red, green, pink, blue and gold are available so far and more may be coming. The stuff is on the shelf in your local supermarket and a 50-foot roll is around $2.00.

Use Balsaloc and light heat to apply and very light heat from a hair dryer held a foot away to shrink. For models with very light framework, use glue stick and only the very lightest application of heat.You could also use canopy adhesive. This stuff is only for very small, light models. It offers an air tight, brilliant colored, transparent covering that can really enhance a simple model.

Cellophane - Gift Wrap

This stuff has been around for decades and is available in craft stores as "Gift Wrapping". It comes in a tremendous variety of brilliant colors, is about 1-1/2 to 2 mils thick, and weighs 2.5 grams per square foot. The cost is around $0.05 per square foot and it is another very low temperature (210° F) shrink material. One source is Highlander Corp of Highland, IL. under the trade name "**Clearphane**".

Hank Nystrom, Harry Murphy and Ron Sharpton have all used the material with good success and have various methods for attaching it. Hank believes it was first used by Bill Hale in Ohio. Besides eliminating dope and providing a non-porous, fuel proof, light covering with integral color, Cellophane is also water proof enough to eliminate that "saggy" effect you get in the morning dew or evening dampness. Since it is airtight, be sure to " pinhole" ribs to reduce "ballooning". The film does not add as much strength to your structure as doped tissue or silk so don't use it on a flimsy framework.

The first step in covering with cellophane is to make sure you know which side has the color. Just wipe a bit of thinner from a Q-Tip on each side of a sheet and see where it takes the color off. Then, mark that side with a piece of masking tape in the corner of the sheet. If you cut out pieces, mark each piece.

Next, decide on which adhesive system to use. Hank Nystrom uses "**Shur-Stick 388 Flammable Contact Cement"** from the

Gibson-Homans Company of Twinsburg, Ohio. He thins it with lacquer thinner to a runny consistency then applies with a Q-Tip® to all surfaces that will touch the film. Allow to dry at *least* 30 minutes (overnight is even better) until <u>all</u> tackiness has disappeared. Now find the lowest heat that will adhere the film - something just under the shrink temperature will usually work. Tack and pull as you would with any plastic film but don't shrink - stretch it around wing tips as you would with MonoKote. Just take out most of the wrinkles and overlap all the edges. Paint some more adhesive on the overlaps, heat and seal and remove excess with a little thinner. Now you can shrink the covering with an iron, <u>not a heat gun</u>. Warps can be heat shrunk out and washout shrunk in. A bit of testing and experience will help you get some astonishing finishes.

Harry Murphy prefers **Pliobond** which is one of the oldest contact cements. Its natural solvent is MEK (Methyl Ethyl Ketone) which is available in many paint shops or chemical supply houses. Thinned 50-50 with MEK, Pliobond becomes easy to brush on. Allow it to dry completely hard then apply with low heat as above.

The "plastic glues" and "canopy cements" used with mylar may allow "creep" with time. Balsaloc requires too much heat. If you try Pliobond with MEK **be sure to ventilate thoroughly**. **MEK is very toxic.** Why not try this "Gift Wrap" technique when re-covering an old free flight model? You may find you have given it a whole new life.

Litespan

Litespan is a plastic film made by **Solarfilm Ltd**. in England and sold by Hobby Supply South and others. It's very close to doped tissue or silk in appearance and comes in nine lovely colors. Litespan has polyester fibers woven into the structure to add strength. This stuff does not need dope after covering so you save weight and time. It is quite airtight and <u>very</u> water resistant and <u>will not</u> sag with dampness. These are <u>terrific</u> advantages for a new covering material and, as the chart shows, with almost no weight penalty over tissue and dope.

One small disadvantage is that Litespan doesn't add much torsional strength to your model as does doped tissue but it's certainly strong enough to use on any model from 30 to 60 inches in span.

In covering an open structure, coat all areas the material will touch with unthinned Balsaloc or Balsarite. You can use a small piece of sponge rather than a brush. Coat any sheet areas all over. Allow at least 30 minutes to dry then tack the Litespan around the edges using the toe of an iron set to about 210-225° F. While tacking, gently pull the Litespan to remove any wrinkles. Don't try for a "Drum tight" finish at this stage. You can reheat and reposition if required. Next, seal the Litespan around all the edges with a "wiping" motion of the iron around the edge. Trim for overlap where required and apply Balsaloc to the area under the overlap, next, iron down the excess using the iron to "crease" over any edges, like the LE or T E You will find that these edges almost disappear.

Shrink the Litespan with an iron set at about 250° F by lightly touching the surface while slowly sliding the iron across it. If warps occur, twist the structure against the warp while reheating. Note that too much heat will soften the Litespan and change it from an "elastic" to a "plastic" material which will cause it to permanently "sag."

As with any new covering material, Litespan takes a little practice and early results may be less than satisfactory but hang-in - there because this is really good stuff and can make your life easier and your models more durable.

Polyspan

Polyspan is a new covering material but certainly not a stranger to anyone who wore polyester leisure suits in the 60's and 70's. It is basically a thin polyester cloth with a slight grain and all the goods and bads of its type. It is quite strong and water proof but shrinks only a bit with heat. Polyspan comes only in white and is available from **Starline**. Apply just like Litespan using Balsaloc and low heat.

Polyspan doesn't shrink as much with heat as MonoKote so go for a fairly smooth covering while applying it. I don't recommend a heat gun for shrinking. That will apply too much heat and soften the material so that it can't' spring back. Just pass your iron over the surface with a smooth wiping motion. Polyester cannot be dyed so you will have to color your Polyspan with some dye dissolved in clear, thinned dope. Don Typond describes this process very clearly in his article in Flying Models 12/94. I haven't gone into much detail about Polyspan because a newer, but quite similar material called **Airspan** has appeared.

Airspan *"Here's a Howdy - do. Here's a thing that's new"*

Forgive the Gilbert and Sullivan but this stuff is actually fun to work with. It's a polyester just like Polyspan but available in eight colors including Cub Yellow and Shocking Pink as well as almost Fluorescent Orange and Black. As a Polyester it has a fiber grain and is waterproof so it can only be shrunk by heat. Available from SAMS in England and possibly from Charlie's in Simi Valley, CA., or Hobby Supply South.

Apply with Balsaloc and low heat, like Litespan (210-225° F), and shrink by lightly touching an iron at 250-275° F to the surface while slowly moving it along. First run a small test on any of these new materials by finding the lowest temperature that will adhere a swatch to a piece of scrap balsa and hold it there after cooling.

Tack Airspan on in several strategic spots while gently pulling it smooth, then adhere it all around with the "wiping" motion described before. Solid sheet areas should be worked from the center towards the edges. With Balsaloc or Balsarite you can soften the adhesive with heat and re-position a few times. Grain, of course should be along the length of the fuselage or the span of the wing. Airspan should be folded over any ribs at dihedral joints or any other areas where only a thin stick or the edge of a sheet represents a turning edge. At a rib, just overlap about 1/4 inch, cut a few slits in the overlap, paint more adhesive on the inside of the rib, and iron the Airspan over the edge and against the surface.

Don't use a heat gun to shrink Airspan. This would heat it too much and soften it to where it won't shrink back. Also, Airspan needs to be sealed with dope. One coat, thinned 50-50 should do it. Apply at the outer edges then work inward.

Patching requires a bit of explanation and practice. If you have to cut out a torn area to replace it, make sure you leave some overlap at the cut. Now you can overlap the edge of the area to be patched, just like a dihedral rib. This will stop the Airspan from pulling back from a thin edge. Any patches need to end on a balsa support. Don't patch Airspan over an open area. This would only result in pull-backs and wrinkles. Once the patch area has been defined, paint a 1/8 to 1/4 inch wide border of adhesive around the patch, then apply it to the wet adhesive just like you would with dope. Don't attempt to iron on the patch like MonoKote. It will shrink up and wrinkle while ironing. After the patch has dried, you can heat the edges carefully with a toe iron.

My first efforts with Airspan were less than perfect but by my second try I was very pleased with the finish. **Fig 5-7** shows my Herr Cub covered with Cub Yellow Airspan, ready for detailing.

Fig 5-7

Silk

Silk has mostly been replaced on large models by the many plastic films available. Doped silk is heavier than many of the new films like Ultracote Light and, obviously, much harder to apply. However, silk is still a wonderful covering for compound curves and adds much more structural strength than the plastic films. Also, there's a use for silk that is still better than anything else around and that's **covering for a balsa propeller**.

Large balsa props on rubber models are right out there in front where damage can happen. Most are carved rather thin and can easily split or crack the first time it hits the ground, particularly if it is still turning under power. Doping and sanding aren't enough protection, and tissue, even Silkspan won't help much. Airspan, Litespan, Cellophane and Mylar all require heat to apply and are tough to smooth around the compound shape of a prop and certainly won't fold over the edge very well.

Silk, when put on wet will follow the toughest curve and shrink drum tight when dry. Just put three or four coats of 50-50 dope and thinner on the prop, sanding *lightly* between the coats with 600 grit. Then lay a piece of wet silk on top of the dry dope. It's very easy to pull the silk tight over the whole surface. It will lay wrinkle-free while you flood thinner through the silk and gently rub it down on the blade surface. Make sure you have at least 3/4 inch extra all around. Don't try to overlap the silk at any of the edges. Just let the thinner dry and make sure you have adhesion all over the surface. Now, using full-strength dope, paint the excess silk all around the blade. This will stiffen the fibers and allow you to cut them with a new, double-edged razor blade right at the edge. Now cover the other side of the blade the same way and trim to the edge.

I use yellow silk and then paint the edges with a yellow Magic Marker. Apply a couple of coats of dope thinned 50-50 on top and you have a prop blade that will last for years.

Silk still compares very well with most of the plastic coverings. It is lighter and just as strong while adding torsional strength to the structure. Covering with silk is supposed to be difficult and is really quite simple. Except for props, don't use silk on any model smaller than 40 inches in span because of its finished weight.

To apply, fill all depressions or irregularities (remember the technique of wetting and heating a small dent), seal your surface with Balsaloc sealer then paint with three coats of 50-50 dope and thinner. Dope *only* the outline of each built-up surface and coat all over on solid sheet areas. Sand thoroughly between coats with 600 sandpaper so the final surface is smooth and uniform. Lay damp silk over the surface and flood thinner through as with tissue or silkspan, while gently pulling taut. Wingtips and other curved surfaces will smooth out easily at this time by lightly stretching the silk around the curve.

When dry, work with two brushes to fold over any edges at LE or TE. Use one small brush with water and the other with dope. Brush water on the overlap, then brush dope on the surface under it. Fold over and rub down. The biggest problem many encounter is filling the silk with dope. It seems to absorb all the dope you can lay on. There are three methods you can try:

1. Use the" toilet tissue trail" method where you wet some tissue with dope and trail it over the surface, wetting more as you go.
2. Add Talcum Powder to your first coat of dope, about a teaspoon to a pint.
3. Add gelatin (get it in any supermarket) to the dope (about a tablespoon of gelatin to a cup of dope), then brush right on.

Silk is really worth trying at least once, particularly on an Old Time Model. You will enjoy just looking at the finish.

Finishing Trim

Trimming with color, graphics and scale effects is covered in chapter 6 **Scale**.

Using The Weight Chart

This weight chart **Fig 5-8** was prepared to give the builder an overview of covering weight and sheet size requirements before starting the job. Each material weight is shown as either **grams per square foot** or **ounces per square foot,** whichever is more convenient for you. Weight of Balsarite, dope, Balsaloc, glue stick or other covering adhesives is, of course, only approximate since each structure will have a unique pattern of wood area that must be covered by the adhesive. This is a very small factor in total covering weight and can almost be ignored.

The chart was drawn from actual weights of models I have built in the past two years as well as manufacturer's information on their products. Of course, tissue from different sources will vary somewhat but this whole exercise is intended to give you some approximate working values on which to base decisions. Since everything is a trade-off, you may be willing to sacrifice a bit of weight for more strength or ease of application or better appearance. This will give you some help in quantifying your decision.

You can easily figure the total area to be covered on your model by using simple measurements and a bit of geometry. A quick approximation is to use **0.7**x **(S)** ^{2} where **S = Span**. For instance, my 31-inch span Jabberwock has about 700 square inches of total covered area. Using the formula you would have S^2 = 31 x 31 = 961 x 0.7 = 672.7 which is within 5% of the true area. My 31-inch Sparky has an actual covered area of 610 square inches so you can see that the formula is only an approximation but a fairly close one. For models under 30 inches in span, take off 10% or so. For models 36 inches and up, add about 10%. You can't really use this formula for ordering covering because the layout, excess and overlap will require at least 25% more area.

Note that 1/4 mil mylar (0.8 gm/sq.ft.) with one coat of dope to adhere tissue (0.6 gms. - non porous) plus tissue (1.2 gm.) plus one coat of dope on top (0.6 again non porous) = 3.6 to 3.8 grams per square foot which compares well with tissue with three coats of dope or Litespan or Airspan.

Dope or Balsaloc used to adhere coverings weighs about .04 grams per inch of span depending on surface area to be covered.

Now you can add up adhesive, covering and dope (where used) to compare total covered weights with different materials. Remember, a **25% reduction in weight will earn a 40% increase in flight time.**

Fig 5-8 **COVERING MATERIALS WEIGHT CHART**

MATERIAL	gms / sq. ft.	oz / sq. ft.	Coats of Dope
Japanese Tissue	1.2	.042	2 or 3
White 00 Silkspan	1.4	.049	2 or 3
Red Silkspan	1.4	.074	2 or 3
Light Esaki Silk	2.4	.085	3
Cellophane	2.5	.088	
1/4 mil Mylar	0.8	.028	
1/2 mil Mylar	1.6	.056	
1 mil Mylar	3.2	.112	
Litespan	3.4	.113	
Airspan	2.5	.088	1
Oracover Light	3.0	.106	
Oracover Standard	5.6	.198	
Polyspan	3.0	.106	
Clear Micafilm	2.4	,085	
Red Micafilm	4.1	.144	
Trans. Colored Monokote	6.8	.240	
Opaque Colored Monokote	8.3	.292	
Black Baron Coverite	7.8	.275	
21 Cent. Super Coverite	7.3	.255	
21 Century Fabric	9.7	.343	

Note: Number under "Dope" indicates recommended coats. First coat of dope on absorbent materials like tissue, silkspan, silk, Polyspan and Airspan weighs **1.0** to **1.2** grams per square foot. Second or third coats weigh **0.5** to **0.6** grams per square foot because surface is sealed by first coat. First coat of dope on Mylar weighs **0.5** to **0.6** grams per square foot (same as second coats on porous materials). Therefore, tissue with 3 coats of dope = 3.4 to 3.6 grams per square foot same as Litespan which doesn't need dope or close to Airspan with 1 coat.

Fig 5-9 Compatibility of Various Finishing Chemicals

UNDER	Vinyl Spackle	Poly Resin	Dupont 305	Aero Gloss Dope	Nitrate Dope	Butyrate Dope	Acrylic Lacquer	Alkyd Enamel	Epoxy Enamel	Acrylic Enamel	Polyurethane
Vinyl Spackle	C	N	C	C	C	C	C	C	C	C	C
Poly Resin	C	C	C	C	C	C	C	C	C	C	C
Dupont 305	C	N	C	N	C	C	C	C	C	C	C
Aero Gloss Dope	C	C	C	C	N	C	C	C	C	C	C
Nitrate Dope	C	C	C	C	C	C	C	C	C	C	C
Butyrate Dope	C	N	C	N	N	C	C	C	C	C	C
Acrylic Lacquer	C	N	C	N	C	N	C	C	C	C	C
Alkyd Enamel	C	N	C	N	C	N	N	C	N	N	N
Epoxy Enamel	C	N	C	N	C	N	C	C	C	C	C
Acrylic Enamel	C	N	C	N	C	N	N	C	N	C	N
Polyurethane	C	N	C	N	C	N	C	C	C	C	C

Examples: Butyrate Dope **is** compatible **over** Aerogloss Dope
Butyrate Dope **is not** compatible **under** Aerogloss Dope

Aerogloss Dope **is not** Compatible **over** Acrylic Enamel
Aerogloss Dope **is** compatible **under** Acrylic Enamel

Applying Color With Dyes

Even though there are now a large number of materials and colors available for covering (also see chapter 6 **Scale Models**), the ability to dye colors may still have some use. Silkspan is still a very useful covering that gives a drum tight finish and adds plenty of torsional strength to your structure. Light Silkspan is usually available only in white but can be dyed any color with standard **Rit** dye available in almost any super market. Rit comes in a huge variety of colors and, following their instructions can be mixed to provide an almost infinite pallette of special shades and tints.

Dye adds virtually no weight to covering and can be used on tissue, Silkspan, silk or any other fabric. It will not penetrate Polyester coverings like Polyspan. Dye works well on wood and can be used on sheet Balsa parts to enhance appearance or add visibility. You can easily mix a dark oak color for a WWI wooden prop that will look a lot better than a painted one.

Rit comes in both powder and liquid form. Use the liquid with very hot water to dye tissue. Just follow the instructions on the package and test a few scraps to approximate dyeing time. If you are dyeing loose sheets, hang them up to dry and iron flat when done. Another method is to tape the tissue to a frame, spray it with dye to the shade you want and allow to dry.

You can also mix Rit with thinner. Pour a small amount of powder in a jar and add thinner. Test with balsa sticks to get the right shade, then add 20% clear dope. Prepare the model with 1 or 2 coats of thin dope before laying on the dope/dye/thinner mixture. You'll get a rich color that can't be duplicated by using colored tissue and is even lighter than sprayed colored dope.

To dye Balsa, sand the surface to final finish level before dyeing. Mix either powder or liquid Rit in very hot water (about 1/2 bottle or package to 1 quart) then simply dunk the balsa part in the warm mixture and swirl it around until you get the desired depth of color. Remove the excess dye with your fingers. (**Wear rubber gloves throughout this operation**) and set aside to dry. Turn the part every 10 minutes or so to avoid warping.

Remember, all these dyes will also badly stain hands or clothes, countertops, furniture. floors and rugs so prepare the area with lots of plastic covering or aluminum foil.

Rit and several other dyes can be mixed with thinner then applied with dope to a finished model. These dyes are inexpensive enough so you can test several different ones for only a couple of bucks. You may want to dye parts of your structure under a clear covering just to get a new effect. Dyes are just another tool that with some practice, can become part of your building system.

Another factor in covering colors is **visibilty**. As your building and trimming technique inproves, your models will fly further and further away. A 24 inch span model at 1000 feet is almost a speck and, if it's not finished in a highly visible color, will disappear very quickly. If you transition to micro R/C you will need to be able to tell if your model is coming or going at long distances, otherwise you may apply incorrect control and crash. **Larry Kruse** published a simple chart some years ago that I believe came from a Cactus Squadron newsletter. It rates colors from most to least visible and can be a handy guide:

Least Visible **Most Visible**

Luminous Orange--
White---
Light Yellow--
Light Orange---
Dark Yellow---
Light Grey---------------------------------------
Light Blue------------------------------------
Light Red-----------------------------------
Light Brown-----------------------------
Light Green--------------------------
Dark Grey-------------------------
Dark Red------------------------
Dark Blue---------------------
Dark Brown------------------
Black------------------------
Dark Green----------------

For R/C, color wing bottoms dark and tops light. A bright orange leading edge on wing and stab will help to orient you as you maneuver the model at long distance. A small piece of highly reflective shimmer material attached to the top of the rudder will help you find your model in high grass.

6

SCALE MODELS

Scale models are among the most popular of all flying types and probably the type of kit that started most of us in the hobby. Of course you wanted your first model to look just like your favorite WWI or WWII fighter or bomber. Unfortunately, scale models are harder to build, a lot harder to flight trim and even easier to destroy with the first crash. That's possibly why many got discouraged and gave up early. Almost everyone I know has told me the a story about lighting the tail of a model and flying it off the roof to "go down in flames".

Therefore, what we all need in a scale model is some way to maintain and even improve scale appearance, add some adjustable features to aid in flight trim and build them a bit stronger to avoid early damage. Since there is hardly ever a free lunch, we'll have to trade off some additional weight for these helpful features. We'll build a bit stronger with heavier wood and change the structure a bit for flexibility.

One interesting feature of scale models is that they come in all sizes from Pistachio (9 inch span) to Jumbo (36 inch span) and up to Quarter Scale (1/4 actual size). Thus the builder can easily choose a size that fits his work board, his car and his field or indoor site. Also, the advent of electric power has opened up a whole new world of scale projects including multi-engined bombers, pushers and canards that were very difficult rubber power projects

I will assume that you have already built and flown some simple models including a stick type or two and a P-30 or P-24 type as well as a scale type cabin model like a Pacific Ace. If so, you are ready to start a scale project. Even if you start with a kit, you need to make some design and construction decisions at the very beginning. I'm strongly *against* Peanut Scale models as a first project. In order to fly at all decently, these small models have to be very light. Their small size makes them tough to flight trim and, if they are a bit too heavy, they fly much too fast for the beginner to analyze trim requirements. Repairs are tough and the slightest warp courts disaster.

For your first scale project, choose a high wing, single engine, tractor (prop in front), powered model between 16 and 30 inches in span. Most of the airplanes from the "Golden Age" of aviation (1929-1941) will do nicely. Their proportions are good for free flight and they will balance and trim more easily. Choose a Piper Cub, Aeronca, Cessna Bird Dog or any similar airplane. Don't be disappointed that your first masterpiece isn't going to be a Mustang or P-38. You will advance to those soon enough and, when you do you will have the skills to really enjoy flying them.

The real secret to scale modeling is *scale detail.* Even a "No-Cal" profile model will look very real in the air if it has all the markings, scale coloring control outlines and other small details that can be included with very little weight penalty. In this chapter we'll cover many ways to include these features, giving the builder choices between simple, flat, "scale-like" appearance and full, three-dimensional details.

Rubber power is the most practical way to start. The model will be less expensive. You need less support equipment and, most of all, your model will be a lot lighter. Rubber power is also infinitely adjustable so your flight trimming will be easier.

Construction

If you are building a conventional box fuselage, use **spruce** instead of balsa for longerons. You can go down a size (if plans call for 1/8 balsa - use 3/32 spruce). Don't go below 1/16" spruce for longerons.

Spruce is tough but can easily be bent into a curve by soaking in hot water with a teaspoon of ammonia. It helps soften the lignin which is nature's glue that holds wood fibers together. Once dry, the lignin hardens again and helps retain the shape without strains that can turn into warps when the structure gets damp or too hot in the sun. I do not favor oven baking and *certainly not* microwave heating to dry anything in modeling. Quick heating can often be uneven and that will leave you with a structure just dying to twist into some unflyable shape. I just pin or clamp the stuff and let it dry overnight. Two of my models spent 3 months each in the woods in all weathers and were returned to me warp free.

Since most real airplanes are streamlined you are going to get involved with fuselage formers, stringers, tapered wings with fillets, elliptical tips on wings and tail and lots of other features that hardly ever appear on a sport or endurance model. Here are some new but simple techniques that can help.

Box Fuselage

Many old time kits and designs started with a conventional box fuselage and added formers to create the true shape. This certainly makes for a heavy fuselage and doesn't add appreciable strength. If you are going to build that way, first make your basic box as rigid as possible by adding gussets (as many as 16) to the corners. The basic box is the area of the fuselage that holds the wing, landing gear and probably your fingers when winding or launching **Fig 6-1**. Sand a nice curve into the gussets. This will reduce weight and actually increase strength by more evenly distributing stresses and shocks.

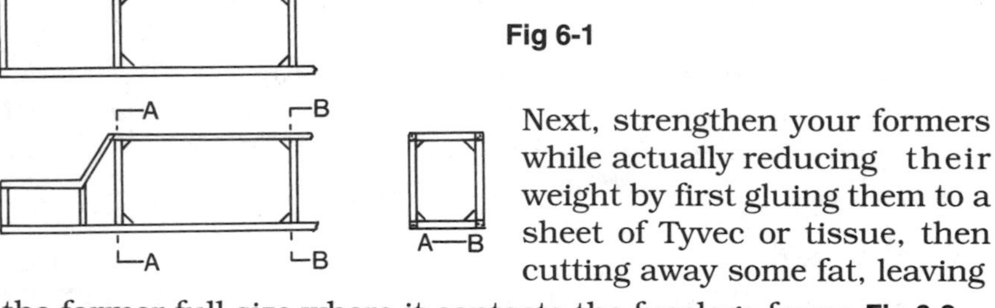

Fig 6-1

Next, strengthen your formers while actually reducing their weight by first gluing them to a sheet of Tyvec or tissue, then cutting away some fat, leaving the former full size where it contacts the fuselage frame **Fig 6-2**.

Wherever possible, notch formers into the fuselage longerons instead of just gluing them to the cross pieces. If you are building from a kit you may have to recut some formers. I hope you have already photocopied all the printwood in case you lose, break or want to redesign some pieces. This will work even with die cut wood sheets. In kits, watch out for formers, ribs or tips that have grain running along the short dimension of the piece The manufacturer may have done this to get better sheet yield but you don't have to live with it. Just recut some from your photo copy.

Fig 6-2 **Fig 6-3**

In most cases, I don't like to notch formers and lay stringers in perfect alignment. It's too hard to get those notches to line up. I mark the formers at each end of a stringer, tack the stringer on at both ends, then glue it to each intermediate former. It's a good idea to assemble matching stringers, to each side, one at a time, in order to avoid unbalanced glue drying which can lead to the dreaded "Banana Shape". If you want to stick with notched formers, sand a recess curve into each former between stringers **Fig 6-3** after assembly.

Keel Fuselage

Most new kits use a keel to form the fuselage. This is cut from hard balsa and outlines the top and bottom shape and often the sides too, **Fig 6-4**. The keel is pinned to the plan and formers are glued to it . This has one disadvantage that troubles me. For one side, you are gluing formers to a shape that is pinned to a solid, rigid board.However, when you build the other side, you are sort of working in midair which typically leads to twists, warps and weaknesses. I suggest you make two identical keels, perhaps of a bit thinner wood. Make sure they match *exactly* . Pin one to your board and glue in the formers. Remove the structure when dry.

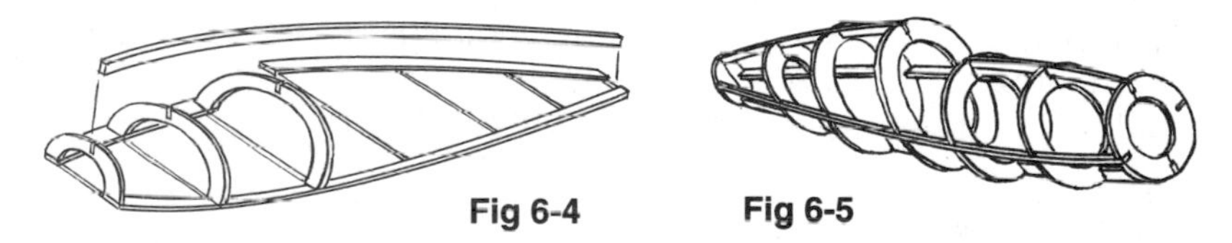

Fig 6-4 **Fig 6-5**

Mark the other keel on the reverse side with exact former locations, pin it down, glue in the formers and glue both keels together. Or, you can build a brace from stiff cardboard to hold the keel rigid while you glue formers to the other side.

Or, lay the plan on a light table, trace the fuselage against a window, rub some baby oil, sewing machine oil or even vaseline on the back - use any easy means of getting the fuselage image on the back of the plan. Build the other side of the fuselage from your new, reversed plan using your twin keel. Just carefully glue the keels together when finished. Basic top, bottom and side keels assembled with formers are shown in **Fig 6-5**.

Before laying on stringers, examine the fuselage for twists or warps. Now is the best time to steam or crack them out. Next, decide where you will need gussets and extra bracing. Carefully examine the rest of the plan and prepare for any of the following: **wing or tail mounting, landing gear mounting, rubber peg, nose block, tissue ending or overlap, wire bracing, windshield, cockpit outline, head rest, fin, fairings for wing roots, struts, dummy lights or guns, control surface outlines or any place else you can think of where tissue should be underlaid by balsa.**

Each of these places will need thin balsa, card stock or heavy paper under the tissue for extra strength and to anchor the tissue.

Once you have provided for as much of the above as you can predict, start adding your stringers. This is not a place to save weight. I use 7-8 pound balsa for stringers, even on smaller models. Remember, your weakest stringer is exactly where your helper will press his thumb when holding as you wind. I like square stock for stringers. On Peanuts you can go as low as 1/32" or even 1/40" square but most models will use 1/16 or 3/32". For those who like to be a bit more tricky, **Micro Mark** makes a steel plate that is used to make *round* sticks from square ones. Just pass the balsa stringer through successively smaller holes to get the size you need. The holes are tapered so they both shave and compress the Balsa which makes it a bit harder. Now you can sand stringer notches with a small round or rat tailed file and actually install round stringers that will contact your covering only in a thin line.

Planking

Sometimes, on a model with a stringered fuselage, you need sheet balsa between the stringers in some areas to support tissue or to strengthen the structure. There is no need to make the planking the same thickness as the stringers. All you need to do is be careful to make the planking protrude just a bit outside the stringers so you can later sand it to a perfect fit. Use light wood (4-6 lb) for planking and be as careful as possible to fit the planks neatly between the stringers.

Once fuselage construction is complete, fill in any spaces with ordinary plasterer's spackle and sand *only with a sanding block.* **Never sand by hand.** You can "raise" any small dents before sanding by wetting the area then heating with an iron. Complex curved and streamlined WWII-type fuselages may need to be covered in strips since tissue won't easily follow a compound (3- dimensional) curve. If you are going to use premarked and preshrunk tissue to cover a complex fuselage (see Dennis Norman's methods later in this chapter), plan your layout carefully before starting. Leave extra room for overlaps and curves.

Windows, Windshields and Canopies

These are the non structural, non-flying details that will have you staring at your model with a satisfied chuckle and piling up scale points at a contest. Don't grab any transparent piece of plastic that's laying around the kitchen. Get hold of some celluloid or Butyrate plastic between 3 and 10 thousandths (.003-.010) thick, depending on your model size. For really small models with flat side windows you can use thin plastic wrap from any food container.

I like to apply my windows *inside* the structure like they are on the full sized airplane. This is a bit harder to do than just gluing some plastic to the outside of the window area after covering but it's really worth the effort. First, cover your fuselage Including the window area. Then cut away the covering in the window area but leave enough to wrap around the sticks at top, bottom and sides of the sticks **Fig 6-6A** . Touch up any open spots with matching thin dope or Magic Marker. Now use a paper template to create the *exact* size of each window insert so it fills the window and has enough overlap to glue to the back of the window sticks. Cut the plastic window inserts to exact size then wash with soap and water and dry on a lint free rag. From here on handle that insert *only* at a corner with a tweezers. Don't lay it down on any flat surface that might deposit sawdust or lint on it. Stick a paper clip into a blob of clay as a temporary holder. A stained or dirty window can destroy your careful scale work.

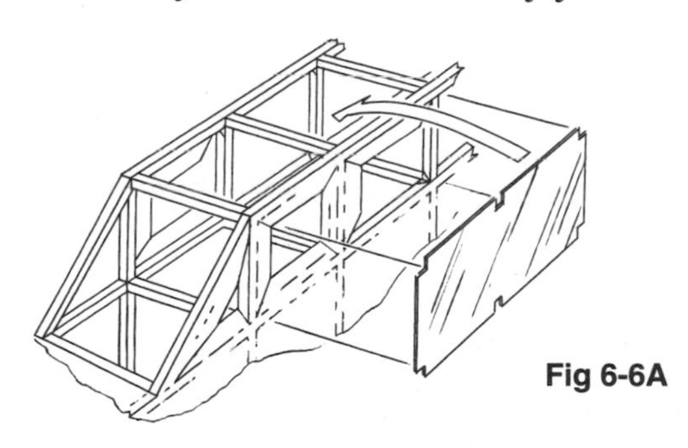

Fig 6-6A

Run a very thin bead of RC-56, or Formula 560 Canopy glue from **Pacer**, on the inside of each stick where the window will touch. I believe some of the craft glues made for vinyl will work as well. Look for glues that are marked "dries clear". Let the glue harden for 5 minutes or so to reduce squeeze out, then using tweezers and toothpicks, press the window on to the sticks **Fig 6-6A**. Any excess glue can be cleaned with some water on a Q-Tip®. Try not to touch the plastic with your hands. Use a tissue when pressing down. Another method is to allow the RC-56 to dry completely then activate it with heat from an iron as you press the plastic on. For Peanut and other small types, food wrap plastic can be applied loosely then shrunk drum tight with a hair dryer.

Front windshields are installed in a similar manner by tucking the plastic *inside* the window side sticks and under the top cross piece **Fig 6-6B**. Some builders don't attach the windshield in front at all, some add tiny points that penetrate the cowling (**RPMA pg 137**). This is about the only way to get good adhesion and permanent location on an open cockpit windshield. A neat touch for old time projects is to cut strips of either tissue colored the same as the fuselage or use chrome colored plastic to simulate the metal strips used to assemble windshields. These strips can be pin punctured to simulate rivets then glued to *both* inside and outside of the windshield Gluing of these pieces must be done with very small amounts of glue and extreme care so as not to stain or cloud the plastic. You can also lay tissue on double-faced adhesive, cut into strips and apply. **Never use Cyano glue for plastic windows**. Its fumes will permanently cloud the plastic.

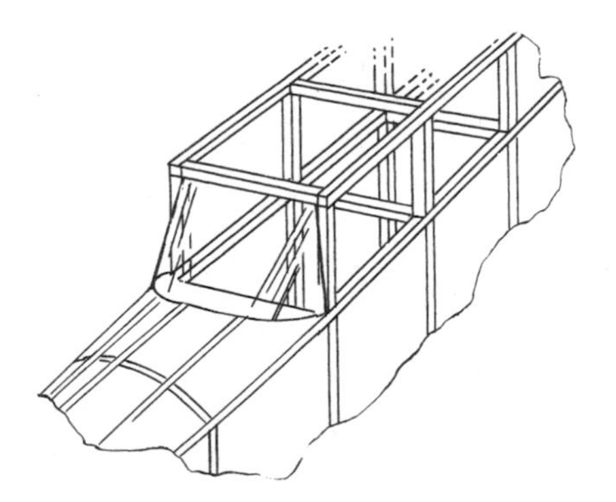

Fig 6-6B

Nose Blocks

One thing you can't have on a scale model is a nose block tilted away from the firewall to provide down or side thrust. That would cancel all your scale efforts. Here are some ways to avoid the problem:

1. Build 2 degrees of down and 2 of right thrust into the fuselage structure. Just angle the first uprights and cross pieces appropriately. Each degree is 1/16 inch at about 3-1/4 inches, so create a triangle 3-1/4 long x 1/8 high and mark off the width and height of your nose block to get the required offset.

2. Build up the nose block itself on one corner by the same amount as in 1 and fair in the sides with scrap balsa.

3. Build in a screw adjustment system **(RPMA pg 42**) and, once the thrust is set, fair in the nose with scrap.

4. Create an adjustable nose block **Fig 6-7**, which allows for infinitely adjustable side and down thrust. The metal strip should be .020 brass or alum can stock with a brass eyelet. Taper the thrust hole with careful carving and a rat-tailed file. Now you can loosen the set screw to slide the rear strip up for down thrust (you probably almost never need up thrust) and rotate it side to side for side thrust. Once thrust is adjusted for maximum power, glue the brass strip to the rear of the block

Fig 6-7

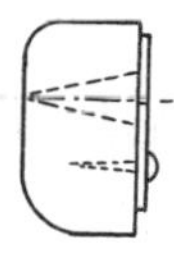

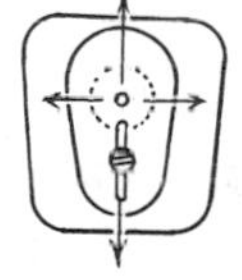

K&P makes a thrust button for small rubber models that contains all adjustments inside the button sleeve. It is sold by SAMS and other supply houses.

Electric, gas or CO_2 models are adjusted for thrust by placing washers under the motor mounts at the appropriate corners. The electric chapter shows several ways to mount motors. Some combination of these with the thrust adjustments shown above will work best for you. Please don't even think about getting away with no thrust adjustment. You are risking destruction of your model.

I agree that a big tilt in the nose block can be a bit unsightly. Two or even 4 degrees will hardly be noticed but you might want to use a smaller diameter or lower pitch prop (with less torque effect) to avoid too much tilt. Chapter 10, **Gears and Warp Drives,** suggests ways to use gears to reduce prop size and Torque. This may be another way to reduce the thrust tilt angle your model needs.

Landing Gear

Here's a subtle area that needs special attention if you are really going to fly your scale creation. Since most flying is done off grass, your model won't touch and roll like the full-sized version. It will glide down until the wheels touch and then will come to an abrupt stop and tilt over on the nose. This type of landing puts direct rearward stress on the gear and tries to rip it loose from the fuselage or wing with appropriate damage. Therefore, you need both strength and flexibility in your gear. If you are converting a rubber kit to electric power, you will need to "beef-up" the gear and its mounting beyond the plan to handle the extra loads which may be doubled !!

Landing gear wire should *always* be sandwiched between braced balsa sheets. Just gluing the wire to a longeron or former simply won't do. **Fig 6-8** shows the basic method. For heavier models, you may want to wrap the sandwich with thread or Tyvek® to add strength. If the gear is installed in the wing as on many WWII fighters, reinforce the wing struts and sandwich the gear the same way. **Fig 6-9** shows a neat way to sandwich the gear and still allow for some spring. For those old time models that had more than one gear wire, Tony Peters has a neat idea. Make and brace the main gear wire as above. Then add the second strut of wood or paper and allow it to slide into and out of a small slot in the fuselage bottom as the main gear wire bends.

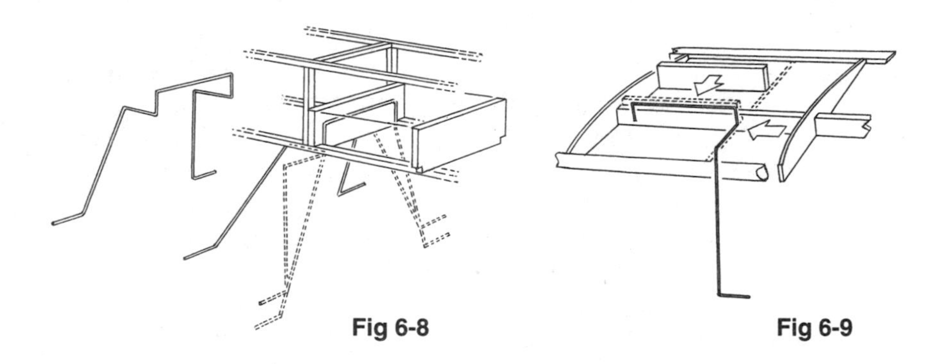

Fig 6-8 **Fig 6-9**

Spinners

A neat spinner adds a lot to the appearance of your model and can even help protect it in a crash. Carving a balsa spinner with a Dremel tool is no problem. Just glue in a 1/8 dowel at the center of the back, chuck it in your tool and grind away. Then hollow out the spinner, cut slots for the prop blades, make a back plate and you're done. Solid spinners can be carved from foam and will absorb some of the shock of a nose crash. Once the foam is carved, cover it with strips of tissue or silkspan laid on with white glue and water. Paint another coat of white glue on top and you can use enamels or even dope right over the dried white glue.

Another neat method for making hollow spinners was dreamed up by a fellow named Mike Evatt some years ago. Make a balsa spinner, as before, on your Dremel. Use it as a master form. Wax it heavily or spray on silicon lubricant. Pull stretch panty hose tight over the form and hold with a rubber band. Spread on white glue mixed with talcum powder and let dry. Make 3 or 4 layers as above. Remove from the form, cut blade slots and make a back plate from ply. Now you can use the same form over and over.

For those who are really handy, it's possible to make those fancy spiral lines that the ME-109 and others had on their spinners. Find some heavy thread of the right color or Magic Marker some in the color you want. Make a small pin hole at the nose point of your spinner. Glue in the thread then wind it around the spinner in a spiral. Wipe with white glue to hold it there and dope over when dry **Fig 6-10**.

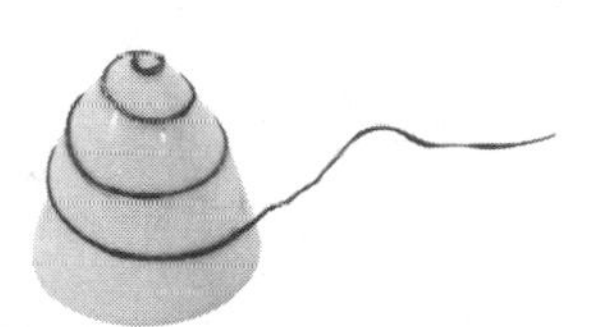

Fig 6-10

Plug in Wings

This feature will not only make transport easier but will probably save your model several times during the trimming phase and almost every time a wind gust hits on launch. It's a rare crash that doesn't impact a wing tip.

Although **(RPMA pg 122)** shows a tongue attachcd to the wing, I now prefer the tongue to be part of the fuselage and the box in the wing. The tongue should be of <u>very</u> hard balsa of at least 8-10 lb. for small models, and spruce or ply on larger models. There are several ways to construct detachable wing systems with wire, tubes or tongues.

Before beginning construction of a plug-in wing system, you have to decide exactly where to separate the wing halves. The obvious spot would seem to be the dihedral break and most of our models are built with that break set where the wing meets the fuselage. We'll work with that idea first but remember that what is obvious is not necessarily best.

Wire and Tube Wing Dihedral Construction Methods

Leo McCarthy uses an interesting method to align his wing and root sections. He builds the wing in three pieces with doubled ribs at the roots of both the wing section and the fuselage center piece **Fig 6-12, 6-12A**. This can be done with either high or low winged models. Instead of gluing the wing to the side of the fuselage in a low or mid-wing model, build a center section and design an opening in the fuselage that will exactly fit the insert .

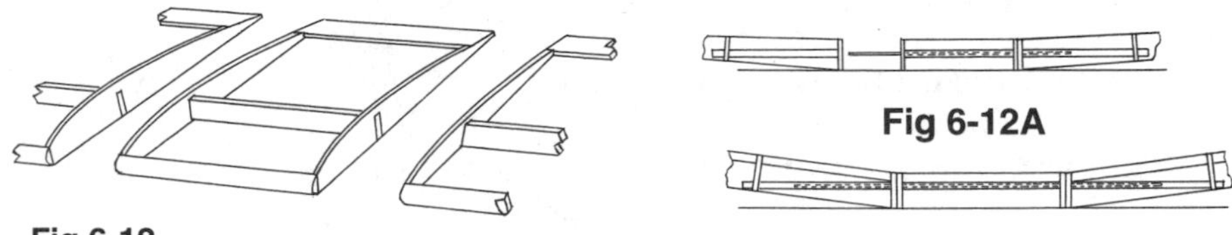

Fig 6-12A

Fig 6-12

While building, tilt the root rib of the wing section inward so it sits flat against the center section rib when the wing is at the proper dihedral angle. If you are scratch building from a 3-view, set the dihedral at 1 inch *on each side*, per foot of span. If a tilt template is not shown on the plan, draw a horizontal line equal to the wing section length **C**, then erect a vertical at one end of the line **B**. Draw another line coming from the base point , also equal to the wing length and tilted so its end is at the correct dihedral height at the tip **B**. The angle shown as **A** is the correct tilt angle for the root rib **Fig 6-11**. For those who like to play with geometry, the tilt angle is equal to 90 degrees *minus* the dihedral angle.

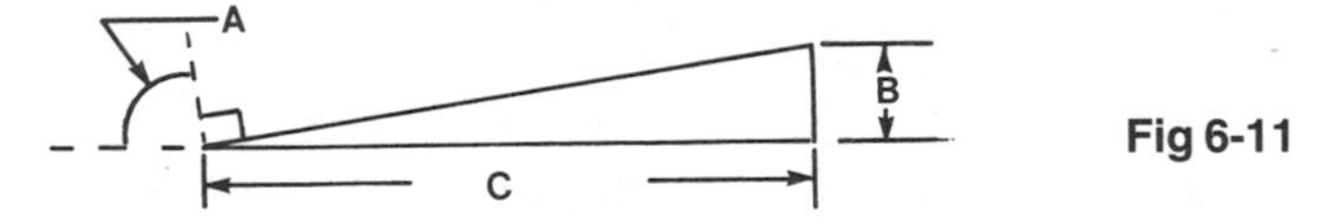

Fig 6-11

Pin the center and wing sections together at the root ribs with the dihedral blocked up. Make a pair of holes through both sets of ribs to accommodate pieces of aluminum or brass tubing .

Put the holes next to a spar if possible. The tubing should have an ID equal to the wire size you will use to pin the wings. I use .045 (3/64") wire for all sizes up to 36 inch span and .062 (1/16") wire for larger spans. Cut the tubing into 4 equal pieces about 1-1/2 to 2 inches long each. Slide a piece of wire about 4" long through two of the tubes. Slip the tubes (with wire inside) into the rib holes. Make sure each tube ends flush with a root rib side. Note that the tube in the wing half is not horizontal but tilts at an angle due to the dihedral. *Firmly* glue each tube half to a spar and through 2 ribs with epoxy. You may have to build a bit of a box from scrap if there's no spar to use as an anchor.

Pull out the wire, slip an Exacto or very thin saw blade between the ribs and separate the tubes where they may be glued together. Clean the tubing edge with a #11 blade. Sand the tube ends flush. Repeat with the other wing. Now rough up the wire pieces with a file and epoxy them into the center section tubes so they protrude 3/4 inch into the wing tubes. You will need 2 tube sets for each wing. You will also need a small hook on each wing section to hold a rubber band running across the inside of the center section to hold the unit together (**RPMA pg 122**).

I prefer a tongue to the wire system. It's a bit harder to set up but allows better break away and lines up the wings very neatly. Before building the wings, cut a slot in all the root ribs about 3/4 inches wide and either 3/32 or 1/8" high depending on the span. Plan the slot to be within 1/8 of a spar if possible. Cut the slot above the center of the rib to allow for the slant in the tongue as in the tubing above. Build the wing in 3 pieces and pin together with dihedral blocked up. Cut a tongue piece from *hard* balsa, pine, spruce or ply so it fits through the slot and reaches the next rib in the center section and extends 3/4 to 1 inch into the wing.

Round the tongue the front to allow the wing to swing back in a crash. Rub candle wax or soap on the part of the tongue that slides into the wing section. Assemble the tongue and glue *firmly* into the center section. Now build a box from scrap balsa around the top, bottom and sides of the tongue inside the wing section **Fig 6-13.**

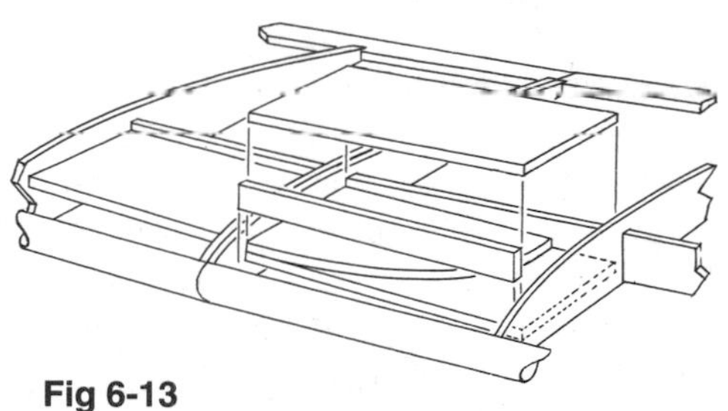

Fig 6-13

Be generous with glue but *don't* use Cyano. It could easily wick through and glue the wing sections together. Some prefer to build the box outside, then install the complete system in the blocked up wing.

If you feel you will have trouble building a plug-in wing system with the tubes or tongue slanted in the wing, then you can simply pre-glue the tongue to the correct dihedral angle (as if it is a small, sheet wood wing). Brace with Tyvec or silk, glue the joint with epoxy and smooth with sandpaper. Now the tongue will slide into the wing exactly parallel with the spar. Assemble as described above, with the wing blocked up to proper dihedral angle, and build the box for the tongue.

The same technique won't work so well with wire and tube. You will have to start with a larger diameter wire (around .062) and carefully bend it to the correct dihedral angle. Then you can assemble the appropriate sized tubing into the wing and root.

There's a way to avoid most of the dihedral break problems in a plug in wing system. That is simply to separate the wing sections at some point **away from the dihedral break**. Take a good look at your model. Is it possible to separate the wing sections at some point **after** the dihedral break ? Remember, most full sized airplanes have little or no dihedral so the amount you require isn't really scale anyway. As a matter of fact, many real aircraft were built with a slight twist to the wings to offset the tremendous torque caused by those great big engines and that doesn't show on your scale model.

Another advantage of breaking the wing a bit past the dihedral point is that your fancy fillet at the wing root of your favorite WWII fighter won't be disturbed. Just build in a couple of extra ribs 1/2 or 3/4 inch outboard of the dihedral joint, anchor your tubes or tongue to the center section and build in a nice, straight slot in the wing section. For those WWII carrier fighters with folding wings, this method will look quite scale. On multi-engined models, like Leo McCarthy's flying boat, you can make the wing break just after the inboard engine nacelle.

Removable wings add another subtle advantage to scale models. Repairs to either wings or fuselage are *much* easier when you can take off the wing. Even a small tissue rip can become a big problem when it's too near the junction to handle easily. Obviously, rebuilding a wing tip or a dented leading edge is a big job when you have to haul the whole model around while you glue in a couple of sticks or a new rib.

Some variation of these methods will fit your profile. You may prefer hardwood dowels or bamboo skewers to mate the wing sections,

Wing Construction

Although I constantly repeat my "Save Weight" refrain in <u>all</u> flying models, scale wings are not the place to concentrate on weight. These are the parts that have to carry the whole load, including fancy spoked wheels, Spandau machine guns, carved foam pilots, etc. In a low-winged model, the wing must also handle landing shocks. If your model is electric powered, the wing load will be *double* that for rubber power. The spars are the load bearing members so they should be spruce or very hard balsa. You can save some weight in the ribs by going to a slightly thicker rib with a lower density. Try 1/16, 5 lb. ribs for 2/3 of the span, then switch to 1/20 for the rest. There's no rule that says all of any component structure must be the same density or even thickness. Remember, the kit manufacturer may have chosen material and direction of grain for economy, not necessarily for best engineering.

Tony Peters adds a strand of Kevlar or carpet thread to LE, TE and tip just before covering. This works on the smallest models. It strengthens the wing and also helps avoid dents and dings. Carbon fiber is an extremely light and strong bracing material but it is black and must be painted over on a scale model. Fiberglass is another fine bracer but too heavy for small models.

Molded Tips

Wingtips are a great place to learn about molded shapes. They are constantly contacting the ground or some other solid object so you want great strength together with some springiness. I have found that very thin spruce (.020" thick), works very well. You can also build up several layers of balsa. Get yourself a plastic tube about 1 inch ID and 38 inches long from a fish tank or golf club store. Cap or cork each end. Fill with warm water and 2 teaspoons of ammonia. Now you can cut lots of balsa strips with your trusty Jim Jones Stripper or buy some thin spruce from Joe Deppe. Soak *overnight* - don't rush this. Cut a form from heavy cardboard, balsa or foam that is just <u>inside</u> the tip outline. Rub the edges of the form with wax, wet 3, 4, or 5 strips with 50-50 white glue and water, and tape the stack to one end of the form leaving at least a 2 inch overlap at the end **(RPMA pg 48)**

Pull the rest of the stack around the form as you tape every 1/2 inch or so. Make sure each strip is tight to the form and the other strips. Once the whole stack is taped, wipe on some more glue and let dry *overnight.* Redesign your leading and trailing edges to accommodate the molded tip instead of the much wider sheet wood tip. You will probably find that the wood strips are tacked strongly enough to the form to do some rough sanding before assembly. Use 2 strips 1/32 x 1/16" up to 18" span; 3 strips 1/32 x 3/32" for 18-30 " and 4 strips 1/32 X 1/8" for larger spans.

Another method pioneered by Paul Kaufmann is to wet the strips then "wick" Cyano glue right through them after bending and taping. This is faster and stronger but requires a perfect fit between strips and can be harder to sand.

Sliced and Cracked Rib Wings

As described in the chapter 1, **Construction,** sliced or cracked rib wings will make your scratch built scale model a much easier project. If you are building one of the newer kits with laser cut parts, then by all means use the kit ribs. These have lightening holes and all are *exactly* the required size. The Flying Aces groups use cracked rib wings which are about the simplest type to make. Don't be too concerned about exact airfoil shape on your early, small scale models. Airfoil has little discernible effect on flight profile on these. Also, consider a wing with full-sized, cut ribs for the inboard part where it separates from the root and cracked or sliced ribs outboard from that point. Just as you can mix and match wood density so the rear of the fuselage is lighter than the front, rib configuration can also be changed to fit design requirements. Get used to experimenting. The guy who designed the kit may have done so in 1955 when many new materials and methods were unknown.

Molded Tail Outlines

As mentioned earlier, saving weight in the tail is important. Every gram saved there can save 3 grams in the nose. But when you go overboard with thin, light tail feathers, the "Potato Chip Stab" may appear. Shrinking your tissue may be enough to cause a warp that will be very hard to fix. Molded tail sections resist warps and also increase strength with almost no weight penalty. The trick is to use a fairly hard and springy (8 lb.) spar with a very light (5 lb.) molded outline. This may weigh even less than the sheet outlines furnished with most kits. Use only 2 strips of 1/32 x 1/16" for small models and 3 strips 1/32 x 1/16" for the larger ones.

Movable Control Surfaces

Since you can't very well change wing or stab incidence on a scale model, you have to provide some way of creating decalage for flight trimming. On your early scale attempts you may want to try attaching the wing *only* at the rear and the stab at the front. Temporary rubber bands can hold the flying surfaces in position while you run your basic flight tests and add shims under the wing LE or stab TE as required. It's a big mistake to glue in wing, rudder and stab surfaces before flight testing. Then, your only way to make flight adjustments is with warps or weights added to wingtips, front or rear. This is hard to control, even for the experienced modeler, and field warps tend to return to their original position after a few minutes.

The best and simplest system for movable controls is to build a double spar in both stab and rudder. Strip one strand of wire from ordinary lamp cord and lace it through the spars **Fig 6-14**(A). The hole for the wire can be made with a fine pin or .012 drill. Leave a card stock gap between the spars and glue the wire to each side. Cover the stab or rudder in one piece and slit the covering between the spars *after* shrinking and doping.

Extreme care is the rule when covering tail feathers. Almost every stage of the covering sequence tends to create strains that lead to warps. Make sure your construction has good fits at all the joints. Loose fits filled with glue will twist the wood when the glue shrinks. Force fits are just as bad. Cut thin sticks with a new blade to avoid crushing the edges where sticks meet. Small gussets in corners will help. Spray a heavy water mix when shrinking and pin the structure flat on support strips so air can circulate top & bottom

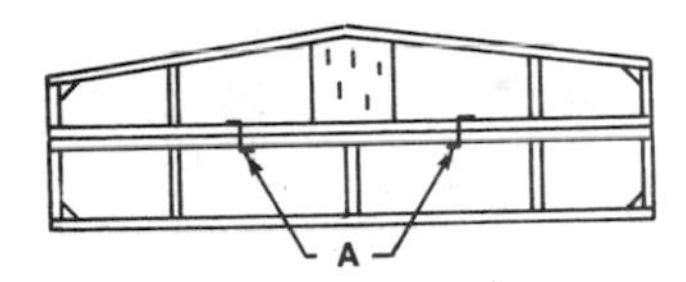

Fig 6-14

Dope with 2 *thin* coats covering top right, then bottom right, then left top, left bottom, then repeat. Pin back in a fixture to dry overnight. **Never** try to force dry either water or dope on tail structures.

Scale Details

Ludwig Mies Van Der Rohe or Karel Capek may have said, "God is in the details" and it's no less true in models than in architecture or robots. Even if you don't compete, those tiny scale details will continue to please you every time you see your model in flight. Things as subtle as a thin line indicating a control surface, a cabin door or a bomb bay add immeasurably to the appearance of your model. Tiny lettered signs and perfectly executed insignia are no longer the exclusive province of the professional builder with a 6 power magnifier, a 1/64" wide brush and a steady hand. The advent of photocopy machines and some simple chemical magic can make experts of us all.

Besides actual scale details like machine guns, wire wheels, radio antennae and engine cylinders, it is **scale markings** that add the essential touch of realism to a model. There are now a great many ways to create extremely realistic scale markings. I have arbitrarily divided the methods into **BEFORE** and **AFTER COVERING**, but combinations of both methods are certainly practical. Study all the methods described and use a few, even if you may not use them on a current project. Learn some of the techniques involved so you can choose which suits you and a particular model.

Before Covering

For any of these methods you will need a couple of frames at least a foot square or the size of 1/2 a sheet of tissue. Make the frames from 1 x 2" pine or aluminum angle iron. Tape your tissue, silk or silkspan firmly to the frames and shrink with water to prepare for marking **Fig 5-2** page 101.

You can actually make black and white photocopies with tissue!! Just reduce or enlarge your copy information to proper size, tape the leading edge of your pre-shrunk tissue to a piece of paper and feed it through the copier. This only works with a **black and white** copy machine ! You can carefully draw panel lines, rivets, lettering, and more *at any convenient size* and reproduce it on your tissue in the correct scale size.

When marking on tissue, remember that the better the surface, the sharper and clearer the marking. Ordinary gift wrap tissue has a rougher grain than the best Esaki Japanese tissue. Good, light tissue has a shiny and a dull side. The shiny side is the smoothest and best to receive marking.

So simple black lines aren't enough for your brand new P-51 flown by the Tuskeegee Airmen. You need that nose art and the colored insignia. Help is at hand. Make a *color* photocopy the correct size using only a **Canon** or **Minolta** copier. Tape the copy face up to a smooth surface like a blotter, lay your tissue frame on top with the smooth side of the tissue against the copy. Now rush out to the local art supply store and buy a **Chartpak Blender**. This is an artist's marker made by **Chartpak** or **Letraset**

The blender is a clear solvent that will allow you to release the image from the photocopy and transfer it to the tissue. You can also color the tissue at the same time by using a colored Chartpak marker. This will even work using several different colored markers (as for a camouflage pattern) that overlap. The transferred image can be either on top or under the tissue or Airspan. If under, it will show through with a slightly dulled or "airworn" appearance which may be preferred.

Make long, even strokes with the marker, always in the direction of the tissue grain. Go over it again if the color is too light. Some practice is necessary here because too much marker will begin to dissolve the image and blur it. For the WWI buffs, lozenge tissue in 4 and 5 color patterns and several sizes can be purchased from **Robert Wells**, Wilmington DE. Reduce this to your scale size, transfer to tissue and finally finish that Albatross.

Most of the research for this process was done by **Dennis Norman** and incorporated into his "**Air Ace**" detail series. Dennis furnishes many specific marking sets complete with lots of panel lines and other details ready to photocopy and transfer. The same method can be used to transfer images on to balsa or other opaque materials by placing the photocopy face down on your material and rubbing the back with a blender. You might also try nail polish remover instead of blender. It works faster when going through the photocopy paper. I have sanded the back of the copy with #400 paper to thin it and roughen the surface to accept the solvent.

If you are going transfer to opaque material, or prefer the image on the front face and your copy has lettering, you will need a *reverse copy*. Many photocopy vendors have machines that will reverse a copy digitally. This may cost an extra dollar or so. If a reverse copy is not available, simply ask for a *transparency*. Turn it over, back it up with a sheet of white paper, and copy it again.

This type of transfer on to tissue also works with Airspan, silk or silkspan since all are porous. To transfer to Litespan or other plastic materials, you will have to work through the photocopy.

Direct transfer of black and white copy is quite sharp but color copies tend to lose some of the sharpness and brightness of the colors. If you find the finished effect too marginal, there are still several ways to use this new equipment to get just the effect you want.

One of the neatest techniques for showing tiny lettering on a model was probably created by Dave Rees some years ago. Dave used **Letraset®** rub on lettering to show all the little signs found on the skin of an airplane. Take a trip to the local private airport and check out the information shown on the aircraft skin. Even a Cessna 150 trainer will have signs that say, "Pitot Tube", "Fuel Cap" , "Engine Access", "Do Not Step Here", "Cowl Release" and many more. How about a neat Hamilton Standard logo right on the prop or a "P" for Piper on the hub cap; or perhaps a pilot's name just under the canopy on a fighter ?

All this lettering can be added using Letraset® while the pre-shrunk tissue is still on the frame. Letraset markings come in a wide variety of sizes from about 1 inch down to .040 and in black and an opaque white. Application is simple. Just burnish the markings through the carrier paper on to your tissue. In addition, die cut, pressure sensitive vinyl lettering sheets are also available in many sizes. This lettering can be colored with magic marker, then applied. Do not dope over Letraset® or vinyl lettering ! Only a thin mist of Krylon® may be used. Practice the technique of overcoating Letraset® on scrap first. It's easy to do but just as easy to spoil if you aren't careful.

For panel lines, rivets and other line markings, use a Micron **PIGMA** marking pen (item # SDK) from Sakura Color Products of Japan and available in most art supply stores. These pens will write *directly* on tissue, silk, Airspan, Silkspan or Litespan without bleeding. The markings will go on over Butyrate dope and can be doped over or sprayed with Krylon for matte or gloss finish. The pens come in Black, Blue and Red and in a variety of line widths from about .030 to .060.

Of course, you can apply Letraset marking, Pigma lines, vinyl letters and even direct color copy transfers on to various coverings *after* they are on the model. However, the chance you take is that a poor application may spoil your covering job and ruin the whole project. That's why I suggest testing the various techniques on scrap materials in order to develop some skill in handling each method. One of the problems with scale markings is that you may do a lot of work on the covering material, then destroy some of it in your first trimming crash. That's probably why long grass was invented! There's a lot more riding on your first toss of a scale model than in test flying a P-30 that's held together with easily snapped off rubber bands. You will simply have to decide how much scale detail to apply before flight trimming.

After Covering

If you plan for some sheet balsa or bond paper support in areas where you are going to add lettering, a lot of the Letraset and Pigma markings can be added later. With careful burnishing and the heat of your finger, Letraset markings will detach from the carrier sheet even on to unsupported tissue areas. vinyl lettering and Pigma markings will also go on easily.

Pressure Sensitive Decals

For those insignia and nose art markings that require bright, sharp colors, there are several methods now available and more will come on line shortly. You can take your color photocopy, sand the back to thin it as much as practical and apply it with white glue. **Chartpak** makes a Design Film that is a clear, pressure sensitive material that can pass through a color photocopy machine. It's called "Gloss Design Film" Cat. No. DGC. It is available in matte (DMP or LCM-10) which is for B&W copiers only. The gloss film can be matted with Krylon. Now you can make your own pressure sensitive decals. Cut the decal close to the edge, immerse in water with a drop of detergent, slide it into place (the water will kill the adhesive temporarily), squeegee out the excess water and allow to dry before overcoating - presto! You now have a permanent colored decal.

Water Slide-Off Decals

We have all used these pesky "Cockamamies" (from Decalcomania) since we were kids. They are still furnished with many kits and, when used properly, are almost indistinguishable from painted markings. Some new materials have virtually eliminated the bubbles, clear borders and glossy appearance. **Micro Mark** sells a set of liquids designed just for decal application. Their #81261 Decal Finishing Set includes Clear Gloss, Decal Setting Solution, Decal Softening Solution and Clear or Matte Top Coat.

With these helpful materials and just a bit of practice, you can apply decals that produce a professional air brushed appearance. Before applying, you may want to paint the surface of the model with Clear Gloss to provide the smoothest receiving surface. Next, don't soak the decal in water!! After carefully cutting the decal from the sheet as close as practical to the edge of the markings, dip it in a cup and allow to stand for a minute. This should soften the adhesive without dissolving it.

Next, apply Decal Setting Solution (sometimes sold as "Solv-a-Set") to the model surface with a soft brush. Gently slide the decal off the backing paper and into position. Use a small, soft brush to move the decal and work out any large air bubbles. Apply Decal Softening Solution over the decal and allow to dry. Decal Softening Solution applied over the decal will make it conform exactly to the surface where it will appear painted. Apply this with a soft brush and allow it to work into the decal and dry thoroughly. Apply a second coat after the first one dries if more "settling" is needed. Now you can overcoat with Matte Clear or Clear Gloss or Krylon matte or gloss. "Feather" your overcoat into the surrounding area or coat the whole component for uniform appearance.

Now you can actually make your own water slide off decals to the exact size you require and even in any color arrangement you like! **Labco** in Warren MI. markets a complete decal system based on a material that can be passed through a color photocopy machine or color laser printer. All you need is a master copy the size and color you want. You can even hand draw your copy in a large size, then photocopy it down as required. The same master can be used in many sizes for future models. As long as your printer uses water proof ink (Ink jet printers won't work). You can make a decal, coat it with lacquer, epoxy, polyurethane or Krylon, cut to size and apply just like a store bought one. The Micro Mark decal solutions will work well with this stuff too. Labco sells a starter kit for about $10.00. Also, by the time this is published, **Brittains** in Connecticut. may have a similar product. As we go to press, Micro-Mark offers their item 81485 clear and 81489 white photocopy decal material.

Glue On Markings

For those who own or have access to computers, plotters and color printers, markings in any size or color arrangement are now almost as easy as printing a letter. There are many Clip Art and CAD programs (even free ones that can be down loaded from the Internet) that have libraries of aircraft insignia and other markings. Both Mark Fineman's 5/96 article in *Model Aviation* and Peter Wank's 5/96 article in *Flying Models* describe interesting new methods for creating and transferring markings. Here's a brief overview along with some of my own ideas.

Enlarge or reduce your markings to the appropriate size, get several color photocopies and either transfer your markings as described earlier or use the photocopy itself. If you intend to attach a photocopy or any other paper printed markings to your model covering, you can enhance the appearance with a few simple steps.

Before cutting out the marking, place it on a smooth *clean* surface and sand the back with 400 or 600 sandpaper. This will thin out the paper. Ordinary bond paper is about .004 thick which is twice as thick as a human hair so the edge clearly shows. Next, you should "edge" the finished decal. **Edging** means coloring the exposed, white edge with a marker of the same color as that part of the decal touching the model surface. This may take as many as three different colors and is needed to make that white edge disappear.

Markings should be applied only with white glue or spray-on pressure sensitive adhesive like **3M** Spray Mount Artist's Adhesive (#6065) It allows repositioning and becomes permanent when dry. Once markings have been applied and are thoroughly dry, seal and overcoat them while "blending" the overcoat into the covering. As you use different materials and method,s or even mix several techniques on the same model, you need to be careful with your covering adhesive and your overcoat material.

Model Paints and Overcoats

With so many colors of tissue, Airspan, Litespan and other materials, it doesn't seem that anyone would want to use paints to color a model. However, some of you will want to create an opaque finish to more closely simulate the real thing and may want to mask and spray or brush trim colors. Here are several ways to do this:

The **Frisket** system is much better than masking tape. Frisket is available in most art stores, can be cut into shapes and is thin enough to follow a curve. It masks closer to the tissue and gives a sharper edge.

For any paint trimming, you should seriously consider spraying. Simple **Badger** Air Brush systems, using a can of propellant, cost under $25, and can get you started. Later on you can get into a $125.00 compressor system that will handle all your spraying needs for years to come.

Instead of dope, you might consider **Floquil Polly S** colors used on model trains. Micro Mark carries a full line and you can match almost any color in gloss or matte. Mix the Floquil with rubbing alcohol or add to very thin clear dope. Acrylics cover very well, are easy to apply, dry hard but are kind of heavy. **Apple Barrel** or **Pactra** brands from craft shops work well. **Grumbacher** makes a brand of Acrylic enamel called **Keepsake** that is water soluble but won't run once it dries.

Again, you must test all these combinations on scrap material before ruining your model with bleeding colors, trim that falls off or covering that fogs or cracks. I suggest you settle on a fine grade of tissue for all models up to about 30 inch span and Airspan, Litespan or Silkspan for up to 60 inch span. Then try some transfer processes from photocopies, lay on some trim lettering and spray on some different overcoats. Never brush on an overcoat. Even if reasonably compatible, a brushed-on coat stays too wet for too long and will soften your trim. Many clear coatings like varnish, lacquer and Krylon are available in spray cans and a few passes with drying in between, work better than a wet coat.

Krylon Kamar Varnish # 1312 (gloss), Krylon Matte Finish #1311, Blair Matte Spray Clear #201 and Testors Dull Coat #1260 will overcoat most of the markings described above. **However, a heavy, wet coat may still bleed your markings**. Build up 2 or 3 thin coats to avoid problems. **Do not** use Butyrate or Nitrate dope to overcoat markings, particularly water slide-off decals. The thinner in dope will act very quickly to dissolve the markings. It's possible to spray a very thin, dry, coat of dope and build up a covering but this takes experience and care.

WHEN USING ANY OF THESE SPRAYS, BE SURE TO WORK IN A VERY WELL-VENTILATED AREA. Spraying is a much more volatile process than brush painting and releases a fine mist of toxic thinner all around the sprayer. Even in winter, take the model into a bathroom, line the tub with newspaper, open the window wide, close the door and spray for a few minutes at a time. Your local paint store has inexpensive paint masks that will help. 3M also has a whole line of filter masks. **NEVER, NEVER** smoke while you are spraying.

I suggest you don't apply any overcoat to your covering until it is permanently attached to the model. Any overcoat stiffens and embrittles the material making a smooth covering job more difficult. Also, with even the best covering job, you may want to try a bit of heat or water-shrinking which will certainly be easier before overcoating.

Once you have marked your tissue or Airspan you will needto use some method other than dope and thinner to attach it. For tissue and Silkspan, glue sticks work well. The technique is described in the covering chapter. A bit of practice will teach you how easy it is to re-position tissue with tacky glue-stick until most of the wrinkles are gone. Once attached, all edges can be sealed with a thin bead of aliphatic glue mixed with water.

Like any good chef, experiment until you are competent enough with all these techniques to create your own combinations. Different methods will suit different models and each technique should be modified to fit your personal building profile. If you are at all interested in scale models, consider that the 12 or 15 hours you spend building can be enhanced many times by adding only an hour or two of scale marking work.

Remember, these are "Techniques" not "Technology". The difference being that a technique gets developed through use, experiment and practice and is usually unique in some way to the practitioner. Technology is a proven system that anyone can use with appropriate equipment and training.

Wheels and Floats

There's nothing like an R.O.G. (rise off ground) for a scale model. No matter how well your model flies, the ability to start that flight from the ground instead of your hand exponentially expands your pleasure. If the model can take off and land on water, you will never forget the thrill. To do these wonderful things you need wheels or floats that not only look like the real thing but also work under free flight model conditions. That means wheels that turn and landing gear supports for floats or wheels that can handle impacts that would destroy their full-sized brothers.

I have previously discussed how to firmly mount your landing gear wires to fuselage or wing so they don't rip loose in a crash. Now let's also give some thought to flexibility so they can absorb some impact without transmitting it to the structure! It's easy enough to design LG wires so they have some "torsion bar" effect **Fig 6-9**. Just add a bend *inside* the fuselage or wing and a small slot for the gear to pass through.

Many types of wheels are commercially available. You can get solid balsa or hard wood, plastic and rubber and even inflatable tires for small models. However, wheels can become a big weight sacrifice if you are not careful. A pair of hardwood or plastic wheels can weigh as much as your propeller. Balsa wheels are simple to make and, if you have a Dremel tool or drill press, yours can look as good as a professionally turned wheel.

Dick Howard has done some interesting things with wheel shapes by grinding contours in single-edged razor blades **Fig 6-15** with a Dremel tool grinder. Dick mounts the contoured blade in a hard wood holder and uses it to cut the shape of the balsa wheel.

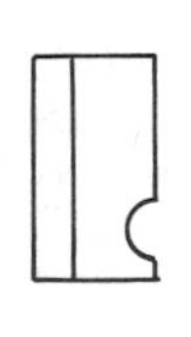

Fig 6-15

You can avoid an unsightly bent wire sticking out of the center by cutting the wire 3/32 or 1/8" outside the hub, retaining the wheel with a drop of epoxy, then glue on an appropriately colored and marked hubcap over the wire end. Look around for plastic tips on pens or pill packages. Cut off the tip for a small hubcap, paint it and stick on a letter or emblem . My Herr Cub has a 1/4 inch high Piper "P" on each hubcap.

A whole chapter could be written about how to make real spoked wheels. Obviously, these appear only on models from around the WWI era and have limited appeal. The Jan. 1976 and Feb. 1977 *Aeromodeller* magazines had two very good articles on the subject. These issues might be available from the publisher. But, here's how you can make decent fake spoked wheels.

With a fine pen, draw a set of radial lines 15 or 20 degrees apart. Make several photocopies on clear material. Cut out disks equal to the *inside* diameter of your wheel. Sandwich the lined disk between two disks of stiff, transparent plastic .005 to .010" thick, using RC-56. Make a tire from black painted, split wire insulation. Insert a short piece of tubing or an eyelet as a hub.

Old Timer Models sells lovely balsa balloon wheels that are great for all the "Between-the-Wars" planes, and, of course, Trexler still sells those real inflatable tire wheels as small as 1-1/4 inch diameter. For balsa wheels, paint the hub in the same color as your covering, then hold a piece of tubing ovcr it to mask the hub while you paint the tire black.

Breathes there a man with soul so dead, he never to himself has said, "Someday I'm gonna build a float plane"? I think not. The special romance of a model that even looks as if it could take-off from water is enough to excite the most jaded scale palate. There are a few kits for float-planes or flying boats. The new, Herr Super Cub-Float plane and the Guillow's PBY are good examples, but if you are to actually going to fly off (and back on to) water you need a few mods to make the system work.

Since floats have a specific angle, spread and track, they are much more rigidly mounted than wheels and, thus can't spring with landing shocks. You need to bind *both* front and rear struts to main fuselage members and brace those members with gussets. On larger models, you will need plywood mounting plates built into the fusclage . On the floats themselves, bend the strut wires (**B**), inward and pass them through a hard balsa or ply spine on top of the float (**F**). Let the wires extend 1/2 inch through the spine. Slip the wires over a picce of brass tubing that becomes the spreader (**H**), and hold it all together with a rubber band across the spread (**G**), **Figs 6-16, 17.** Do this on the front and rear struts

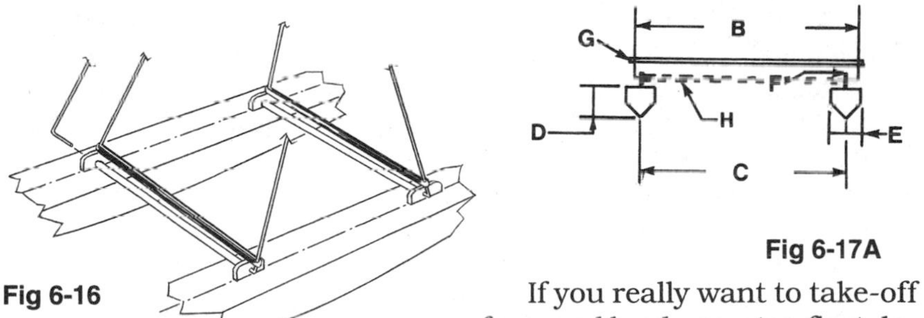

Fig 6-16

Fig 6-17A

If you really want to take-off from and land on water, float design and placement becomes critical. You will probably need to modify your kit somewhat. Since you are adding lots of weight and drag to your model, the wing will have to develop some more lift at low speed to get the model off. The usual solution is to tip the front of the float *down* 2 or 3 degrees. Thus, when the float is horizontal, the wing is at a slightly higher angle of incidence, adding some lift. On landing a FF though, the front tip of the float may dig in causing the model to flip. Most of our FF models have such a high power to weight ratio that they will get off with a parallel float-wing combination.

Float length (**L**) should be 70-75% of fuselage nose-to-tail length and the floats should extend 1/2 the prop diameter in front of the prop (**A**). The step should be directly under the c.g. and the float spread (**C**), should be 20% of the span. Float width (**E**=L/7), and float height (**D**=L/8) (**Fig 6-17A**) . Of course, the float should clear the prop circle by 1/4 " min. which makes for long struts on rubber powered models. Consider a 3 bladed prop which can cut the diameter by 20% and still deliver close to the same thrust. A small (1 in. sq.) water rudder is a must because the floats must track straight as speed increases and the model "goes-up-on-the-step"

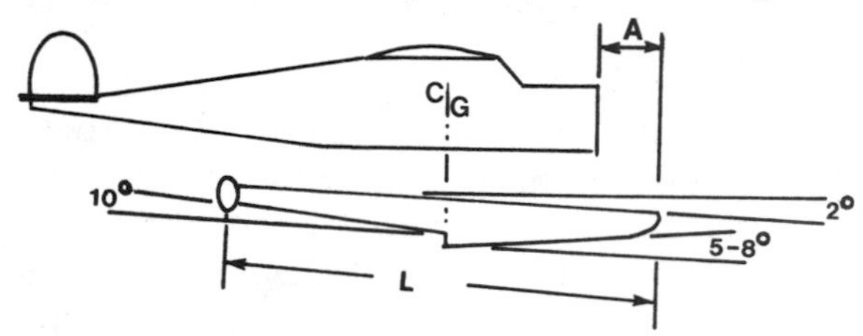

Fig 6-17

For those who like calculations, multiply your model weight in oz. (including floats) by 1.8 to get cubic inches of float displacement . **Fig 6-17** shows basic float dimensions and mounting angle. The 2 degree down float tip angle will make takeoffs easier but may dig in a float tip on landing if your model tends to nose down in the glide. However, the float extending past the nose may save landings. Test your model over long grass before any water flying. Short grass landings can rip off a float.

Floats can be constructed like keel fuselages with a sheet keel down the middle. Cover with silkspan or Airspan, dope with 3 coats and spray on furniture wax. Larger floats can be all sheet covered, then tissued. Or, you can carve the whole float from foam (1-2 lb. per cu. ft. density). Cover it with tissue put on with Aliphatic glue, paint with 3 coats of glue and water. Color with Acrylic enamel. Even if you don't fly off water, here's a model that you can fly in morning, dew wet grass.

Shoes & Ships & Sealing Wax

One of the great fun things about scale modeling is the scavenger hunt for those odd items that greatly enhance scale appearance. The drink stirrer that is just the size for a Spandau machine gun barrel, the 1/4 inch piece of wire insulation that makes a perfect shock absorber on an Aeronca landing gear, and the black painted aspirin tablet that just fits as an ammo drum on a WWI machine gun. They all add tremendous realism and lots of fun when you show them to the gang at the field.

There is no end to the every day items that can be used. Visit some shops that cater to model railroad and doll house buffs for special "I" beam or "angle iron" wood strips, small plastic lights and maybe even neat decals you can use. Collect drinking and mixing straws of all sizes for LG struts, cabanes, interplane struts on biplanes, guns and shock absorbers. For the type of airplanes that had "V" shaped landing gear, Tony Peters uses wire only for the front strut and a straw for the rear. He allows the straw to slide into a slot in the fuselage when the gear flexes.

Williams Brothers makes neat plastic molded engine cylinders in many sizes. You can turn your own from balsa disks, even tapered cylinders can be made this way. Also, thread wrapped around a balsa cylinder or tube will do. Don't forget to add spark plugs, rocker arms and exhaust tubing to your cylinders using bead headed pins and thin aluminum tubing. For aligning cylinders we again go to Tony Peters. Make a cylinder alignment pattern on cardboard so it extends beyond the outside of the nose block. Tack glue or plug it into the nose and use it to align the cylinders. Remove when complete.

Dressmaker's elastic thread can be colored with Magic Marker and used as rigging and radio antennas. It won't sag in dampness. Also, you can find all kinds of swell eyelets and hooks at a dressmaker's store. They are handy as turnbuckles and rigging points on those old time aircraft.

One of the most useful items I have found is plain, ordinary grass. The stems of many weeds are hollow and grow in many different diameters. Cut them when next at the field, dry out until winter, then cut, paint and apply. The stuff is, of course, incredibly light and quite strong, and will take almost any paint or glue.

Tom's Modelworks has a wide variety of tiny etched brass parts in 1/32, 1/48, 1/72 scale that can be assembeld into prop hubs, machine guns, turnbuckles and many other items to add realism to a scale model.

Water soak and heat grass stems to get nice bends which accommodate almost any shape. Some stems even grow sort of oval just like a streamlined LG or interplane strut. (Jeff Anderson)

Lots of over-the-counter pills are packed in sheets and retained with little plastic blisters. These make neat gun blisters. Stop throwing away the blister packages from things you buy. Look at them in a new way as a supply of vacuum molded parts for models. Even sunflower seeds can become rocker arm bumps on a cowling when split in half and painted.

There's a lot of use for split tubing as in cockpit coamings, windshield edging, window frames and shock absorbers. I use wire insulation, stripped-off, slit and painted. Don't slit the stuff by hand. You will end up with crooked cutting and frustration. Check **Fig 1-17, page 27** for a tubing slitter. Since wire comes in an almost infinite number of sizes, you can get insulation to fit any application.

Carved foam is great for pilots and many other items. For small models you can carve the wheel pants, *including* the wheel in one piece, coat with white glue and paint as desired. Even a crudely carved pilot is better than none. You can hollow out the pilot for lightness, carve in goggles and other details. Jim Kaman likes to turn the pilot's head slightly to get rid of that "frozen stare ahead" look and it really works. Even if you use a thin paper pilot, you can twist the head slightly and glue it in place. Why not add a tail gunner to the Grumman Avenger you are building ?

To better illustrate how fine detail and great photography can create a scale masterpiece of Smithsonian quality, check Bob Bender's RE-8 **Fig 6-18**, at about 30 inch span. Matt McCarthy took the photo and the puddle reflection certainly adds to the beauty. Bob's model has *incredible* detail including rigging, turnbuckles, engine and prop, and almost all can be done using the methods discussed above. Break the total impression you want to make into lots of small details and work on them one at a time. Although I don't recommend Peanut Scale models for beginners, they can be made to look very realistic with just markings added by pen. **Fig 6-19** shows my Aeronca Peanut with panel lines, door outlines and registration numbers added with a **Pigma** pen. The Aeronca logo on the rudder was photocopied right on to the tissue and the wing tip lights are red and green pin heads.

Fig 6-18

Fig 6-19

Fig 6-20

Profile (No-Cal) Scale

An interesting way to get started in scale is the profile or "No-Cal" model. This is a model with only a two-dimensional (flat) fuselage that uses a motor stick or tube to carry the rubber motor. Wings and tail are single surface covered and, for competition, span is limited to 16 inches. There are hundreds of profile plans around and you can easily create your own from a magazine three view. Weights of 3-5 grams and flights of over 2 minutes are common, yet you can easily include lots of scale markings and details. Some builders roll a 1/64 balsa tube about 3/8" diameter which supports the rubber motor on the *outside* of the tube. This is less than half the weight of a 3/32 x 3/16" or 1/8 x 1/4" motor stick. Props made from plastic or foam cup sides are almost indestructible and covering is not shrunk or doped. These models are great indoor fliers and fine projects for a winter weekend. **Fig 6-21** shows my Japanese Shinden with plenty of light scale markings and details.

Fig 6-21

For pure scale detail it's hard to beat Guillow's line of multi engine kits that includes a P-38, a B-24 **Fig 6-23** and the wonderful DC-3 **Fig 6-20**. These kits include lots of plastic molded parts for cowlings, cabins, wheelwells and more that will add a lot to scale appearance. Although these are billed as "display" models, by adding some of the modifications (added strength, spruce bracing and detachable wings),as discussed here and in Chapter 3, **Electric Power,** they are flyable as either FF or Micro RC. **Fig 6-22** is another view of Leo McCarthy's Boeing 314 with the parts disassembled and the wing tongues showing clearly.

Fig 6-22

Fig 6-23

Figs 6-24 and 6-25 are instrument panels and engines you can enlarge, add color and additional details, then reduce to fit your model. For even the smallest models, try a bit of transparent plastic over each instrument face. A flat piece will do for very small models, and for the larger ones, just drill some holes in a piece of 1/16" ply, heat the plastic and "bulge it" through an appropriately sized hole to create a "bullseye" instrument face. Use canopy cement for a clear bond.

For scale detail information including colors, markings, engines, armaments and a host of other details, check Dr. Lyle F. Pepino's **Scale Plans and Photo Service;** 3209 Madison Ave-Greensboro, NC 27403; (910)-292-5239. He has thousands of aircraft listed as well as scale plans for many. An equally fine scale documemt source is Bob Banka's **Scale Model Research**; 3114 Yukon Ave-Costa Mesa-CA 92626, (714)-979-8058. Both can supply color photos, 3-view line drawings and documents. Probably the most comprehensive listing of plans, kits, scale drawings and components is **Model Warplanes 1996** by John C. Fredriksen, Ph.D, 461 Loring Ave-Salem MA., 01970; (508)-745-9849. His 5 volumes list over 10,000 items including 1250 aircraft types.

Bombs from drinking straws, torpedoes from pencil lead holders, antenna mounts from toothpicks, hubcaps from pill packages, tail-wheels from painted pills, maps photocopied to 1/24 size and placed in the cockpit, - it's all up to your imagination.

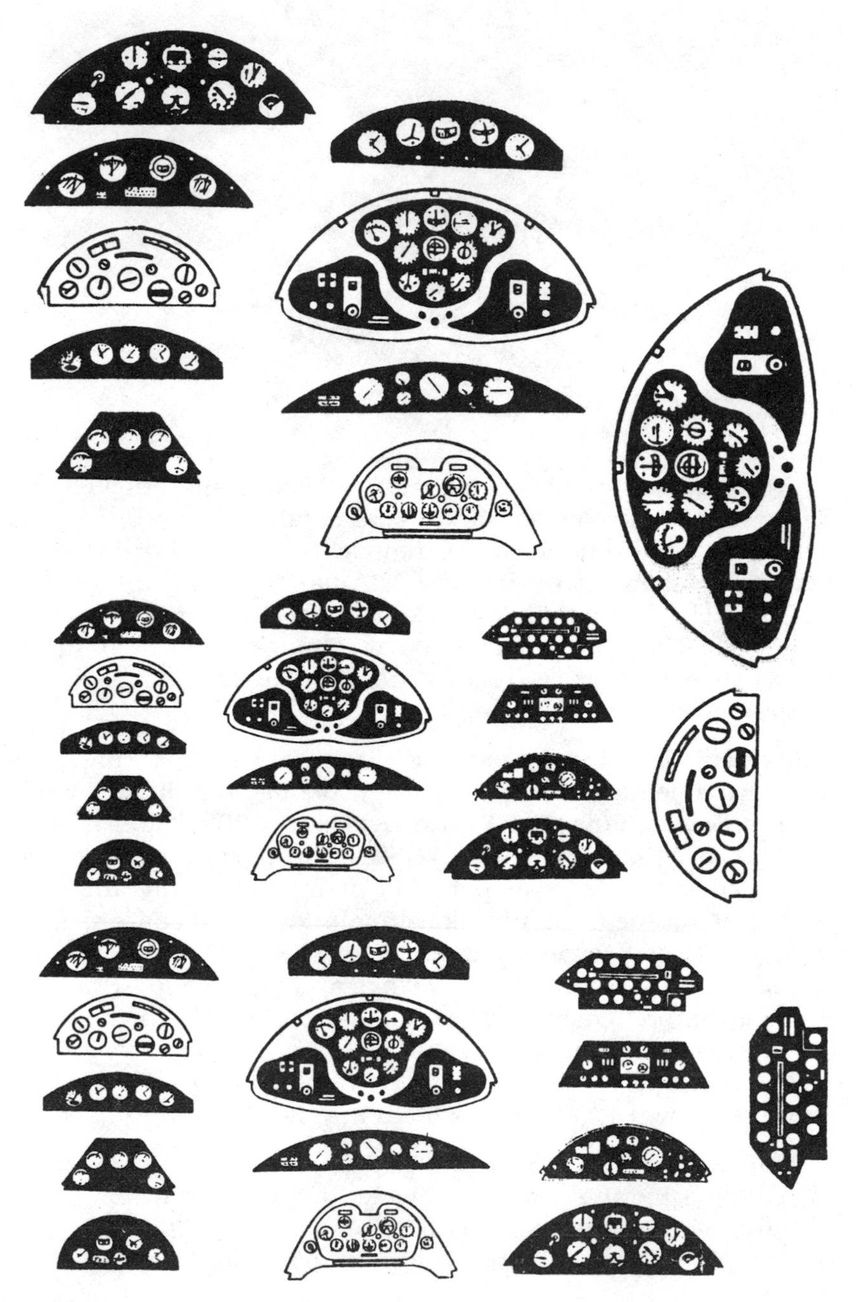

Fig 6-24

Fig 6-25

7

SHEET FOAM CONSTRUCTION

Hot wire cutting of wings and other structural parts from foam blocks is common in larger models built for R/C and C/L. The use of sheet foam for FF is still rare and not clearly understood,yet foam has some neat advantages over sheet balsa. When properly used it can result in a lighter model. It won't warp or even be affected by dew or rain, it's very easy to repair and foam flying surfaces can be bent for flight trimming just like cardboard.

If the pictures of Tony Peters' great Sikorsky S-42 **Fig 7-1**, and Dornier DO-212 **Fig 7-2** (both about 18 inch span), have got you excited about trying foam sheet, let's get into the what and the how.

Fig 7-1

All foam sheet is **not** the same.There are different chemical components and *very* different densities.Most of us are familiar with Styrofoam which is Styrene plastic foamed when molded and formed into sheets or blocks. This is the stuff you find in big sheets several inches thick in building supply stores.It comes in blue and white *and* is probably available in 1 and 2 lb. per cubic foot densities. You can also get it in art supply stores in higher

densities. Two lb. is about as light as you should use f[illegible]
tural strength.Here's a good way to compare sheet foam and Balsa.

A wing from 1/16" balsa sheet of 6 lb. density would weigh the same as a 3/16" thick sheet foam wing of 2 lb. density. If the foam sheet is only 3/32" thick (which should be stiff enough) you will save almost 1/2 the weight of the wing.Of course, neither will be as light as a built up stick and tissue wing but they will certainly build faster. I have tried out lots of designs in sheet foam before building as stick and tissue.It's easy to reduce a rudder size or change a wing planform with a scissors right on the field.

Fig 7-2

I'll first discuss how to cut foam sheet from blocks, then construction methods and finally, the various sources and types of commercially available sheet.

Paul McIraith has come up with the simplest possible Foam Slicer **Fig 7-3**. Paul's article in *Aeromodeller* (Feb. 1996) gives a lot more info. Except for the SIG .015 Nichrome wire, all the parts are probably laying around your shop. Construction is easy and results are almost guaranteed. You can slice foam sheet down to 1/16 thick and get a nice, smooth surface on top and bottom. **Don't try to run this slicer from a normal AC outlet.** You <u>must</u> use a **DC source.** A 12-volt auto battery charger, or one that you use with an electric power battery will do just fine (see Chapter 3-**Electric Power**).

Start with a block of foam (**A**), Make sure the bottom of the block is as flat as practical.(**B**) are ordinary alligator clips attached to SIG Nichrome wire of .015 diameter (**E**).(**C**)and (**D**) are screw, nut and wingnut assemblies used to hold the wire a specified distance above the plywood base. This assembly is shown in the breakout detail where **(J)** is the plywood base, **(K)** is a spacer to control the thickness of the sliced sheet, and **(L)** is the hot cutting wire.**(F)** is an "S"-hook that joins the hotwire and a rubber band loop **(G)** which is a tensioner (approximately 3 lb. tension) .

(H) adjusts tension on the rubber band. **(K)** can be one or more washers, .032 thick. Lightly tighten the wingnut nearest the tensioner to allow the wire to slide. Glue the screws into the bottom of the board. Use a 6-or 12-volt DC battery charger, 2 or 3 amps required. Slide the alligator clips to adjust temperature.

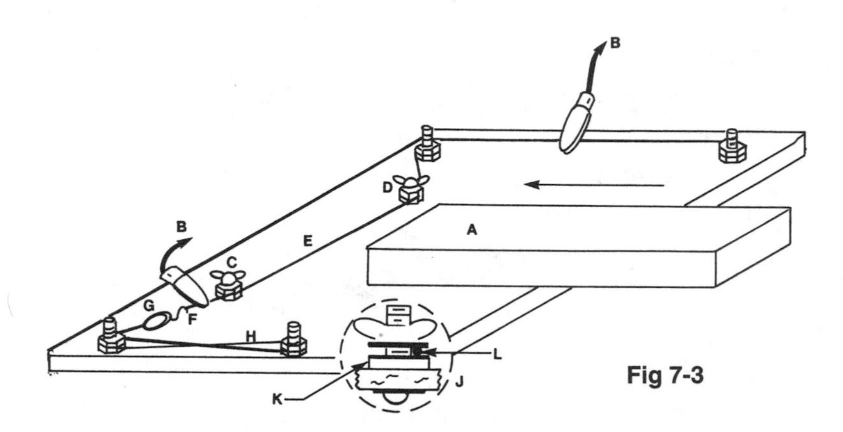

Fig 7-3

Feed the foam block at a uniform rate and sand the finished sheets on both sides with a block to remove glue adhesion.

Once you have foam sheets of the proper thickness, cut wing and tail outlines with an X-Acto knife as you would with balsa. A bit of sanding to round the edges will have the tail group ready to decorate and attach.Undercambered wing airfoils are easy to form and will hold their shape nicely. Create a center rib and "work" the sheet with your hands to form the airfoil. Hand heat alone will work on 1/16 or thinner foam. If your foam is stiffer or thicker, form it with an iron. Since foam shrinks when heated, apply your iron to the bottom of the undercamber. Iron heat is critical here and the best way to find the correct temperature is to drag the iron across a piece of scrap foam as it heats up. When the iron starts to "drag" on the foam, you have reached the right temperature range.

Another way to form foam wings is to create a slicing tool **Fig 7-4** that will make a thin cut about 1/3 to 1/2 the depth on *top* of the foam sheet. Bend the wing sheet over a rib form with the slits on top. Glue the wing to the root rib and wipe white glue into the slits.When dry, the wing will hold its form and will never warp.

Fig 7-4

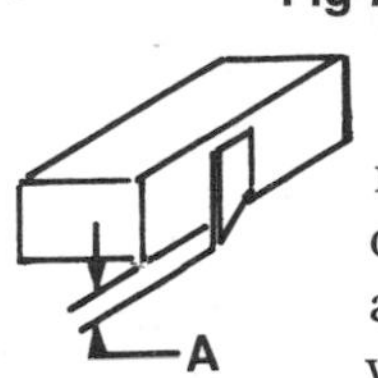

Leading and trailing edges of wings can be sanded with 220, then 400 grit to get a nice entry radius and knife edge TE. For protection, glue a strip of Tyvec, tissue, silkspan or Airspan of the appropriate color to the L.E. You can do lots of decorating while the parts are still flat.It's easy to use a ball point pen to make a groove indicating ailerons, elevators or rudder and the groove will act as a good hinge point when you bend the controls for flight trim.

Dope is not usable on foam. It will dissolve the foam as fast as you paint it on! It is possible to use colored dope by first carefully painting the foam with at least two coats of white glue and water (50-50), then doping on top. First, test this on scrap foam. Also, there are many water based paints that work well on foam. An easier way to get color trim is to simply apply light tissue with white glue and water. Lay damp tissue on the foam, then paint over with 50-50 white glue and water then smooth down.

Foam is a very good material to use on prototypes or experimental designs. Make a foam profile model of your new electric idea and "fly-it-to-death" while finding answers to engineering features without having to build a stick and tissue structure.

Tony Peters' Gee Bee, 16-inch span foam profile model

Fig 7-5, is one of the few of this design that I have seen really fly well.

Fig 7-5

Foam can also be used to create whimsical flyers like Matt's Bat **Fig 7-6**, designed and built by Matthew Silbermann.

Fig 7-6

Unfortunately,thin foam sheet of the proper density is not available in local hobby shops at this time. Order by mail or slice your own from building supply blocks. Check the density of the block , as discussed in Chapter 2, **Compound Interest**. Simply multiply the width, height and length of your block in inches. This will give you the cubic inches of volume of your block. Divide this by 1728 (the number of cubic inches in a cubic foot) to get the cubic feet in your block. Weigh the block and convert to pounds. Divide the weight in pounds by the cubic feet to get the pounds per cubic foot density. Anything over 2.5 to 3 lbs/cu ft is too heavy.

There are a few good sources for sheet and block foam as listed below:

Paul K. Guillow, Inc.- 40 new Salem St.-Wakefield, MA. 01880 781-245-5255 (3/32 thk. sheets 12x18 or 12x24)

Kenway Microflight- P.O. Box 889-Heckettstown, NJ 07840 908-850-9571 (6 lb density x .039 thk, 11x17 shts, 10/pk

Opitek- 7 West Rd-Woolston, Southampton, SO 199A England Various thicknesses & colors

Aerospace Composites- 14210 Doolittle Dr-San Leandro, CA. 94577 - Rohacell 1.9 lb. density, .118 thk, 3.1 lb density .039, .079, .118 thk.

SIG Mfg- 401-7 S. Front St.- Montezuma, IA. 50171- Flight Foam- 1 lb density- 3x12x12 blocks

Peck Polymers- P.O. Box 710399- Santee, CA. 92072 - 619-448-1818- 1/16 & 1/8 sheet

Of course, there is always the "Doggie Bag" food container you get at restaurants. Some have large flat areas on top and bottom that are perfect for building. Try your local delicatessen or food market for samples. "**Hefty**" dinner plates are very good. Be sure to buy the "uncoated" type. Many are 1/16 or 3/32 thick and big enough for a half wing section. Peter Kaiteris has discovered **Dixon Ready Markers** available in good art stores, which can mark foam without damaging it. Heavy application gives opaque colors, with a quick wipe for transparent colors.

Peter Kaiteris has come up with a neat flying modification. For his small (12-24" span) scale models, he makes flat wings with no airfoil. The wings are mounted with 2-3 degrees of incidence. A 1/32x1/16" strip of balsa is glued with the 1/32" side against the underside of the wing along the bottom of the trailing edge Fig 7-7. This acts like a flap and induces an airfoil like action that slows the flight and lengthens the glide. Taper the strip towards the tip to get the best glide.

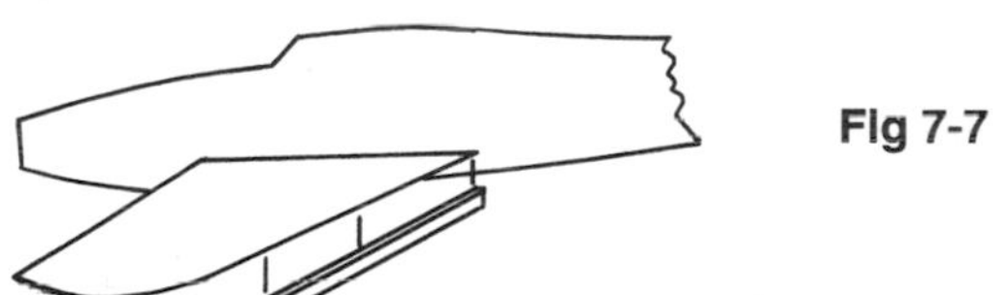

Fig 7-7

Our British friends have an entirely different technique. They start with foam blocks then carve fuselage or nacelle outlines, split in half and hollow out to 1/16 or less wall thickness. Wings are 3/32 or 1/8 carved like HL glider wings. These models are light enough (1 or 2 lb foam) to be painted and decorated with many scale features. Indoor, multi-engined rubber or CO_2 powered bombers are standard features at their meets. A very fine short book called "**Indoor Foam Scale Flying Models**" by David Deadman, Peter Smart and Richard Crossley is available through Aeromodeller. Also, David Deadman's "how to" articles in Aeromodeller September and October 1997 explain these techniques with many hints for scale detailing.

For more detailed information and lots of clever building techniques in sheet foam, try Tony Peters' fine article, "**Fun With Foam**" in the 2/98 issue of *Flying Models*.

There's no reason you can't combine foam, balsa and stick and tissue construction for the best strength and appearance. Difficult front cowlings , wing fairings, wheel pants or float shapes are easy to carve in foam, cover with tissue and color to order. Once you begin to use foam sheet and block it will become an essential part of your building system.

8

VACUUM FORMING

Although vacuum forming is used mostly on scale models, I feel it should have its own chapter because the process is little understood and yet useful on almost any type of model. Besides scale details like pilots, wheels, guns, bombs, canopies and interiors, you might consider whole hollow wing tips, spinners, fillets, access panels or cowlings. The main advantage of molded parts is that they are **repeatable** and **identical.** Once you have created a mold master and learned the simple techniques involved, you can have an endless supply of spinners that will all fit the same props. Molded parts are often stronger than carved balsa or foam.

The basic principle of vacuum forming is to soften a sheet of plastic material until it "sags" or becomes formable, then place the sheet over a carved form while vacuum pressure sucks the sheet closely against the master before it cools. When the sheet cools it will retain the shape of the master. **Fig 8-1** shows the three basic steps of **heat, drape** and **form.**

In order for this system to work we need to fill in a few details.

1. Correct choice of plastic material and thickness.
2. Proper heat source and control.
3. Means of holding plastic sheet during heating and forming.
4. Carved master form.
5. Means of sealing sheet over master so vacuum can be drawn.
6. Source of vacuum pressure.

Like most engineering problems, once you separate the elements, individual solutions become simpler and the whole problem is easier to deal with.

Instead of long, detailed explanations and illustrations, I'll cover some simple systems and then refer you to **Douglas E. Walsh**'s very fine book "**Vacuum Forming**". Doug takes the reader through many different systems from the simplest and least expensive through complex variations capable of the most detailed and varied forming.Doug also manufactures one of the very best vacuum forming systems around. His machine will satisfy almost any forming requirement you are likely to find and yet is quite affordable, simple to use and rugged.

If you have never worked with or seen vacuum forming then perhaps the best way to start is with something you can do in your home at no cost and with very little effort .Tony Peters has been using this most basic method to produce canopies, cowlings and spinners for quite a while.

The material is all around you. Almost every day you buy some product that has been packaged in a clear, molded plastic bubble pack. Toys, tools, office supplies, computer parts and almost anything else you find on a "point-of-purchase" visible rack has been packed by placing the item on a cardboard sheet, covering it with a hot plastic sheet and vacuuming the plastic down to surround the item. **This is the stuff you can reheat and reuse.** For the very lightest items, the sheet can be as thin as .015 but this will have little strength. Look for something about .020 to .025 to start with. Cut a section out of the blisterpack several inches larger than what you estimate you will need to cover the mold.

Next, get yourself a test mold master. A spinner or nose block or quickly carved canopy shape will be fine. If you are carving a shape from balsa, sand it but don't polish. The fine channels created by sanding will help. Cover with a couple of coats of dope, then spray on some furniture wax. To test the process and get rid of your fears of something new, use anything around the house as a master. The tip of a tool handle might make a rounded spinner. Use your imagination.

Mount the mold master on a piece of dowel a couple of inches long and clamp the bottom end in a vise. Avoid any "undercuts"in the mold master which would make removal of the sheet almost impossible.

Using oven mitts, just hold the plastic sheet over your stove gas flame or electric burner. Stay at least 6 inches above the heat source. Practice this a few times to see how long it takes for the plastic to start to "sag" in your hands. If it happens almost immediately, you are too close to the heat. The plastic should soften within about 10 to 15 seconds. Immediately move the plastic to your mold. (Have it in the same room as the heat source). Lay the plastic sheet over your mold and watch it sag right into shape. Try this a couple of times, then next time use your fingers (still in the oven mitt) to "shape" the plastic even closer.

Although the above won't make you any finely shaped wheels or pilots. it will prove how easy it is to heat and shape plastic sheet and how much control you have with even this crude system.

The next step **Fig 8-1** is to carve a mold **(A)**, mount it on a sheet of ply, then create a frame from wood or metal **(B)** to hold your hot, sagging plastic sheet. Cut another sheet of ply with the outline of your mold **(C)**, about 1/16 bigger all around. Heat the plastic sheet as before, lay it over the mold and force the "shaping sheet" down over both.You probably won't get very good molded parts this way but it will serve as a good introduction to the next step which is real vacuum molding.

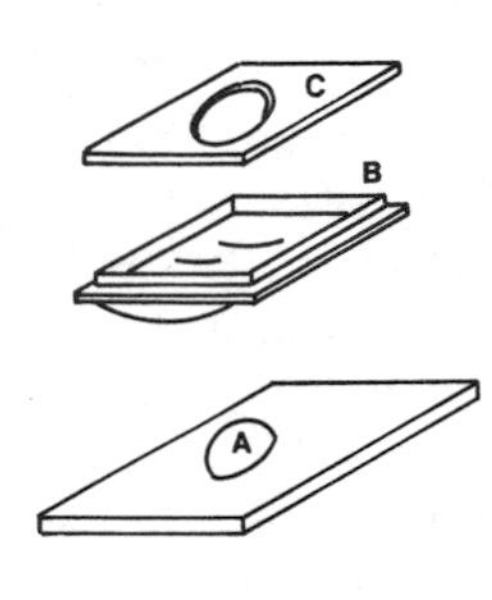

Fig 8-1

Once you have practiced a bit with hand molding and feel confident enough to continue,we can begin to consider more exact molding systems. The plastic materials you will probably use are shown in table **Table 8-2** along with the approximate molding temperatures:

Fig 8-2

Material Type	Temperature Range
ABS	300-350 F
PVC	255-355 F
Polycarbonate	350-400 F
PET-G	260-300 F
CAB	265-320 F

Most of these are available in local plastic supply houses and their data sheets will tell you more about their strength, temperature range, hardness and UV resistance. The stuff you get from bubble packages is usually Polystyrene and is fair for shatter resistance and strength. If you want to use packaging material, test it with a few whacks against the corner of your work table. That's close enough to what the industrial labs will do.

A new source for plastic sheet for molding is "**The Builders**" in Chesterfield, MI. They sell most types of plastic described above in various thicknesses.

If you are satisfied with the results of your first practice molding steps then you can consider whether to build your own simple vacuum forming system or to buy one tested and ready to use. For years model mags and newsletters have touted a toy vacuum forming machine once made by Mattel. Sometimes these can still be found at garage sales. Don't waste your time. The work area is very small (around 2 x 3 inches) and the vacuum is drawn by a tiny hand lever where the rubber seal has probably dried or rotted.

Instead, by using scrap wood, less than $5.00 worth of metal angle, a household vacuum cleaner and a few other odds and ends you can build a quite serviceable vacuum forming system that will handle parts up to 6 x 6 inches and 1 inch or more deep. Doug Walsh's book shows several simple home made systems using a box or cake pan for a vacuum chamber, weather stripping for a seal,aluminum angle iron for a holding frame and pegboard for a vacuum platform. **Fig 8-3** shows a typical setup. Ron Williams' plan for a simple, home built vacuum form machine appeared in the April 1976 *Model Builder* magazine.

Fig 8-3

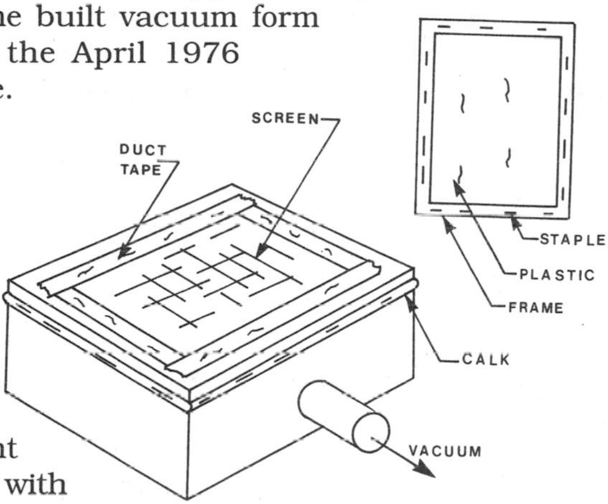

This type of system is limited by the amount of vacuum you can draw with your household vacuum cleaner which probably won't form plastic over .032 thick.You can significantly enhance the strength of your home vacuum (a tank type "Shopvac" is best) by removing the dust bag and sealing around any hose connections, the top of the canister and any other possible leakage areas with duct tape. A few practice passes with this type of system should start you off on a whole new career of accurate vacuum forming.

Doug's book shows how to expand your home-built system and increase vacuum by adding a simple hand pump and check valve. This is really an introduction to an almost professional system like the one Doug sells.

The best way to enhance your home-built vacuum forming system is to carefully trace the airflow and seal every possible leak no matter how small. Then, use the smallest volume container that will do your job. If you use a 6-inch deep box or pan, you will have to evacuate twice as much air as if you use a 3-inch deep pan. If your aluminum holding frame is twisted, bent or poorly clamped, the plastic sheet will not sit firmly on the edge seal when you are forming. This will also cost vacuum pressure.

The edge seal on your vacuum box can be nothing more than 1/4 or 3/16" wide Self-Adhesive Sponge Rubber Weather Stripping available in your local hardware store. A bit of silicone adhesive at the corners to insure good contact will also help.

Ordinary office paper clamps **Fig 1-3** are just fine for clamping the top and bottom of your aluminum angle iron frame. Make good, sharp bends by cutting out a corner . Use some "liquid metal" type of glue at the joint and, if you really want to be neat, fit a square piece into each cut corner, glue and file smooth. Now you have a frame that will hold your sheet steady and will fit smoothly and seal properly.

Pegboard makes a good platform for the top of your box. Make <u>sure</u> to seal the edges where the pegboard contacts the box sides. A few small blocks to support the pegboard will complete the job.

Now you can begin to explore the world around you for mold masters. Toy dolls make great pilots, wheels on toy cars, toy guns and lots of other little items can become part of your mold master stock. Remember to make sure that there are no undercuts to complicate your mold. For instance, mold a wheel in two parts. You can simply sink the wheel or pilot figure into a small block of clay. The part that protrudes will make a one side mold. This home made molding system may satisfy your requirements for years. If you feel you want to mold more complex parts, look into Doug's two-stage machine.

Once you have begun vacuum forming some parts, you will find more and more applications for this new skill. Choosing the right plastic material for your particular use is the next step.

Styrene is the most commonly available plastic and is used by the hobby industry to form bodies for cars and boats. It is available from .010 to 1/8 inch and is usually found in white. It's paintable and can be glued with ordinary model cement. Practice a bit with styrene because as you heat it, you will see it get wavy then taut before it begins to sag. Form as soon as it sags because if you wait too long, it will soften too much. You can get really detailed forms from styrene.

Butyrate (cellulose acetate butyrate) made by Kodak as Uvex®, is available from SIG in clear sheets in various thicknesses (.008 - .040"). It is also available in translucent colors from plastics distributors. It heats and sags quickly and is one of the easiest materials to form with. It is fairly impact resistant but not as good as ABS.

Polycarbonate is about the toughest plastic sheet you can use but one of the hardest to mold. Also, it is made in so many types that choosing the correct one is more than I can cover in this book.

Local sign shops are a good place to go for plastic sheet suitable for molding. They may be quite willing to give you some scrap to try and may even help you with molding technique.

Molds

The most important things you need to make a mold work well are:

1. A good surface that will release the plastic. A surface that is too polished will not have the fine air channels that a sanded surface will have. Just sand with 400 sandpaper, then wax.
2. A proper draft angle so the plastic will slide off. A perfect cube would not be a good mold because the plastic shrinks when it cools and would hold fast to the sides. Therefore you need a small (about 5 degrees) angle slanting in towards the top so the plastic will slide free.

An interesting way to duplicate a plastic part is to make a plaster cast from the part, then use that as a mold master. I have smashed several cowlings on my Electra sailplane and now can make new ones at almost no cost. Just create a frame to hold the plastic part, then carefully pour in ordinary Plaster of Paris (available in any hardware store). Check the mixing directions in case you want a slower cure to help fill a large mold. In some cases you may want to add Vinegar to the mix to slow down the process. Air bubbles are the worst enemy of plaster molds.

Make sure the plaster is well mixed and use a piece of wire to push out any bubbles. If your plastic piece is transparent, look for bubbles in the mold near the outside. These will certainly show up on your finished part. You can use **Durham's Water Putty** to correct defects in the mold. Be sure to let the plaster dry overnight before sanding. Doug's book has much more detail on how to modify and correct molds.

If you want to mold a toy, like a doll, for a pilot, remember to check for undercuts. It's easy to sink the plastic part into a bed of clay so only half is exposed. This will give you a "flange around the part that will have to be trimmed. Then you will be able to join the two halves of your molded part together. Hobby shops have special glue for this type of plastic.

Forming

Once you start forming parts you will develop your own techniques just as you have with covering or finishing. One good habit is to test the plastic for the amount of droop while it is heated and before placing it over the mold. You may want a lot of droop for a tall mold like a wingtip and only a little droop for a shallow part like a wheel half. If the plastic droops too far for a specific mold, you may get webs that ruin the appearance. A simple cure for some webbing problems is to raise the mold up on a dowel or block. This will drop the webs below the mold line where they can be discarded.

Another area that may need extra work would be any depressions or recessed pockets in your mold. This kind of spot will be hard for the vacuum to reach. Drill a small (.025) hole in the recess all the way to the bottom of the mold so air can pass through.

Once you are ready for your first molding test, make sure all your equipment is nearby and ready. Place the plastic sheet in your holder and clamp it solidly. Start your vacuum cleaner, then put the holder with plastic sheet into your preheated oven so that the plastic rests over a cake pan or some other structure which will allow it to sag freely.Watch for the slight sag, then maybe some tightening, then the final deep sag. As soon as the material sags enough, remove it from the oven, (using gloves, of course),and place the frame over the seal. Let the plastic rest directly on the rubber seal and watch the vacuum pull it down. Leave the vacuum running until the plastic gets firm. Poke it with a finger at the rubber seal to test. When it is hard, turn off the vacuum and remove the frame from the box.

Remember that the single vacuum cleaner, even with all the leaks closed and taped will only pull a vacuum of 4-6" of Mercury out of a total of 29" (about 20%). Thus you are limited to smaller and more shallow parts and thinner plastic sheet. This will *certainly* do for a start but you can make *vast* improvements at little expense.

The next step to improve your vacuum forming system is to add a mechanical or electrical means of pulling more vacuum pressure. The very simplest addition is a hand pump with check valve. This is available with an already built-in check valve from Doug Walsh for around $15.00. I don't recommend using a cheap bicycle pump. They usually have welded seams and no check valve. This type of pump can be added to your vacuum chamber by epoxying in a tube at the bottom corner. Doug's Deluxe Hand pump (at about $70.00) can actually draw 26-27 inches of vacuum and will put you in the professional class.

Using a secondary pump is simple but requires some alacrity or a helper. The idea is to start your hand pump **immediately** as you place the heated plastic sheet over the mold. Your vacuum cleaner will already be drawing some vacuum and will pull the sheet down on the mold. As soon as you have placed the sheet (in its holder) over the mold form and sealed it to the rubber edging, quickly grab the hand pump and pull 2 or 3 strokes. With a stroke length of about a foot and only a 16 pound pull, you can draw 26 inches in 2 seconds or less.

You may want to have a helper around the first time you do this. The helper can begin stroking the hand pump as you place the sheet over the mold. This will ensure that the plastic has no time to cool before being fully drawn.

As you progress, you can use either an air vacuum pump run from a compressor or an electric vacuum pump that is automatically actuated. Doug sells lots of components like clamp frames, valves, gages, screens and, of course, **plastic sheet for molding.**

Doug also has books on mold making and casting complete with source and material references. His book "**Vacuum Forming**" is a complete text and guide to forming from simple, beginner's projects to the industrial level. An important feature of Doug's larger machines is the ability to plug in a sheet size adapter to use smaller sheets. This saves plastic and speeds molding. Three sizes of Doug's machines are shown in **Fig 8-4**.

If you intend to get serious about modeling of any kind, I strongly suggest you consider learning some vacuum forming techniques. The equipment is not expensive and the uses will expand every day as you take on more modeling projects. Special pushrod exit guides for R/C, servo covers for inset aileron and elevator servos, rudder and elevator tips, whole ailerons with molded in control horns; there's really no limit. One thing the ability to mold parts gives you is the chance to have a **different model** from any other at the field. If you build scale models from plans or scratch, you need to be able to mold your own cowlings, canopies and details. Some molded parts and sheets made by Doug are shown in **Fig 8-5**.

Another neat feature is the ability to mold *several* parts at the same time. Why not make two or three mold masters and form all the parts at once ?

When you can buy a *complete* 6 x 9 inch *two stage* Vacuum Forming Machine from Doug, ready to use for about $60.00 or build one for $15.00 and add a second stage for $13.00,this interesting and useful process is within the reach of every modeler.

Vacuum Forming by Douglas E. Walsh
272 Morganhill Road
Lake Orion, MI 48360

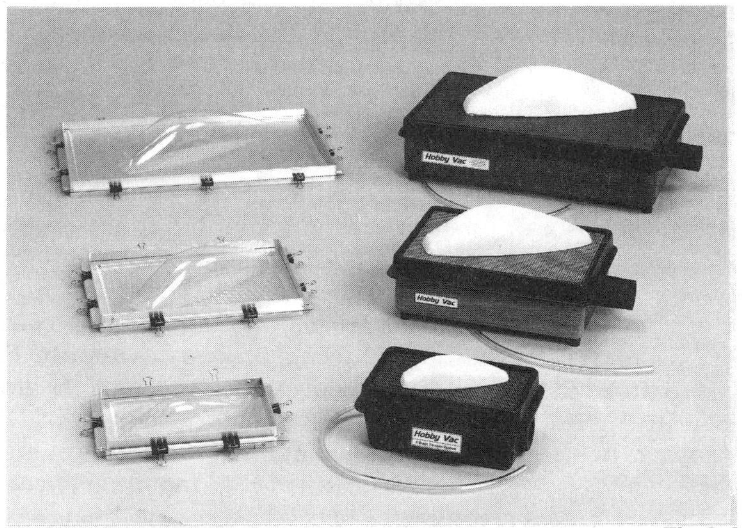

Fig 8-4

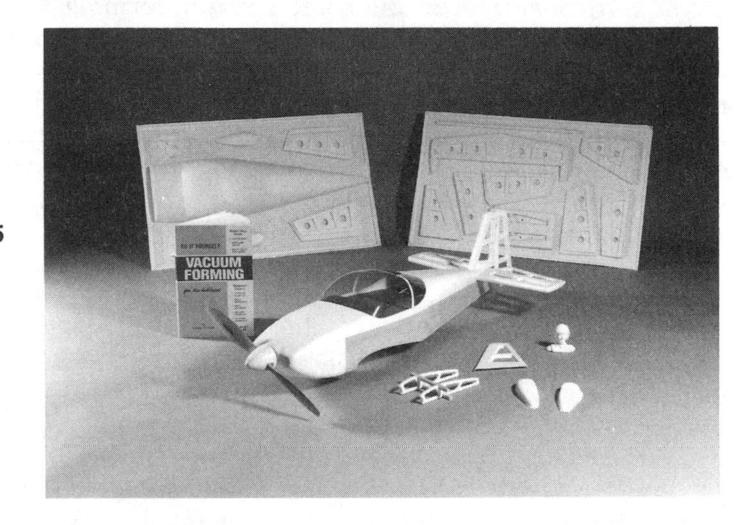

Fig 8-5

ABOUT RUBBER MOTORS

Rubber is still the lightest and simplest power source for model airplanes. It will fly an all balsa beginner's stick model, a 1 gram, 30 minute indoor model, or a complex 300 square inch unlimited outdoor winner. By merely changing rubber size, length and number of strands, almost infinite power and duration variations can be realized with no high tech on-board equipment. Flight trim with rubber power can be modified by starting with just a few turns then working up towards maximum power as the flight pattern stabilizes.

Since the 1930's, Pirelli Rubber has been the standard and has maintained a very reliable range of energy delivery. Unfortunately, the company stopped making this material quite a few years ago and the formula was lost . Serious modelers hoarded their supplies and many contests were decided by who had the best rubber, not the best model.

A few years ago, Ed Dolby of **FAI Model Supply** embarked on the enormous task of developing a new rubber to replace Pirelli. His efforts over the next years are to be commended by every modeler, kit manufacturer and columnist. After probably hundreds of tries, Ed developed **Tan** rubber. The first batch was labeled **Tan I** and quickly became the standard. Continued experimentation has produced **Tan II** which, in many ways, is actually superior to Pirelli.

Rubber energy is classified by the foot pounds of torque that would be available if an entire pound of rubber was wound to maximum turns. The target established by Pirelli rubber was in the neighborhood of 3000 foot pounds and **Tan II** often exceeds that figure. I mention the 3000 ft.-lb. figure only as a general classification since the average sport flyer will probably never want to run such tests. Theoretically, a pound of rubber wound to 3000 ft-lbs. would lift itself 3000 feet in the air. Friction and aerodynamic losses limit this to about 50% of the theoretical figure.

While the average sport flyer may not need to test every batch of rubber he buys, anyone wanting to become a serious contestant will have to learn something about testing and will need some additional equipment.

Five Basic Factors That Affect Rubber Energy:

Storage

Rubber is a natural material that will deteriorate when acted upon by ultra-violet light. Therefore, store your rubber in the dark. I store mine in plastic bags inside a cake tin. Also, heat will tend to embrittle rubber so cool storage is very helpful. Most users have found that refrigerator storage keeps rubber in good shape for years. I still have some 1940's Pirelli in the fridge that's in decent shape. I have heard that some plastic bags and paper envelopes give off vapors that may hurt rubber. I have no specific information on this so I can't comment positively.

Break-In

Again, as a natural substance, the molecules in your rubber are arranged in a sort of random fashion with a general orientation along the length of the strand. For best energy transfer and least likelihood of early breakage, follow a stretching procedure to orient these molecules into alignment. This is a simple procedure requiring stretching then resting of the rubber. Set up some sort of very solid anchor which will hold your rubber under pressures that may exceed 50 pounds. If you are going to use a door-knob for a multi-strand motor, you had better seriously test the strength of the knob and the door before starting. A nail in a board is also a poor anchor since repeated uses will rock it loose. Set up a big screw hook (2 inch diameter) into a solid support column. Mounting to a plasterboard wall is also a "No-No". Of course, for 2-to-6 strands of 1/8 rubber, you don't need to moor the QE II.!

My setup is simply a few big screw eyes mounted 2, 3 and 4 feet apart in a 2 x 8" in my garage wall. I can stretch motors to almost any length by winding them around some combination of screws. For instance, to stretch a 20-inch long motor three times its length (20 x 3 = 60 in. = 5 feet), hook it at one end on the 3-foot hook then over the base hook and back to the 2-foot hook.

Break-in procedure is to stretch your motor to three times its resting length and hold for 2 minutes. Then allow the rubber to rest for 15 minutes and stretch again to 4-5 times resting length and hold for 4 minutes. While the rubber is stretched, rub in lubricant. Don't be in a rush and skip the break-in. When properly done it will not only increase the maximum turns and life of your motor but will also help guard against catastrophic failure at high winds, which can totally destroy a model.

Knots

Obviously, you will want to knot your motor before break-in but I wanted to make sure to emphasize the break-in procedure by covering it early. In **RPMA** , I detailed two different types of rubber knot and there are probably ten more in use. The usual method for starting a knot is to thoroughly wet the ends of the rubber with saliva.

Lately, though I have begun to use a procedure that I think adds stability to the knot and helps eliminate the little nicks near the knot that may lead to a break. The major ingredient is ordinary **talcum powder**. First dip 2 inches or so of the end of the rubber into talc. You can do this even with already lubed rubber . Then tie an overhand knot at the ends leaving at least 1-1/2 inches excess. Pull the knot fairly tight. Now you can either pull on the strands above the knot to shorten your loop or below the knot to increase it. That way, you can create a loop of exactly the correct size. Once your loop is set, pull the knot as tight as you can, then tie a square knot on top and another square knot in the opposite direction right on top of the first one. Pull all knots as tight as you can and cut the excess short. You may then want to put a drop of instant glue on top of the knot. Instant glue is hard and may have a sharp edge that can easily tuck under during winding and cut your motor, so make sure you use only a tiny drop and always keep the knot right over the rear peg or tube so the knot can't become part of the winding **Fig 9-1**. You can eliminate the Cyano glue step if you wish. The knot will hold well without it. Just make sure to test the knot *before* winding the first time.

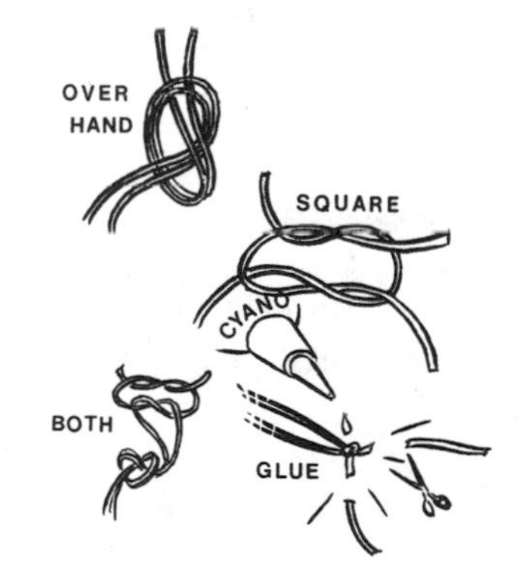

Fig 9-1

Lubrication

Unlubed rubber is **very** dangerous to wind. It can break at any time because knots simply won't slide over each other. Old time lube was glycerin and green soap which did a good job but also tended to slurp all over the inside of the fuselage during the motor run, staining the tissue and weakening all glue joints. Commercial lubes are about the same and the only advantage seems to be that they are water soluble and can be washed off the motor for storage. Lately, many of us have begun to use preparations made to restore vinyl or rubber. About the best of these is **Son - of-a-Gun** sold in auto supply stores in spray or liquid. Just slosh some in a plastic bag, insert the motor and rub it around until fully coated. You can also put a few drops on a motor already inside your model and rub them into the strands. Another choice is one of the silicon greases used in VCR's and other electronic equipment. **Dow #33** is a good one. It is rather expensive but a very little goes a long way. These lubes won't come off during the motor run *or any other time*. Once applied, it stays on. That's why I like the talc knot idea. If you break a single strand during winding, you can tie it and continue. Just carry a little 35 mm film can filled with talc in your field box.

Some other successful lubes are **Plumber's Silicon WG-1** available in hardware stores and **Syl-Glide** available in NAPA auto stores. Also, Kent Le Mon has discovered **Harvey's Silicon Grease** made by Wm. F. Harvey Co. of Omaha NB. It's available in plumbing supply stores at about $1.00 for 1/2 oz. (a two-year supply).

There is some data that indicates that rubber lubed with Son-of-a-Gun can be wound to 110% of maximum winds before breaking. I have no tests that prove this yet, but it sounds interesting. Also, my rubber stored with Dow #33 on it, shows no deterioration or lowering of strength.

Winding

Approach rubber winding just like love with a porcupine - very carefully !! There's no mystery involved and practice will soon get you right up there with the experts. The first rule is that rubber *must* be stretch wound. The only way to get an even distribution of power is to get an even pattern of single , double or triple knots in your motor. Sounds reasonable, doesn't it ? Even if you are just flight testing with 100 winds or so, stretch the motor and wind in smooth turns.

First, anchor your model in a good stooge and insert your winding tube. **(RPMA pg 87, Fig 10-3)** describes this procedure in detail. Then, if you are using Tan II, stretch the motor to 4 times its resting length. Tan I might feel tight at 3 times so stop anywhere between the two that feels comfortable. Then wind in 50% of the target turns. Wind in the final 50% as you slowly walk in towards the nose. A bit of practice will allow you to end the winding just about at the nose block. During the winding, watch for big knots, frayed strands or breaks. Massage the motor to smooth out the knot pattern as you go.

For the serious competitor, try backing out an extra foot or two after the first 10% of turns are wound in, massage the knots and continue to wind.

Most beginners wind rubber to a specific number of **turns** based on some fraction of **maximum breaking turns** taken from a chart. Certainly, this is a good way to get started as long as you are conservative and work to no more than 75% or 80% of charted turns for a particular width of rubber and number of strands. Later, we'll get into some more effective ways to wind for maximum energy delivery.

Rubber is usually supplied in standard widths of 1/16, 3/32, 1/8, 3/16 and 1/4 inch. The thickness of all these sizes is the same at about .045 inches so we can make all our calculations based on width of strip alone. Also, for ease in manipulation, we consider the **total width** of all the strands in a particular motor as the **Total Face Area.** This allows us to lump several motor sizes together for good approximate results. For instance, four strands of 1/8" rubber (two loops = 4 x 1/8 = 1/2) will have close to the same values as two strands of 1/4. (one loop = 2 x 1/4 = 1/2).

Fig 9-2 shows the breaking **turns per inch** of various cross sections related to size and number of **strands**. Don't confuse loops with strands. All charts shown here use strands. A loop is **two** strands. If your motor is 16 inches long and you are using 4 strands of 1/8 rubber (4 x 1/8 = 1/2 = .500) then max. breaking turns will be 76 turns per inch so for your motor, 16 x 76 = 1216 turns. 75% of this would be 912 turns which would be a safe maximum number. Although a similar motor made up of two strands of 1/4 inch rubber (2 x1/4=1/2= .500), would have approximately the same characteristics, the numbers will almost never match exactly.

Fig 9-2

Rubber Turns and Torque

Number of Strands x Width	Approx Equal Motor	Cross Section Area (A)	Square Root of (A)	$A^{3/2}$	Break Turns per in.	Break Torque in. oz.
2 x 1/16		.125	.354	.044	145	.88
2 x 3/32		.187	.432	.081	119	1.72
2 x 1/8	4 x 1/16	.250	.500	.125	107	2.70
2 x 3/16	6 x 1/16[1]	.375	.612	.229	84	4.35
4 x 1/8	8 x 1/16[2]	.500	.707	.353	76	6.50
6 x 3/32		.562	.750	.422	70	9.00
10 x 1/16		.625	.790	.493	65	10.00
6 x 1/8	12 x 1/16[3]	.750	.866	.751	60	14.50
5 x 3/16	10 x 3/32	.937	.968	.907	56	18.00
8 x 1/8	4 x 1/4	1.000	1.000	1.000	52	22.00
6 x 3/16	12 x 3/32	1.062	1.030	1.093	48	24.00
10 x 1/8		1.250	1.120	1.404	46	28.00
8 x 3/16	12 x 1/8[4]	1.500	1.224	1.834	44	40.00
10 x 3/16		1.875	1.369	2.566	39	46.00
16 x 1/8	8 x 1/4	2.000	1.414	2.827	38	56.00
12 x 3/16		2.250	1.500	3.375	37	70.00
20 x 1/8	10 x 1/4	2.500	1.581	3.952	35	74.00
24 x 1/8	12 x 1/4	3.000	1.732	5.196	29	90.00

(Approximate equivalent motors to those indicated by small 1-4 above)

1. 4x3/32   2. 2x1/4   3. 4x3/16, 8x3/32   4. 6x1/4

Note: 8 strands 1/16= 32 sides, 32 corners. Approximate equivalent 2 strands 1/4 = 8 sidses, 8 corners. Obviously the 1/16 has somewhat greater friction.

. Please note that the chart figures are based on tests of only two batches of Tan II rubber supplied from Tony Peters' stock and mine. It's quite possible that another batch would give different figures so the chart is intended only as a general guide. Any nicks or tears or sharp edges that affect the rubber can change these calculations with a bang.

Based on the above actual tests, my **K** (Turns Constant) came out between 51 and 54, The **C** (Torque Constant) came out between 18 and 21. Both well within 5%. The best way to get the most energy out of rubber strip is not by counting turns. The experts work with a force called **torque**. I'm sure many of you have heard the term and may have decided you didn't need such high tech parameters to enjoy modeling. You may be right but let's explore the idea just to see where it goes.

Torque is nothing more than a **twisting force**. It is measured the same way you would compare the power you can apply to a stubborn nut with a 6-inch wrench or a 12-inch one. If we assume that the force your arm applies is the same in both cases, then the difference will depend on the **leverage** you are getting from the longer wrench. If we assume that you might be able to apply say 20 pounds to the end of the wrench, then the **torque** on the 6-inch wrench would be 6 x 20 or **120 inch pounds**. Obviously, the 12-inch wrench would provide 12 x 20 or **240 inch pounds**. We usually express torque in inch-ounces so we can convert the above figures to 1920 inch-ounces and 3840 inch-ounces by simply multiplying each by 16 (16 ounces in a pound).

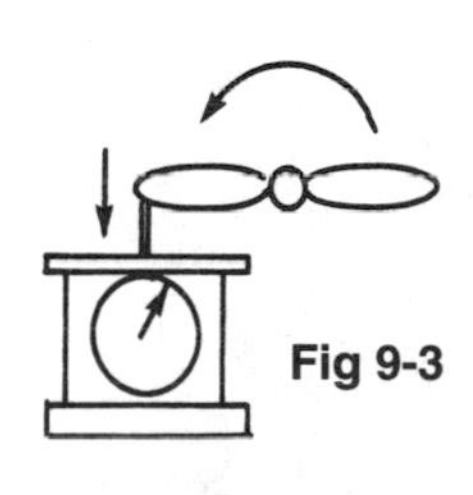
Fig 9-3

Now picture a fully wound rubber motor with a 2-inch diameter prop attached. Each tip of the prop is only 1 inch from the center of the hub. If we place a scale under one tip of the prop, Fig 9-3 we can measure the twisting force that motor will apply. This would be the **inch-ounces** of **torque** of that particular motor. It is possible to build a device that does exactly that by twisting a piece of wire against a calibrated dial. This is called a **Torque Meter.**

Most experts agree that torque is a much more accurate way to assess rubber motor energy and maximum winding . Torque meters are available commercially for rubber from indoor sizes (.040 - 1/8") right up through unlimited motors of 16 strands of 1/4 inch rubber.

They can measure torque up to 150 inch ounces. **Fig 9-2** also shows breaking torque of various motors but the reader is cautioned to be sure to *calibrate* any torque meter against an accurate scale *not* by comparing it with another commercial meter. **(RPMA pg 94)** shows how a torque meter can be built. The meter reading is based on twisting the wire between the rubber and your winder. A twist of more than 180 degrees might permanently deform the test wire. Therefore you would need several different wire diameters to accommodate a full range of motor sizes. A set of three or four torque meters can cover everything from indoor, single strand .050" motors up to 12-strand 1/4" motors for unlimited models.

Fig. 9-4 shows a basic **Torque Meter**. Wire sizes and deflection for various torque ranges are shown below:

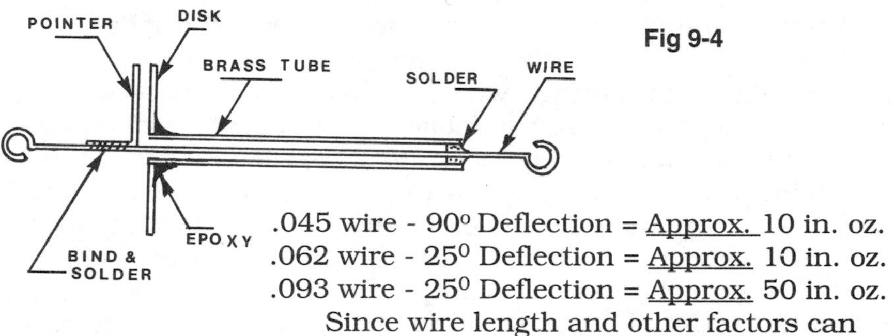

Fig 9-4

.045 wire - 90° Deflection = Approx. 10 in. oz.
.062 wire - 25° Deflection = Approx. 10 in. oz.
.093 wire - 25° Deflection = Approx. 50 in. oz.

Since wire length and other factors can significantly affect deflection, calibrate your torque meter with an accurate scale and a measured lever arm. My simple calibration setup is shown in **Fig 9-5**.

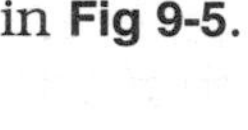

Fig 9-5

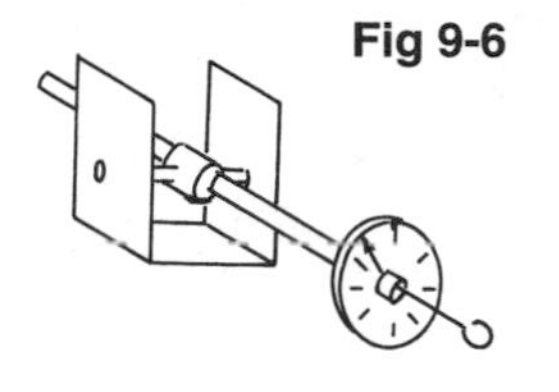
Fig 9-6

For indoor use, the Torque Meter would be mounted directly on the work table **Fig 9-6** and the motor wound "in the air". Both **Indoor Model Supply** and **Micro-X** sell such meters. A stop hook is mounted at the exact motor stick length from the Torque Meter hook andthe motor is transferred to this hook and then to the model. Also, some winders are made with a brake so when max winds are reached, the winder can be locked while the motor is transferred to the stick model.

All other models where the motor is wound inside the fuselage need a winding tube to protect the structure in case the motor ruptures. **(RPMA pg. 87)** The Torque Meter is then placed in series between the rubber and the winder and read as winding proceeds. Note that you can reduce the torque by moving in as you wind. This is part of the technique that comes with practice. I suggest you set up a hook and wind some motors similar to the ones in your model. Wind them right to destruction and watch the torque and turns. Safety glasses are a good idea here. You won't believe how far a piece of rubber motor can fly "without the model" until you see it happen.

Mechanical winders are available for all sizes of rubber motors. The advantage of a mechanical winder is that it is geared to give you several turns of the rubber for each turn of the crank. Imagine winding 1500 turns into an indoor motor - *one turn at a time.* Winders for small, thin motors from one loop of .040 rubber to perhaps two loops of 3/32" are available from **IMS**, **Peck, Micro-X, Sig** and others. The cheapest are geared 5 or 6 to 1 and for a few dollars more you can get one geared 16 to one.

Wilder makes a fine, all metal 20:1 geared winder and a torque meter that can be mounted right on the winder. Next is the Scalewinder from **HiLine** which is geared 10 to 1 and will handle two loops of 1/4". As you graduate to larger models and more rubber you will want the Sidewinder from **FAI** and others. It will handle up to 120-inch ounces of torque which is more than any sport rubber motor you are likely to use. It is available with a built in counter and can accommodate a torque meter in front.

Here's where I caution you, **Do not use a hand drill without modifying it to hold a hook !!** Inserting a cup hook, screw hook or wire loop into the chuck of a drill press can end in **disaster**.

As you build up torque, the chuck wants to twist and loosen. After a few windings, the hook can blast loose, destroy your model and possibly injure you severely. If you want to use a drill, remove the chuck (it unscrews), drill a 1/16 or 3/32 hole through the shaft, insert and bend a 1/16 or 3/32 music wire hook, bind with wire and solder, **(RPMA pg 90**). Now you can concentrate on the rubber and your model.

Winding stooges come in as many varieties as poker hands and each has its fans. The **Simplestooge** (FAI, Peck, and others) **(RPMA pg 89)** is the Cadillac of stooges and will handle almost any model. For indoor use I simply clamp a bent aluminum sheet to the table top. The sheet stooge has several holes in the sides to hold the wire that runs through the rear motor tubing holder **Fig 9-7** For outdoor use, I still favor my "Car Door" stooge which simply straps over the door and can handle almost any size model.

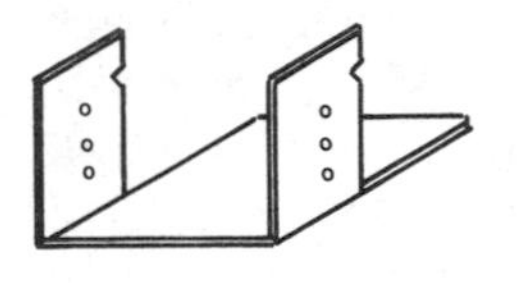

Fig 9-7

Rubber is sold in enough different widths to satisfy any outdoor requirement. However, indoor flying represents a different sort of problem. Instead of rapid, high climb, you are looking for a long cruise in a tight circle that won't impact ceiling or walls. Thus for each model you may want to come up with a very specific rubber size. Where 3/32" is just a bit too strong you may want a motor that measures .080" (between 1/16 and 3/32"). For this you need a "Rubber Stripper". This is an expensive tool that will put you in complete control of the power delivery of your rubber motor.

Just as it sounds, a rubber stripper will cut standard rubber widths to almost any dimension you choose. Usually consisting of some sort of adjustable holding groove for the rubber, a set of rollers to keep the strip straight and compressed and a rolling knife powered by a hand crank, good rubber strippers can cut to tolerances of .005 inches when handled properly. **Ray Harlan** and **Robert Opegard** sell fine rubber strippers in the $100 range. Although most beginners won't need such precision tools at first, if you fly indoors you will quickly see how fine control of rubber width can result in longer flights and fewer crashes.

How much rubber is too much ? Once, in the days of souped up cars, I drove a "Fordalac". For those of you born after 1950, that's a Ford with a Cadillac engine grafted on. The funny thing about that combination is all you really got was the wonderful throaty growl of 350 hp idling away. About two gallons to the mile, zero-to-60 in 6 minutes and cruising at over 50 was dangerous because of all that extra weight in front. Yes, Bucky, it's possible to have too much power.

As a *very* general rule, rubber in a sport model should weigh somewhere around 25% of the total weight of airframe and rubber combined. A model that weighs 30 grams without rubber can carry 10 grams of rubber so the total weight is 40 grams and the rubber weighs 25% of that total. Thus, rubber weight is 1/3 of model weight approximately. Some scale models have motors that weigh 50% of of the total of model and rubber (usually called AUW).

Rubber location is just as important as length and weight. Many old time plans call for the rear peg to be located at the very rear of the fuselage. This is bad for balance and will probably require lots of nose weight to correct the c.g.. Instead, locate the motor so that half is on each side of thec.g.. This is not always possible but moving the rear peg a couple of bays forward will help. If your motor is much longer than the fuselage, braiding will keep it from sloshing back and forth when unwound, **(RPMA pg 92)**. Start with a motor about 2 inches longer than hook-to-peg for beginning trim. Once you establish a stable flight pattern, add length until the motor is 1-1/2 times the hook-to- peg distance. Braiding and considering width and number of strands will help here.

Your model may fly better with a 10-gram motor made up of four strands of 3/16" rubber 24 inches long than the same 10-gram motor made of four strands of 1/4" x 18 inches long. Both motors weigh the same but the 1/4" motor has 1/3 more cross section. (3/16" x 4 = 12/16 = 3/4 in. total , 1/4" x 4 = 1 in. total), and will therefore have a shorter run with more initial torque. Start with 1/8" rubber. That will allow finer adjustment than 3/16" or 1/4". You can go from four strands of 1/8" (4 x 1/8 = 1/2 in. cross section) to six strands (3/4 in. cross section), but going from four strands 1/4" to six strands 1/4 is too big a jump.

Remember, when you add rubber, you add power but you also add weight. At some point, the stop watch becomes your best tool for deciding on rubber weight, size and length. Most contests specify the amount of rubber allowed as well as the maximum model weight and often the wing area. Where you can make these decisions yourself, you will have to consider, climb, cruise and glide which add up to flight duration. For instance, an indoor model needs the longest possible cruise. Climb higher than the ceiling is useless and glide means you didn't have enough rubber. Outdoor models need to get as high as possible for the longest glide. This is not always accomplished by a skyrocket climb. A longer motor run and a climb "on-the-wing" results in a much longer flight. For more detail see Chapter 11 **Flight Trimming.**

How Many Turns

Here's where the fun begins. The obvious answer, often called out at the field just after a motor bursts is, " Back off two turns". To win contests, the expert will try to wind his rubber to just under the absolute breaking number but the sport flyer can be content with something less and safer. Unfortunately, since each batch of rubber is different there's no *absolute* maximum number of turns for any particular rubber motor. **Fig 9-2** will give you a **close approximation** of maximum turns that you can use only as a guide! For sport flying, wind to 75% - 80% of the turns shown and for contest flying, test each batch.

Before you get turned off by the math that follows, I promise you can do it all on a $2.00 calculator by punching only two keys.

The simple way to closely predict the max turns for any specific batch of rubber requires only two or three short test motors from one batch and a quick calculation. With the help of **Martin Millman** this simple formula was derived from original data prepared by **Charles. Sotich** in 1976, and plotted based on cross sectional area by **G. J. Alaback** some years later. The theory simply states that the maximum winds per inch on any motor will decrease as the *total cross section* (the width of a strand times the number of strands times the thickness of a strand) increases. In other words, the more strands of rubber, the fewer max. winds. Since all the rubber we buy is the same thickness (about .045"), then we can disregard thickness and assume winds are proportional to the width times the **number of strands** which we can call **Cross Sectional Area = A, Fig 9-2** (expressed as square inches in decimals, i.e., two strands of 1/8 = 2 x 1/8 = 1/4 = .250). Hang-in-there, it gets *very* simple from here on.

The only thing we need now is some way to make the formula work for each individual batch. For that we need something called a **constant** which changes with each batch. Here's how it works.

The basic formula is: $\mathbf{T} = \frac{\mathbf{K}}{\sqrt{\mathbf{A}}}$

T= Maximum Turns Per Inch, **A**= Cross Sectional Area which equals width (1/16, 1/8, 3/16, or 1/4") times number of strands. **K** = Your Constant for that particular batch.

We can re-arrange the formula to solve for **K** for any batch: **K=T X √A.** That symbol indicates "square root" which you can easily obtain from your calculator or from the table. Now make up two motors from your batch, each 10 inches long, one of two strands and the other of four strands. Break in and lubricate both and carefully stretch wind each to breaking. You will feel each motor get very *stiff* just before breaking. Move in and out a bit to relieve this as you wind. Record the number of turns as the motor breaks. Simply solve the formula for **K** in each case. For instance, if you used a 2-strand, 10-inch motor of 1/8" rubber it might break at 1000 turns or 100 turns per inch (1000 turns divided by 10 inches) My actual test (shown on **Fig 9-2**) is 107 turns per inch on that size motor. The **Cross Sectional Area** of your motor is two strands x 1/8" width = 1/4" expressed as a decimal = .250. The square root of .250 is 0.5, the formula is expressed as:

$$\mathbf{K = T \sqrt{A}}$$

K = 100 x 0.5 = 50. Now you can use 50 to predict the approximate breaking turns for that particular batch of rubber. On the batch I tested, K = 53. Simply apply the formula to any motor. For instance, four strands of 1/4" rubber, basically equivalent to 8 strands of 1/8", (C.S. Area = 4x1/4 = 1 inch) would be: **T=K/√A** **T**= 50/1 = 50 turns per inch. My test came out at 52 turns per inch. You can now use this constant to predict a much closer **Maximum Turns** for your specific batch of rubber.

If you run a few tests you will find that **K** varies slightly. Just average three or four **K** values to get a working constant. For your convenience, **Cross Sectional Area (C.S. Area)** and its **Square Root** are shown on **Fig 9-2** along with **Maximum Turns** and **Torque** from my tests.

The Importance of Torque

Winding to 75% or 80% of Maximum Turns will be enough for the beginner to get decent flights from his first rubber powered models. Later, as you look for increased performance, you will need to learn about **Torque** which is the real key to maximum rubber performance. **Torque** is simply the twisting force on wound rubber expressed as a force (ounces) times its distance from the center (inches). For instance, the torque applied by putting 1 pound (16 ounces) of pressure on the end of a 1 foot (12 inch) long wrench would be 1 foot-pound or 12 x 16 = 192 inch-ounces.

Breaking torque on a rubber motor can vary from a fraction of an inch-ounce (1 loop = two strands of 1/16") to over 100 inch-ounces, (10 loops= 20 strands of 1/4"). Breaking torque is much better than Breaking Turns as an indication of maximum stress on your rubber motor. Since stretched rubber does not always return to its original length after winding, it makes sense that after a while you are dealing with a longer motor thus will get more turns before breaking. Also, winding technique (walking in and out as you wind, massaging the motor) can raise or lower torque changing maximum possible winds.

Experienced flyers use **torque** as their winding guide and get very repeatable flight performance. This is important even when flying a simple contest model like a P-30 with only 10 grams of rubber. Winding to torque of course requires a **torque meter** which is a simple device that can be calibrated to read directly in inch-ounces. The simple torque meter shown in **Fig 9-4** is based on the twist in a specific length and diameter of music wire.

Fig 9-5 shows a neat device for calibrating your meter with an accurate digital scale. You will certainly be buying an accurate scale relatively soon if you get serious about weighing balsa sheet and model parts. If not, try stopping in at the local Post Office or "Mailboxes" during slack time and calibrating your meter with their scale. Here's the formula for Torque

$$\textbf{Torque} = C\,(\sqrt{A})^3$$

For those who have a more advanced calculator, simply take **A** to the 3/2 power. For the others, look up the square root of **A** and multiply it by itself 3 times. For example, if **A** = .25 (2 strands of 1/8") then the square root of **A** = .5 and ($\sqrt{A}^3$ = .5 x .5 x .5 = .125). **Fig 9-2** shows $(A)^{3/2}$ in the column next to $\sqrt{A}$.

Already calibrated indoor Torque Meters are available from **Indoor Model Supply** and **Micro-X** while fine outdoor meters in various ranges are available from **Rex Hinson** and **Wilder.** Remember, it's not a good idea to calibrate one Torque Meter from another. The possible error range is too wide.

With a Torque Meter you can now expand your breaking tests to include Torque as well as Turns. You can also use this information to Predict **Breaking Torque** in a batch of rubber by testing two or three motors as you did with Breaking Turns. You will need to establish a constant **"C"** for Breaking Torque just as you did before. This constant **C** will *not* be the same as the **K** you calculated for max turns.

The formula for **Breaking Torque,** which was first established by J. P. Glass way back in the Zaic Yearbook days is:

$$C = \frac{\text{Torque}}{(\sqrt{A})^3}$$

Now you can predict a fairly accurate Breaking Torque for any motor in your batch. These formulas are most accurate in the middle of the range of motor sizes, say from two strands of 1/8" to 8 strands of 1/4. As you wind by Torque instead of Turns you will see that your winding technique can affect Torque. You may be able to pack in more winds by moving in slightly to reduce Torque or massaging the knots in your motor. All this is even more reason to wind models only in a very stable stooge while you are doing all this manipulating all of this.

For those who enjoy working with math, Len Sherman has done a great deal of testing on TanI and Tan II which resulted in some interesting formulas. Len's equations may allow you to predict the behavior of a batch of rubber without pretesting. Our results differ so you may want to test a batch and compare formulas to see which works best for you.

$$\text{Turns/in} = \frac{(160)(1-2W)}{\sqrt{N}} \qquad \text{Torque (in.oz)} = (.45+10W)(N)^{1.38}$$

Where **W**=width of strand in decimals, **N**= number of strands. You can get 1.38 power from your calculator. Interestingly, Len reports that Herb Weiss (one of the early rubber power greats) uses a similar formula with **N** to the 1.5 power which corresponds to $(\sqrt{N})^3$.

Odds & Ends

Two often neglected areas in rubber motor handling are the loops at the ends. These are the places where breaks will usually develop first since they bear the most stress and rub against hard surfaces like the front hook and the rear peg. On larger models, you *must* cushion the front hook somehow. The easiest method is to cover the hook area with rubber or plastic fuel tubing. A better system is to use a **Crocket Hook** as shown in **(RPMA pg 87)** with a rubber band around the motor. This allows you to wind the motor *without* the prop assembly which is a much safer system. Crocket hooks are available in several sizes from FAI, Peck and others.

Another important advantage of a Crocket type hook is that the rubber won't "climb-off-the-hook". This is a strange phenomenon that can occur during flight and can destroy your model. With a motor torqued near maximum and a slippery cover on the hook, the rubber can actually twist right up and over the hook, collapsing the fuselage . This can also happen with a poorly bent "S" hook that doesn't mate properly with the prop hook.

In smaller models you can bend a prop hook to diminish the climbing problem. **(RPMA pg 90)** shows how to do this.

(RPMA pg 92) covered "Braiding a Rubber Motor" and this is a very important technique as you begin to use longer motors. Obviously, a long motor can tend to bunch up somewhere in the fuselage and will upset the balance of your model. Unfortunately, since most fuselages taper sharply towards the rear, a bunched-up motor settles there, adds weight to the rear, and causes a sharp stall which can lead to a crash. Braiding collects the motor strands into a shorter "Braid" while still allowing almost the same turns.

To braid, open the motor out to twice its length (four loops opened out to two), wind in 2.5 turns counter clockwise for every inch of finished motor length. Grasp in the middle, double back to four loops and allow the motor to "jump" together. Massage the motor into a smooth braid and put a tight, small rubber band around each end. This takes less time to do than explain and can save your model. Another way to braid is to put the motor into the fuselage, hold half the loops on your wrist, wind the other half of the loops 2.5 turns/inch of length *counter clockwise* and hook all loops back on the Crocket Hook with a rubber band to hold them.

Store motors in glassine, not Polyethelyne bags.

What can you do when a strand breaks in a wound motor? Unwind the motor, put some talc on each end of the broken strand and tie the same knot you used on the original ends. Tying a knot while the motor is still wound is not for the faint of heart but I've seen it done at a mass launch.

Learning to get the most out of your rubber motor can easily turn a "Turkey" of a flyer into a better than average performer and may add 20 - 50% to your flight times.

10

GEARS AND "WARP" DRIVES

Since they were introduced in the early 1930's, a controversy has raged among modelers about the use of gear drives on rubber powered models. In theory, it's hard to dispute that gears offer some definite advantages. In practice, workable gear systems seem to be restricted to the top builder who has some machine shop experience. Perhaps the introduction of new materials like epoxy and CyA gluc will tip the balance and allow you to turn frustration into longer, more realistic flights.

The first gear systems were simply return gears used to double the length of a competition motor **Fig 10-1**. Equal-sized gears **(A)** were free to rotate. Two separate rubber motors **(B)** with one hooked to thc prop and the other hook anchored in the noseblock **(C)**. Bearings and washers allowed for free motion **(D)**. I believe a Swedish model placed or even won a Wakefield competition with such a system in the 1930's. However, you had heavy gears at the rear of the fuselage and lots of rubber to carry. Today's competition models can exceed three minutes in still air time with only a single, braided or tensioned motor and that's plenty of time to go OOS in even a 5 mph wind.

Later on, folks like Leon Bennett, R. Wetherell, Bill Warner and Bob Meuser explored gears more fully and were able to quantify definite advantages.

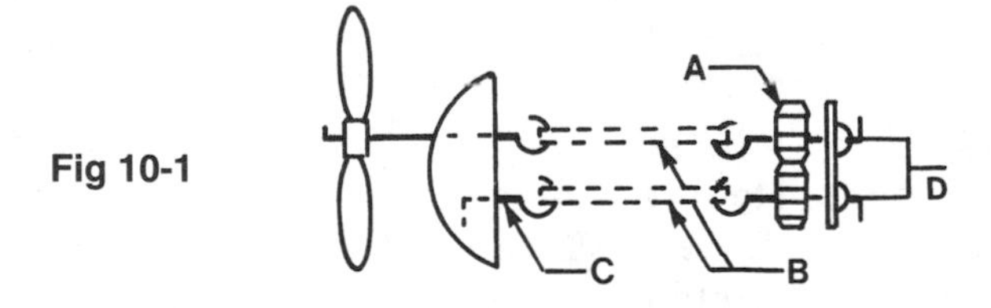

Fig 10-1

Reduction Gear

This is a system that uses a larger gear on the rubber motor and a smaller one on the prop shaft **(A)**, **Fig 10-2**. Both shafts are free to rotate with proper bearings and washers **(B)** and all are enclosed in a Gear Box **(C)**. With a 2:1 ratio, your prop will rotate twice for every time the rubber turns once. This will reduce torque by 40% and almost double your prop run time. Also, you can use a smaller, more scale like prop and shorter landing gear with a shallower but longer climb and cruise. Ratios of up to 5:1 have been successful. In addition, you can use a thicker, shorter motor for better balance. Gears are available from many small parts suppliers. Be sure to order all the gears for a system from the same place and of the same group. Gears vary not only in the number of teeth but also in the tooth design so you need the same group to insure good meshing.

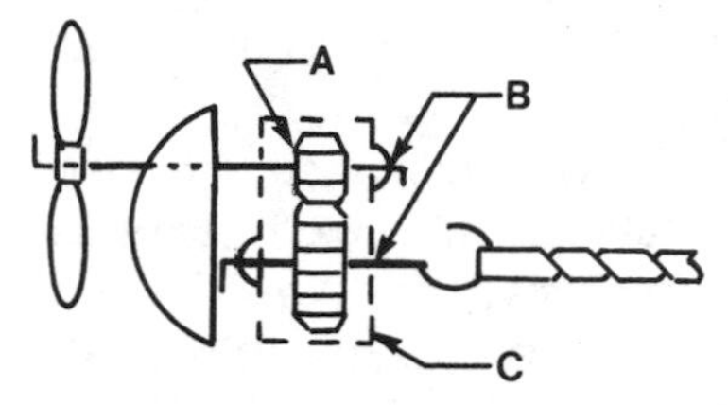

Fig 10-2

The best way to build a gear system is to make a gearbox (**C in Fig 10-2**) out of 1/16" ply with brass bushings and ball bearing rollers. For outdoor models, gears come with a collar molded or machined on the face. This can be drilled and tapped (some come that way) to take a small set screw to grab a notch filed in the shaft. You can now reduce a 12-inch prop to 8 inches, add two strands to your rubber motor (or increase the cross section) and shorten the motor by 25%.

The shorter motor improves balance and moves weight to the nose while reducing strength requirements at the rear. Your gear-box must be strong enough to hold the moving gears and with-stand the pull of fully wound rubber motors. It must also mount firmly in the fuselage in perfect alignment with the rubber motor. Bushings like the **Peck** thrust buttons must be used to anchor the shafts and allow free rotation.

Gear systems can be built with two separate motors driving the same prop shaft **Fig 10-3** which allows for two thinner motors equaling the torque of the single motor but providing more total turns. Thus you can combine a reduction gear with a two-gear system to carry two, thinner rubber motors. Back in 1946, Don Foote (of Westerner fame) described a system created by Harry

Roderick that actually shifted gears on a rubber FF model . Those courageous enough to try that will find drawings in the **9/46** issue of *Model Airplane News*, **page 37**.

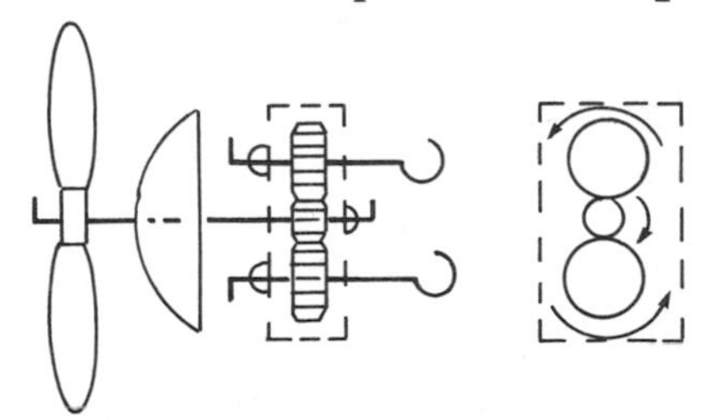

Fig 10-3

The best application for geared rubber motors seems to be on large (40 to 90 inch span) scale models where the gear box is large enough to work with and the gears, shafts, bushings and bearings are more easily handled. I suggest starting with a 2:1 or 3:1 gear ratio and a single motor to test the concept.

At the other end of the scale, Mark Allison and Jack MacGillivray have had great success with gears on indoor models. Indoor scale model flight is almost completely under power, and long cruise rather than swift climb is the rule. Gear systems satisfy these requirements extremely well, offering flights well in excess of 2 minutes. You will find small gears in all kinds of products. Discarded cameras, servos and toys are good sources. Care and light building are still necessary but the rewards are worth the effort.

For those interested in the technology and numerical advantages of various gear arrangements, see Leon Bennett and R. Wetherell's articles in *Flying Models* **10 & 11/88**, also Bob Meuser's article in *Model Airplane News* **7/65**.

Note that for clarity, washers and prop bearings are not shown, but should be added to any rotating system.

Gearless Transmissions

Sometimes called **Warp Drives**, gearless transmissions offer almost the same advantages as gears but can be built with a bit less skill and no special materials. As shown in **Fig 10-4**, two or more rubber motors turn the outside cranks, **A&B** which move the center plate **(C)** in a circle thus "cranking" the prop shaft around.

This arrangement *does not* provide any turns increase as a 2:1 gear ratio does, but it does allow you to divide your motor into two or more sections. This will give you a lot more turns which can result in longer flights. Obviously, you will get more turns from 2, four strand motors than 1 of eight strands. Such a system can be lighter than gears and can easily be transferred from one model to the other. Just build your nose blocks to accommodate the crank case.

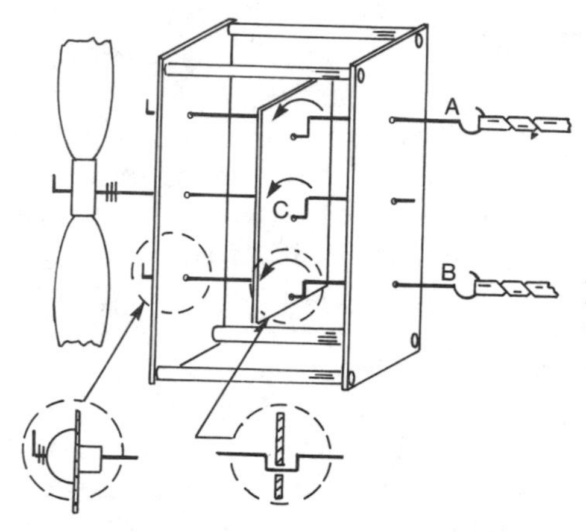

Fig 10-4

Two motors in parallel will produce 30% less torque and 40% more turns than the same two motors made into a single one of the same length. It's possible to parallel more than two motors in a warp drive. I have seen four motors arranged in a square around the prop shaft and Bob Meuser in a 1970 article says he once tried 15 motors but couldn't bend all the wires exactly enough.

Construction is easier than a gear box. Drill both aluminum outside plates and the inside crank plate together. Insert brass bushings and ball bearing washers on the motor cranks and carefully bend all cranks exactly alike. Insert dowel spacers and build the whole thing into a nose block.

The biggest problem in Warp Drive use is winding the motors. Unhook the motors from the drive hooks and, using hooks, wind separately and hold with a pin. Then, hook up the nose system.

Although the above may be interesting, the advent of small, electric motors capable of 2-3 minute runs changes the equation.

Contra - Rotating Prop Gears

The idea of contra-rotating props on a rubber powered model has fascinated me and many other modelers for a long time. Imagine a **Macchi Castoldi** Schneider Cup racer or one of the great W W II fighters in only 24-30 inch span built really light and sporting a pair of contra rotating 6-or 7-inch, maybe 3-or even 4-bladed props, driven by a single rubber motor. Of course such a system requires some gears and a gear box to contain them which is enough to discourage all but the most dedicated tinkerer.

Bill Hartwell created a nice, light system with brass gears but it is a bit hard to build and align. **Leo McCarthy** also designed an angle geared system but it never had extensive use. Then, at Middle Wallop in England in the summer of '96, I met **Roy Tiller** who showed me the best idea yet. It is his version of a **John Cooke** design using simple plastic angle gears obtainable from **Lego** (the toy makers). **Fig 10-5** shows the layout. Follow the drawing from right (the hook end) to left (the prop end). The hook wire **(A)** is soldered to brass tube **(B)** (nearest to right) and the same tube **(B)** is also glued to gear **(D)** (nearest to right end). Gear **(D)**, of course drives Gear **(E)** (on top) which, in turn drives Gear **(F)** (left end) in the opposite direction.

Gear **(F)** is glued to brass tube **(G)** which is also glued to prop **(H)** (nearest to right) The driving (hook) wire passes through tube **(G)** but is not attached to it so it can drive prop **(C)** only directly from the rubber motor. Prop **(H)** is driven only by gear **(F)** and tube **(G)**. This will give you contra-rotation with very little loss in power if you are just a bit careful in aligning and pinning the gears. The gears used in Roy Tiller's system are the ones Lego uses in their motor driven assembly sets. Lego gears are available through Lego Inc. P.O. Box 1221, Enfield, CT. 06083 - 860-763-4011
They are called: Item 5229 "Gears & Differential" You get 23 pieces for $4.50.

Believe me, seeing one of these items fly is worth all the building effort and, after you build one, you will see that it is as easy to create as a good folding prop or DT system.

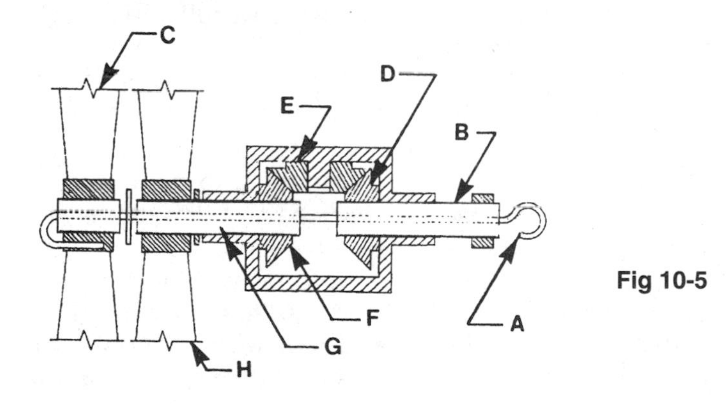

Fig 10-5

11

FINDERS - KEEPERS ?

Reward.

In the past 15 years at our heavily weeded field in Galeville, NY, I have lost 13 models and gotten 11 of them back, some, three months later and from six miles away. Yet, when I walk the line at a field, half the models aren't identified. I make up fancy colored nameplates to match each model but a simple address label will do. Stick it on the rudder or under the nose. If you feel it will detract from the appearance of your masterwork, slip it behind the windshield or between the wheels. Some FAC scalers simply write the info in small type along the T.E. Don't wait until you have finished flight trimming. I lost a P-30 on 50 hand winds while showing the glide to a friend. Rich Fiore put a HL glider in the top of an 80 foot tree with a wrist flip from shoulder height. Remember, most thermals start at the ground .

Dethermalizers

These are devices that will cause a model to descend after a pre-determined interval. Dethermalizers work by upsetting the aerodynamic balance of the model. Over the years, many different systems have been tried. Swinging weights, parachutes and even a spool of thread released from the fuselage to unroll and pull the wingtip down have been tried and discarded. Most systems today either tilt the stabilizer up 40 or 45 degrees at the rear or release the wing entirely. The tilt stab is most common and is easy to install, see (**Fig 11-1 and RPMA pg 55**)

The stab platform should be solid and rigid to hold position and still allow for tilt. The crosspiece needs to be at least 1/2 x 1-1/2" hard balsa or 1/32" ply. Make *sure* you compensate for the extra height of the front crosspiece so the stab does not have positive incidence. Add a piece of dowel or hard 3/32" as a stop at the front of the stab and epoxy in hooks and rear wire as shown. You can extend the hooks under the stab as an angle stop or simply tuck a limiting thread under it. You should always add a **fuse snuffer tube** at the rear of the fuselage (**Fig 4-16, pg 95**). Many fields are dry in summer and it's very easy to start a big fire with a little fuse. The fuse sits between the rear wire hooks which are held by a small, thin rubber band. Several suppliers sell orthodontic bands for this purpose.

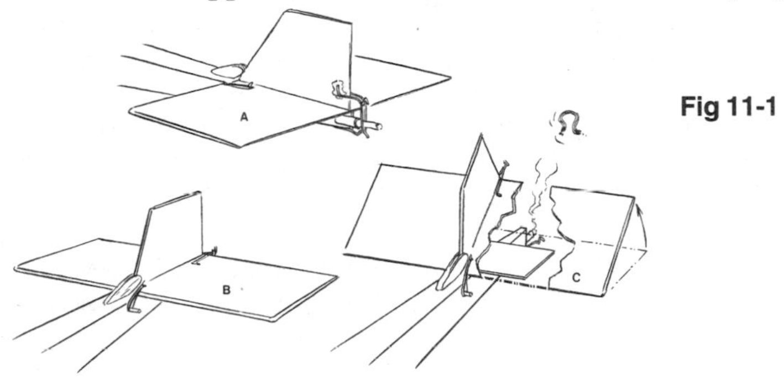

Fig 11-1

Test your fuse for burn time and mark each package with inches vs. minutes. This type of DT should work smoothly and should always return the stab to its proper position and angle when reset. Since most of us have quit smoking by now, another means for lighting fuses had to be developed. Matches are a poor choice and may be dangerous to model or surrounding dry grass. One of the new, hot coil, flameless cigarette lighters will do a nice job.

While the fuse is probably the simplest and lightest trigger to use, it is not the most reliable or the easiest to set. There are several new devices available that are fairly accurate and easier to set. One of these is the Silly Putty timer, **Fig 11-2**, page 190, where a spring (**A**), pulling at the top of the pivot (**B**), forces a wire (**C**) through a putty filled groove (**D**). Another wire (**E**), is held under the pivot wire (**B**) until it moves far enough through the putty to release the end of (**E**) which then pivots in a tube until it releases the rubber tensioned DT line. The spring (**A**) can be anchored in a series of holes (**F**) which control its tension and, therefore the timing. The left drawing shows the system at the start of the flight and the right drawing at the moment of DT release. **Fig 11-2** shows a sketch similar to one that used to be sold by Gary Buddenbohm. Those of you who are creative and handy may want to design one. You can transport the whole system from one model to another rather easily. One drawback of Silly Putty is that it is rather sensitive to temperature fluctuations which can change your time setting by 25%.

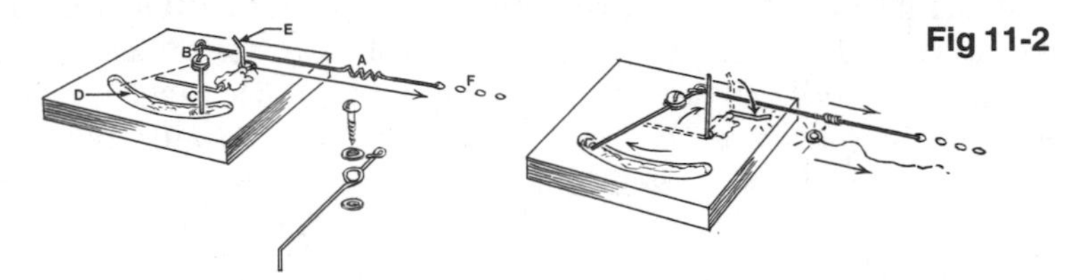

Fig 11-2

Another, similar system is called the **Badger Fig 11-3**, and is sold by **Wheels & Wings** and **EMP**. The Badger consists of a small, sealed cylinder (**A**) filled with a heavy grease. There is a shaft inside the cylinder that has a vane (like a paddlewheel) attached (**C**). The shaft (and vane) are forced to rotate in the cylinder by a tension rubber band that leads to the DT release. The tension band is looped over the pin and wound around the outside wheel (**B**). The amount of rotation controls your time. This unit is easily transportable and much less sensitive to temperature changes. Devices similar to the Badger may be found in electronics supply catalogues as "dampers" for VCR doors or other devices. Clockwork timers are still available but their weight makes them usable only for larger models.

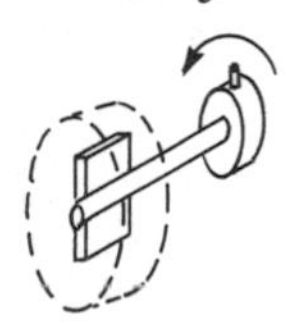

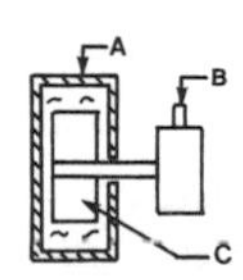

Fig 11-3

Probably the most common timer in use today is the ubiquitous **Tomy**. This is a spring actuated timer extracted from a common wind-up toy. The name comes from the toy company that first produced the little critters but toy and novelty stores now carry lots of types. Just look for a very light, small wind-up toy that has a little white knob sticking out. Prices are often under $1.00 and these toys can sometimes be found in the $0.59 discount bin near the store entrance. Look for "Pencil Pets", "Pocket Pets", "Marching Bands", or "Get-Along-Gary" made by Tomy of Taiwan.

The modifications required to turn the toy into a reliable DT timer are very simple and can be done with standard tools and minimal skills. The results are really worth a bit of effort and will surely save an airplane for you.

First, be careful to remove the timer from the toy intact. Some toys have a hat or head that can be taken off, then the body splits into two pieces. Some are two shells fastened by molded tangs.

Just slip a single-edged razor blade under the tang, pry outward and split the shells. Sometimes you will need *very* careful action with a Dremel saw blade. Just avoid damaging the timer.

Once you have released the timer, identify the **Winding Shaft (A)**, the **Pawl (C)** and the **Drive Shaft (B)**, **Fig. 11-4**. For DT purposes, you can cut off the drive shaft close to the case with diagonal pliers. Next step is to add some weight to the pawl to slow the mechanism from about 35 seconds run on six turns of the winder to 5 or 6 minutes. Dave Hipperson has written a pair of fine articles in **Aeromodeller 11/86 and 12/86** where he describes this mod. Dave suggests making 2 holes in the Pawl with a red hot pin then installing a pair of bent, ball headed pins as shown. The pins will snap in and hold if bent correctly. You can also CyA a single pin into the Pawl and add different sized beads to the end until you get the speed you want. Mark the winding knob with a dot, count in five or six full turns and time the unwinding.

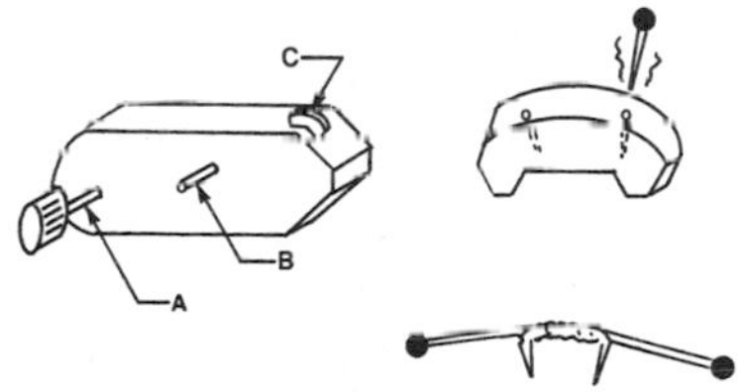

Fig 11-4

I find the simplest way to actuate your DT is to drill an .030" diameter hole in the side of the winding knob, insert a 1/4 inch length of wire with the end ground very smooth and hold with a drop of CyA. Now you can hook the DT cord over the wire and wind it around the knob as you wind in the appropriate number of turns. With a small rubber band in the line to maintain tension as the knob unwinds, you can release the DT as the loop slips off the wire retainer on the knob. If the winding knob is too small to easily accommodate several turns of line, remove it and substitute a larger piece of plastic rod or even a 3/8 or 1/2 dowel.

This method retains the spring inside the timer and does not require any disassembly. Other proponents suggest opening the case of the timer with care and removing the spring. Now you can use a stronger rubber band wound around the winding knob to power the system. The advantage here is that you have a more positive action on the DT since the driving rubber is opposing the hold down band in the front of the stab. Obviously, the disadvantage is the problem of careful disassembly of the motor.

Some builders cut a small groove in the winding knob to retain the DT cord. I like this idea because vibration of the model can easily slip the cord off the knob and on to the shaft, thus partially releasing the stab and adding lots of negative incidence and a dandy stall. Perhaps the best of the simple mods is to remove the winding knob by holding the shaft with a needle-nose pliers while working the knob loose. Then replace the knob with a length of 1/4-20 nylon screw drilled and CyA'd to the shaft. Now you have a *graduated* retainer knob and can use a wire loop that will simply ride up the thread until it releases.

Once you have started fooling with Tomy timers you will begin to see lots of other possibilities. Instead of removing the drive shaft, you can use it as another release scroll for a separate function.

With a weight of only 2-3 grams and capability of hundreds of runs while eliminating any fire threat, the Tomy timer is certainly worth a bit of experimentation. If yours gets dirty or lands in mud, just wash it out in water. The nylon parts are water proof and self-lubricating.

Lost Model Locators

Even if you can see a model DT, it often disappears into grass, trees or bush. When they go beyond the tree line it's very easy to drift away from a direct chase line and lose your model. Before we discuss sophisticated electronic locating systems, let's explore a tried and true system that was probably finding models in Penaud's 18th century time.

The tools are simple. A compass, a rough sketch map of the field with North marked in, and a couple of poles 8 or 10 feet high. Mark your launch point on the map and stick one pole in the ground. Watch your model with compass in hand, (the military type that has a sighting reticule is best) and mark the compass heading on your map. If you tend to follow the model in flight, check the compass as you go and be sure to get a good heading when the model goes down. Take the other pole with you and use it to sight between the two for a true heading. If you fly with a friend, he can wave you right or left by watching your pole. A walkie-talkie is also a neat helper as you go further into high grass or bush. Even if your model has gone "out-of-sight" you can follow a compass heading and have a good chance of spotting it as you walk.

At Galeville, which is very heavily overgrown with waist high bushes, a model can be within 10 feet and still be lost. A good compass heading can be accurate within a couple of yards. Usually, you underestimate the distance to the landing spot. Try walking another 200 yards along the heading.

Sound Locators

The next step up in locators are those that emit a sound actuated by the DT or a timer, or buzz continuously from shortly after launching. These are relatively inexpensive ($15.00 - $35.00) and are quite effective. The human ear is a very good direction finder and a high- pitched beep can be heard for several hundred feet. Coupled with a compass heading, an audio finder can do a good job. Often you will see a model go down in high grass or corn and have an approximate location. An audio finder can then lead you right to the model even if it is invisible. I lost the Beautiful Bess in a field of 8-10 foot high corn at Geneseo in 1995. Four of us started with a double sighted heading and still spent over an hour in 100 degree heat often within 10 feet of the model before we found it. A beeper would have saved a lot of frazzled tempers.

Since I haven't tested all of these locators, either audio or radio, I won't attempt to classify them as to efficiency or durability. A simple description may help you choose the one best fitted to your modeling habits. The following are listed in order of weight. Almost all are transferable from model-to-model.

The Cricket

Sold by **Charles Ribak** for about $15.00 this weighs 3.5 grams and puts out a solid tone. Range claimed to be 250 feet.

The Tattler

Sold by **John Watters** of **Triple J Products** this one weighs 8 grams and has a 9-minute delay after launch. Then, it emits beeps at 10 second intervals. This sells for $32.50 and is said to operate for 12 hours.

Estes Transroc II

Made by **Estes** as a rocket finder, it weighs 16 grams, sells for about $30.00 and emits a high-pitched buzz.

Screamer Beeper

Sold by **Bill Turner**, this one weighs 18 grams and uses a 12-volt electronic cigarette lighter battery. It sells for about $20.00 and would probably (due to the larger battery) have a longer audio range and life.

Radio Shack Do-it-yourself

Radio Shack sells some very tiny buzzers that can easily be mated with a battery. All you need for a switch is a piece of card stock slipped between the battery positive end and the case.

Rich Fiore has done some interesting experiments with the guts of a singing greeting card mounted under the stab actuated by the DT. You should look at a model finder project as a new kit you want to build. Invest a few hours and save a lot of hot sun searching time.

The Bionic Ear

An interesting addition to an audio finder is an amplifier that will enhance the sound emitted by the locator. This can considerably increase the range of the locator, then you can use your own ears when you are close to pinpoint the exact location. **Edmund Scientific** sells a "Bionic Ear," part # 33595, at about $149.00. This is a hand held, battery powered sound amplifier. It will help you hear your locator up to 1000 yards away. One drawback is that these sound amplifiers will also hear crickets, trucks, airplanes and crowd sounds so you may have to practice for a while to develop a good technique. Estes also makes a sound amplifier to go with their Transroc II.

Radio Trackers

The most advanced (and expensive) tracking systems use radio beams which have a much longer range and can be more easily pin pointed by checking signal intensity as you head towards your model. These systems require an antenna and a sensitive receiver and vary in signal strength depending on how your model landed and the antenna location with relation to the ground. I have not tested most of these systems so I will simply list them with some of the features of each. If you intend to become or are a serious free flighter, this type of system can more than pay for itself by saving a model that may have taken months to build and trim. Most of these systems are small and light enough so they won't affect performance and they can also be moved from one model to another. Prices are approximate as of 1997.

Jim Walston Retrieval System

Used by many Northeast flyers, it weighs 4 gms, is $335 for the Rx, $135 for the Tx,. It has a 20 mile air range and a 2 mile ground range. A <u>directional</u> Yagi antenna at $80.

Airtek

Designed by **Ken Bauer,** this unit also weighs 4 grams with battery and has a 48 hour output life. The Tx is $95, the Rx $250 and the directional Yagi antenna is $80.

700 West Model Beacon

Moe Whittemore's unit weighs 4 grams too, but is designed to work with almost any CB receiver, saving considerable cost. The Tx unit in the model costs $50 and a decent Rx in the 27 MHz range, Citizen's Band, will cost $30 or less. This unit is not directional so the Yagi antenna is not required, however you need to know the general direction of your model in order to get close. Range in open country is 1 mile.

Gino Ursicino

This unit may soon be available from Italy. It is said to weigh only 2 grams and is usable with any standard FM receiver. It has an extra long battery life with range of over 1/2 mile on the ground and 5 miles in air. Tx cost around $150.

Falcon Xtr

Originally designed to track falcons, this unit weighs 4.5 grams and costs about $100. It can be used with the Walston Rx and has a range similar to most of the other units.

The simplest, cheapest way to reduce permanent loss is to **mark the model with your name, address and a reward offer**.

Locator Sources

Airtek-Ken Bauer-2306 Turquoise Circle-Chino Hills CA 91709-909-393-1104
Bionic Ear-Edmund Scientific-101 E Gloucester Pike-Barrington NJ 08007
609-573-6879
Cricket-Chas. Ribak-187 Swanson Terr-Staughton MA 02072
Falcon XTR-Bob Johannes-5117 Silver Lake Dr-St Charles MO 63304
Jim Walston Rerieval Systems-725 Cooper Laqke Rd-Smyrna GA 30082
404-434-4905
Moe Whittemore-2348 S 700W-New Palestine, IN 46163
M. Ursicino-Via Porrara 27/a-02100 Rieti- ITALY-39-746-205601
Screemer Beeper-Bill Turner-3025 Rutgers Ave-Long Beach CA- 90808
310-425-6866
Tattler-Triplet Prod-PO Box 1232-Battle Creek MI 49016
Transroc II-Estes-1295 H St-Penrose CO 81240-719-372-3419
Wheels & Wings-PO Box 762- Lafayette CA -94549

12

CO_2 POWER

In this book we've been talking about many different types of power. Rubber, CO_2, electric, and even compressed air. As you will see, there is no best power source. Each has advantages and disadvantages and each might be chosen for a specific task. Don't become wedded to any particular system. Use several. You will find more fun and knowledge as well as a different kind of flying with each new arrangement.

CO_2 has two of the advantages of rubber power. It is fairly light and it is infinitely adjustable. At about 1/3 the weight of a comparable electric system, CO_2 can fly very small models. Usable both indoors and out, CO_2 is a good choice for either duration or scale. Among the disadvantages of CO_2 is the drop in performance at low temperature or high humidity. Most CO_2 engines will operate best between 60 and 90° F. Also, since the tank is attached to the engine with a fairly rigid tube, you are restricted in tank location.

To better understand a CO_2 motor, compare it to the old time steam "Donkey" engine used for almost 100 years to pump water out of deep mines all over the world. The "Donkey" operated on the principle that water heated in a boiler would turn to steam and expand. If the water was heated and contained in a boiler, the pressure would build-up and when released through a valve, would push a piston as it expanded. When you hear the whistle blow on an old time steam train in a John Wayne movie, it's not necessarily to greet Wayne. The engineer may just be "Letting-off-steam" to reduce the pressure that built up in the boiler while the train stood still.

If expanding steam will push a piston with enormous power, then any expanding gas will do the same thing. **The power will be in proportion to the gas pressure** (we'll *expand* on this idea later on). So what's the key to getting the most power or the longest run from your CO_2 system?

First, let's explore the engine, tank and charger so we can get the best performance from the system **Fig 12-1** The engine is similar in construction to almost any internal combustion system. The expanding gas (Carbon Dioxide, CO_2) , climbs out of the tank and runs through (**A**) into the cylinder head (**B**). There, it pushes down on the ball (**C**) which jams itself into the head valve (**D**), stopping the gas from reaching the piston. As you flip the prop, it turns the crank shaft (**H**) which pushes up the piston (**F**). On top of the piston is a short stub (**E**) that pushes up the ball at the top of the stroke. As the ball rises, it reaches into the wider part of the head valve (**D**) and allows gas to escape into the expansion chamber on top of the piston. The piston moves down until the gas can escape through the exhaust port (**G**). The crankshaft keeps turning, bringing the piston up for another cycle. This little waltz happens over 1200 times a minute inside your engine. That's one reason why lubrication is a good idea. Use sewing machine oil and put a drop in each exhaust hole and on the prop shaft.

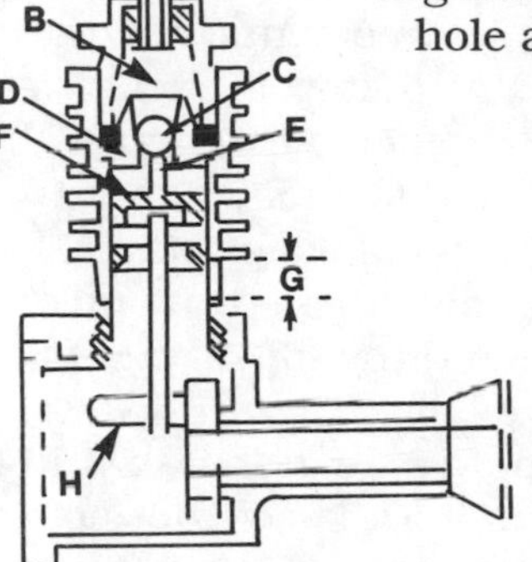

Fig 12-1

This is a somewhat simplified explanation of the engine operation but it will serve to clarify this type of power for the beginner. We all owe a big debt of gratitude to **Fritz Mueller** for his many articles on CO2 power and the basis for most of my sketches.

The motor's tank is just a reservoir with two tubes at the top. The "Loading Tube" also has a spring loaded ball at the mouth of the tapered insert. Higher pressure from your cartridge or large tank pushes the ball up the tube slightly allowing gas to enter your motor's tank. Once the pressure is *equal* between the charger and motor tank, the ball returns and seals the tank. This is an important note to remember when you want to get maximum charge into a system. The other tube from the tank is attached permanently to the engine and has no restriction on the gas until it reaches the motor's top ball.

If you start with the standard soda charger, understanding its construction will help you get maximum power and longer motor runs as well as reducing maintenance problems. The little soda cartridges you buy are loaded to a pressure of almost 800 pounds per square inch !! Although they are used by the millions, that kind of pressure still deserves your respect. Keep the cartridges cool and always check for damage to the outside or the top seal. **NEVER** allow the cartridges near any sources of heat.

The cartridge holder has a gasket at the neck as well as a needle that punctures the cartridge. As you advance the thumb screw , the cartridge first seals itself against the gasket then the needle extends to puncture the top. The needle is tapered so you then have to back-off slightly to retract the needle enough for gas to get into the tube **Fig 12-2.**

Fig 12-2

It's a good idea at this time to check your cartridge holder for leakage. Just load the cartridge, screw in the thumb screw, back off a bit, then immerse the whole thing in water and watch for bubbles. Most will leak for a few moments when new. Advance the screw 1/4 turn to stop the leak. If a leak persists, you may have a defective holder. Also, get in the habit of checking for leaks before any flying session. Now check the motor for leaks by making up a solution of soapy water. Fill the motor's tank from your cartidge holder, then paint on the soap solution around the tube entrance and the top of the cylinder as well as at the engine tank neck.

Once your system is up and running, you can install it in a model either upright or inverted. The motors leave the factory with the speed set at a medium level. In the Brown engine, speed control is achieved by simply screwing the cylinder into or out of the base. Screwing it in (or clockwise) will add speed and screwing it out will slow the rpm. No more than **3/4 turn** covers the whole speed range. The Gasparin motor works basically the same way but you need to turn a nut on the front of the engine. See the instructions with each unit.

Now let's discuss the stuff in the tank. CO_2 (Carbon Dioxide) can be a gas or a liquid. Obviously in the liquid state, you are going to get more of the stuff into any given volume. Under the pressure found in the cartridge, your CO_2 is almost all liquid. As it expands into the motor's tank, you get a mixture of liquid and gas. At first, fly with only a gas charge to minimize crashes and flyaways. To do that just hold the charger upright when attaching to the motor tank tube **Fig 12-3A**. As you progress, you can use a partial liquid charge by simply pointing the charger down while loading **Fig 12-3B**. This will extend your motor run but may scare you at first because the liquid CO2 may expand so rapidly that it causes some ice to form in the engine making it "sputter" and run rough.

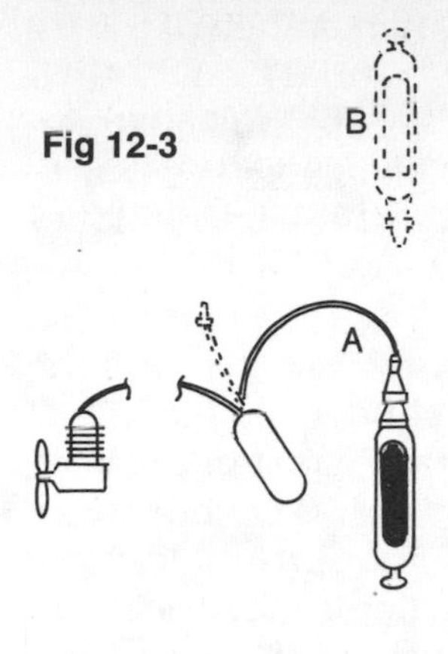

Fig 12-3

Let's talk a bit about this liquid - gas - pressure - temperature - volume stuff. Nature, being pretty smart, has made these two states and 3 properties interdependent . You can't change one without affecting *all four of the others.* If you compress a gas you raise its temperature and, of course, reduce its volume. Apply enough compression, which is equivalent to a reduction in volume, and many gases change into liquids.

Compare this to a hot air balloon which we have all seen. As you load the bag with hot air, the volume increases and the hot air now takes up more volume than it did when cold. When the bag is filled, the volume of air inside simply weighs less than the volume of air outside, so the balloon rises.

Therefore, if you could manage to cool the motor's tank while loading it from the charger, more liquid CO_2 would be delivered. In other words, you would get many more molecules of CO_2 as liquid into the tank, resulting in **a longer motor run**. There's an equation that covers this interaction. It goes something like this:

PV=rT Where: **P** = Pressure, **V**= Volume and **T**= Temperature **r** is a constant, depending on the fluid, but not important to us in this discussion. If you play around with this a bit, you will see that by increasing **P** or **V** you must increase **T**; or an increase in **T** will automatically increase **P** or **V** to balance the equation.

Therefore, if we can decrease **T** (by cooling the motor's tank) while loading, we will decrease **P**. That means we can get more volume in the same size tank. If the above hasn't turned you off yet, let's try one more exercise. If you suddenly increase **V**, the pressure drops very quickly. The product, PxV, is lower, so the temperature drops to balance the equation. When a gas expands suddenly its temperature will drop. That is how your room air conditioner works.

This can have a troublesome effect on your CO_2 system. The expanding gas from a liquid charge can actually form ice as it enters the motor. This will cause your system to "sputter", clog and even stop. If the motor sputters and continues to run, then hold the model for a few seconds until the it "smoothes out", then launch. If the ice stops the motor, let the whole system warm up and try again. On a particularly humid day, the ice problem increases because the rapidly expanding gas cools the surrounding air and condenses moisture which freezes instantly. We often fly in a steam heated auditorium and the drop in power is quite noticeable.

Ice formation can be reduced by mounting the engine tank almost upright or at a slight angle leaning forward. Also, coil the feed tube from the tank to act as a trap for condensed liquid.

To increase motor run time you can certainly install the largest tank that fits (Brown makes tanks from 3 to 50 cc) but that's not as efficient as simply getting the motor tank to hold more CO_2. Since most of the CO_2 in our charger is liquid, the trick is to keep that liquid from expanding into gas as you fill the tank. Earlier I noted that at lower temperature, both pressure and volume decrease. We can use this principle with a simple procedure to get more "Bang for our Buck".

If your motor tank is exposed as on a contest model:

1. Apply a liquid charge by pointing the charger down at the tank fill nozzle.
2. Remove the charger.
3. Cool the motor's tank with ice or a cooling spray (found in electronic stores).
4. Recharge immediately with another liquid charge.

If yours is a scale model with a hidden tank:

1. Apply a liquid charge.
2. Release the CO2 from the engine tank by pushing the back end of a #71 drill bit against the filler nozzle ball. This rapidly cools the tank inside the model. (Don't use the pointed end of the drill as it can scar the ball that seals the nozzle.)
3. Recharge with a liquid charge.

If you are still using a soda cartridge charger, you may wonder if the charge decreases as the cartridge is emptied. It certainly does. As pressure decreases in the soda cartridge after three or four charges, the pressure transferred to the engine tank also decreases giving you shorter runs. You will probably now start considering larger and more expensive charging systems. That is not necessary yet. Some years ago, the CO_2 flyers came up with a clever system to get the most out of a pair of soda chargers. Here's how it works:

Use two cartridge holders labeled **A** and **B**. Start your charging with **A** and use it two or three times. On the next charge, start with **A** and charge again with **B**. This way, as the pressure in **A** lessens, you can make it up with the higher pressure in **B**. Use the system for three more charges then discard **A**. Now **B** becomes **A** and you load a new cartridge in **B**.

Depending on your tank size, you will get anywhere from three to six charges from this arrangement before you have to discard an "**A**" capsule. Once you have set the speed for a particular motor- model combination, you can tell a lot by the sound during a power run. Of course, a tachometer is a good tool to have when running any sort of engine. A "Tach" is a simple device that can be held in front of a running prop to read rpm directly on a liquid crystal display. There's no high tech knowledge required Once you can compare rpm of different settings or different motors, you can start experimenting with prop diameter and pitch.

You may want to swing a larger prop at slower rpm for a particular model. **Henry Pasquet** of Missouri has run CO_2 models with props up to 9 inches for flights up to four minutes on models in the 30 -36 inch span range. Many are also R/C. Both Gasparin and Brown offer a range of prop sizes from 4-5/8 to 7 inches. For larger sizes, rubber power props are effective and available up to 9-1/2 inches.

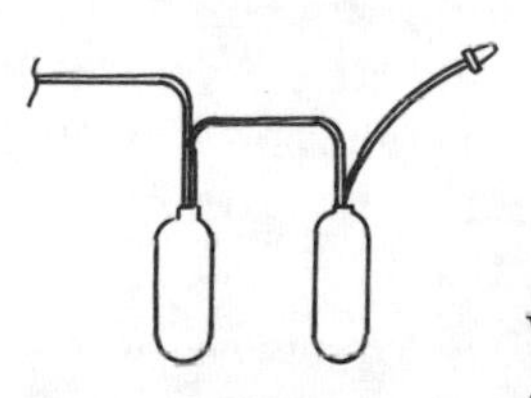

Fig 12-4

Tanks for CO_2 motors come in sizes from 0.5 cc to 50 cc and can even be ganged up with a manifold for extra long runs, Fig 12-4. With such a broad range of tank sizes, almost any motor-model combination can be flown successfully. As you progress with CO_2 power you will probably want to move up to larger loading units. The best next step is a 2-1/2 or 5 lb. aluminum tank. These are used in fire extinguishers and are available from Peck, Brown, Davis, SAMS and other sources. I fill mine only once a season at a local fire extinguisher service place for $7.00 or $8.00 and get hundreds of good, uniform flights.

The advantage of infinite speed adjustment with CO2 really shows up when you switch from outdoor to indoor flight. Just slow the engine down (or try a smaller prop) until you get a nice circle below ceiling height. This can be a challenge with electric power.

For the larger models, Davis Diesel has evolved a series of conversion systems that replace the heads on .010, .020 and even .049 Cox type glow-plug engines. Of course, with their much larger displacement (the volume of the cylinder swept by the piston) these engines need larger tanks for any decent run time. I use 2 - 20 cc tanks in series on my Davis .020 conversion.

I have tried the Telco and Shark systems and found them not as good as the **Brown** or **Gasparin**. The plastic piston used by Telco wears quickly and becomes oval thus losing a lot of compression. The Brown unit is very dependable, but at the time of this publication Bill Brown, Jr's illness may have caused the company to temporarily cease production. Many mail order houses carry the Brown motors and they can advise on availability. The Gasparin motor is an extremely well built and durable unit that has gaineds popularity very quickly. It is easy to adjust and very rugged. "O" rings are used instead of solder at the gas line connections and around the piston. These make the connections more flexible and may need replacement from time to time. Steel instead of brass tubing also adds ruggedness. Altogether, the Gasparin system is practical, user friendly and available in many sizes and even multi-cylinder configurations.

The Herr Ryan ST **Fig 12-5**, is powered by a Brown B-100 (100cc) engine with a 20 cc tank and an 8 inch Peck prop. The model has a 30 inch wing span and weighs about 100 grams (approx. 3-1/2 oz.). I later added a 12 gram CETO R/C unit to the Herr Ryan and get very satisfactory 2 - 3 minute radio control flights.

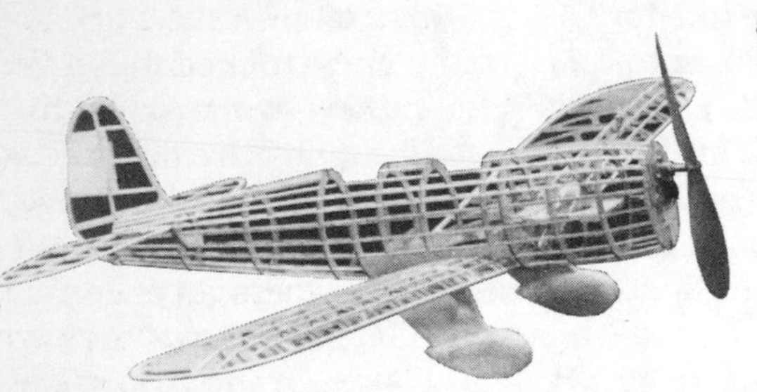

Fig 12-5

One of the best features of CO_2 flying is the ability to avoid high power crashes while flight trimming. Simply adjust the power for a sort of lightly powered glide to the ground straight ahead, then add power slowly as the flight pattern develops. We managed to adjust Robin Marin's first flying model to make neat, safe circles inside the Floyd Bennett hangar in only five flights with not a single dent or tear.

When using a rubber power prop on a CO_2 motor, be careful to square off the back of the prop or else it will not only wobble crookedly under power, it will eventually bend your prop shaft screw. A small disadvantage of CO_2 power is that you can't easily freewheel the prop after the engine run as you can with either rubber power or small geared electric motors. I'm working on a modification of the Superior Props Free Wheel Hub that may accomplish this for larger 8 to 10-inch props. If you decide to test this, remember that the blades are *detachable* so take proper precautions. You wouldn't want a blade running at 1200 rpm to suddenly fly off.

CO_2 is an interesting power source for both multi-engined scale models and pusher types. Like electric motors, you can run a CO_2 motor in either direction so a pair of contra-rotating props on a twin engined DC-3 or a pusher prop on a Vickers Gun Bus are simple to do. Also, like electric motors, two or more CO_2 engines running off the same tank or series of tanks will stop at quite close to the same time.

Now you know more about the advantages and disadvantages of CO_2 power and some of its uses. With the tricks described above, you can get consistent, long power runs and smooth flights. Use the soldering techniques described in Chapter 3, **Electric Power** to modify or repair.

If you are anything like me, you may want to use a lot of different power sources just as you like to fly a lot of different models. CO_2 is certainly worth trying, particularly if you have flown only rubber or gas up to now. You can easily convert almost any rubber or gas model and can also change the motor from model to model in a few minutes. Most P-30 kits convert easily. The **Guillow's** Arrow and Lancer are good subjects as well as their 300 series of scale models. **Al Lidberg** sells a whole series of plans and kits for scaled down old time gas models that are just about perfect for CO_2 or small electric power. The **Herr** laser cut kits are proven performers as are many other scale models from 16 to 36 inch span. **Fig 12-6** shows my own design CO_2 R/C model in a competition pylon high thrust configuration with the CETO unit mounted in the pylon. This uses an old P-30 wing and tail with a 1/32" balsa rolled tube fuselage tube and a 1/32" sheet balsa hollow pylon. It is shown with a 6-inch prop but lately I have been flying it with an 8-1/2-inch rubber power prop and getting 3 minute flights on a 20 cc tank. The engine is an old J70 Brown twin. The newer Brown B-100 twin will produce even more power with a very small weight penalty.

FIG 12-6

Grab an old rubber or gas job, chop it up, glue a 1/16" ply plate on the front end and screw a CO_2 motor to it with a couple of your smallest wood screws. Hold the tank on with a rubber band or a piece of duct tape (until you find the correct location) and go flyin'.

Dan Baird is a possible new engine manufacturer who may take over from Brown. Dan lives at 3529 Koln Lane, Knoxville, TN 37931. He will not be active until possibly late in 1998 but you might check with him for Brown parts or motors. Hobby Club and Henry Pasquet may also have replacement parts for both Brown and Gasparin motors.

13

COMPRESSED AIR POWER

Compressed air power has been around almost as long as modeling itself. Early motors made with carefully hand machined cylinders and wire wound tubing tanks were very successful. Many of these were multi-cylinder engines flying models of six foot span and more. Dave Stott regularly flies a large, multi-cylinder compressed air free flight model at New England Flying Aces meets.

The principle of compressed air power is quite similar to that of CO_2 as described in the previous chapter. Air is compressed to anywhere from 50 to 100 pounds per square inch pressure by anything from a bicycle pump to an electric compressor used to inflate auto tires. It is pumped into a tank which is directly linked to the engine. The rest of the operation in the cylinder, directly follows the CO_2 system with a ball check valve, a piston activating point and side port exhausts. To some extent, compressed air power is also affected by temperature and humidity according to the same laws for fluids and gasses.

Right now, there are three sources for compressed air motors. **Bert Pond** (one of America's most prolific collectors) has books, plans and articles for many types of engines including multi cylinders. His book, "**Expansion Engine Powered Model Aircraft**" is a *must* for anyone interested in the subject. Plans for both engines and aircraft are included. Bert also has finished parts like check valves and control valves for sale. He is the distributor for "Z" Models of Italy who make the Powermax-Z engine.

The Powermax-Z is a new development in compressed air power that brings the whole concept to beginner level and will get you into the air almost immediately. The engine comes complete with tank, prop and pump. It has the added attraction of a transparent plastic cylinder so you can watch the action while it runs.

This engine has two amazing new features that make it more efficient and longer lasting. The first is a diaphragm at the top of the cylinder that allows air to vent as the piston comes up. Thus, the piston finds no pressure resistance as it comes to top dead center (an improvement over other piston opened head valves as in CO_2 motors). The second is an arrangement that allows the crankshaft to separate from the piston as tank pressure drops. This opens the valve for a longer period admitting more air to the cylinder. These design advantages greatly increase the efficiency of the system providing longer motor runs at good rpm.

Fig 13-1 shows the basic parts of the engine. The arrows show air escaping from under the diaphragm (at the top of the cylinder) as the piston begins to rise. A much more complete description of operation and application is contained in the **Doug McHard** article in *Aeromodeller* April 1990. Doug describes the engine operation and several possible model designs including some nice scale efforts. Also, the article describes the **Jonothan** which is a neat, all Balsa ARF that is capable of OOS flights.

Fig 13-1

Of course, the system needs a tank to hold all the air. The tank is 2-3/4 inches in diameter (it swells to almost 2-7/8 under pres sure), and just over 11 inches long. This requires a fuselage large enough to hide it in a scale model. The motor will fly models up to 40 inches in span if built light. Certainly, a wide bodied Lacy or Fike at 36 inches would be a great subject. Doug McHard describes his Piper Super Cruiser at 40 inch span and 6 oz. AUW as capable of 1-1/2 to 2 minute flights.

A full charge of 100 psi gives a motor run of about 1-1/2 minutes which is plenty to lose a light model. The total weight of tank and motor is 49 grams. Note that weight increases by 6 grams when the tank is pressurized. Did you think all that air was free?, Make sure the bottle is roughly at the c.g. Propeller rpm depends directly on pressure so try to get a pump with a pressure gage so you don't suddenly find you have a runaway model that zooms higher than you expected. There is a safety valve in the tank cap set to open at 117 psi but the tank is not supposed to be filled to more than 103 psi. The rpm at 100 psi is about 4000 which falls to 2500 after about 1/2 minutes. This is plenty for long free flights with the large prop furnished.

The instructions and notices refer to pressure in **bars** which is simply shorthand for "one atmosphere of barometric pressure". Thus air at sea level has a pressure of 14.7 pounds per square inch which would be **1 bar** . The **7 bars** pressure limit would then be:

7 X 14.7 = 102.9 psi

A new motor, quite similar and a bit smaller is available from: **Spin Master Toys**-250 The Esplenade, 4th Floor-Toronto, Ontario, CANADA-M5A 1J2. The motor is built into a foam RTF FF airplane with a 22" span and delivers 4000rpm at 90 psi to a 6-5/8" prop. The motor may soon be available as a separate item.

For the scratch builder, put any spare set of wings and stab from an old coupe together with an arrow shaft fuselage to make a fine first entry into compressed air power. **Fig 13-2** shows my granddaughter Karen with my "Bottle Baby". It flies a consistent 1-1/2 minutes at 90-100 psi. At 110 psi, it climbs an extra 50 feet to do almost two minutes.

I recommend compressed air power to any one who wants something new, safe, almost soundless and with a very scale-like flight profile. These motors require almost no maintenance. My Powermax-Z has lasted 3 seasons of steady flying.

If you are an experienced machinist and like new projects, Bert Pond's plans for multi cylinder engines are also a must. There are also more than a dozen plans for C. A. models inserted in Bert's book.

Bert Pond - 128 Warren Terrace- Longmeadow, MA 01106-413-567-5346

Fig 13-2

14

FLIGHT TRIMMING

In **(RPMA pgs 96-116)**, I call Flight Trimming the toughest chapter in the book, both to write and understand. That is even more true in this book because we're talking about models powered by other means than rubber, thus considerably complicating the issue. For instance, electric powered models are heavier and will fly a lot faster than rubber powered models, therefore we need even more flight trim care and knowledge. Even R/C models should be trimmed for stable free flight to perform properly.

Since this book is meant as a companion to **RPMA**, I will repeat only a little of the material in it, and will add new information that pertains to larger, heavier models.

The **RPMA** chapter started off with a discussion of **Wing Loading** as a means to evaluate the potential of any model for stable flight. Wing Loading is simply the grams or ounces of total weight of the model (This includes the complete airframe and the power source - motor, batteries, etc.) **divided** by the Total Area of the Wing. For simplicity, you can simply measure the wing including the part that is on top of, under or through (as in a shoulder wing) the fuselage. For instance, a wing of 30 inch span and 4 inch chord would have an area of:

30 x 4 = 120 Square Inches

If that model weighed 60 grams (which is approximately the weight of a P-30 model including the 10 grams of rubber allowed), the **Wing Loading, (WL)** would be:

60/120 = 0.5 grams per square inch.

To convert this to ounces per square foot, go back to **Chapter 2, Compound Interest** for the method. Multiply 0.5 by 144 (square inches per sq. ft.) and divide by 28.35 (grams per ounce) to get 2.54 ounces per square foot. Wing Loading is *very* important.

Your model will climb and glide better as you lower the W L and *certainly* the inevitable crashes will cause less damage with low W L. **Fig 14-1** shows some approximate values for W L. for various sizes and types of models. This is only a guide! If your W L is reasonably close then you can proceed with standard flight trimming procedures. If it is way too high then you may have to reconsider what flight performance you can expect and you will also need to find some real tall and soft grass to test over. Adding power to a heavy model rarely helps. There's no free lunch. Adding rubber power also adds rubber weight. Adding electric power requires more batteries to increase voltage. The max suggested WL may also be considered the point of diminishing returns for that particular model.

Fig 14-1 **Wing Loading**

Type	Span (in)	Power	gm / sq in	oz / sq ft
Peanut	13	Rubber	.5 - .7	2.54 - 3.55
Small FF	16-20	Rubber / CO_2	.6 - .9	3.05 - 4.57
Med. FF	18-30	Rubber / CO_2	.7 - 1.0	3.56 - 5.08
Elec. FF	18-36	Electric	1.0 - 1.4	5.08 - 7.11
Micro R/C	24-40	Elec / CO_2	.9 - 1.5	4.60 - 7.62
Small R/C	50-72	Elec. / Gas	1.4 - 2.0	7.00 - 10.0

Calculating the wing area for a wing that is not rectangular in planform can be challenging but is worthwhile. You can break up the wing pattern into rectangles, right triangles and semicircles then add up the results. The formula for the area of a right triangle is: height times width divided by 2. For a semicircle use π x D x D all divided by 8, where π= pi or 3.1414 and D is diameter. In *all* models including R/C you should try for a wing loading as low as practical without sacrificing strength. Chapter 2, **Compound Interest** , suggests several ways to do this.

Remember that your FF model climbs, cruises, glides and thermal hunts with no one at the controls. It must recover from upsets caused by gusts, bad launches or power surges, while maintaining a steady flight profile. Frankly, I had trouble doing that in the early stages of both my full-size and R/C flight careers. Yet we expect to spend four weeks or more building a model, then maybe two or three trim flights. Assuming your model is warp free, within W L limits and balanced at the correct c.g., a dozen trim flights over two or three days is a reasonable flight trim program.

Probably the most important lesson to learn about flight trimming is that almost all adjustments are interdependent. Bend the rudder for a turn and the nose will drop. Move the c.g. back for better glide and you change the climb as well as the turns. Bend an aileron for turn and the speed increases while the model stalls more quickly. The point is that while I discuss trim adjustments individually, always be aware that each may affect others in sequence. That's why you should keep a record of adjustments and effects with any new model.

In Chapter 2, **Evolution**, I created a piece of doggerel to list adjustments and the order in which they should be applied:

Why Be In Far Germany To Trap Some Whales

Warps -Balance-Incidence-Flat Glide-Thrust-Turn-Stop Watch

The reason adjustments are made in a certain order is the very interdependence I mentioned before. For instance, if you attempt to improve your glide by increasing wing positive incidence *before* the model is balanced at the correct c.g., you take the chance of creating a *violent* stall during the climb. Therefore, let's make sure we understand all the terms and adjustments before discussing their effects.

Warps

This was discussed at length in Chapter 1, **Tools and Construction** and Chapter 6, **ScaleModels.** Besides weight control, this is probably the most important yet least understood area in flying models. Consider the effect of a 3/32" deflection in a 1/2 x 1/2" tab on the wing tip. It can result in a "death spiral" under power. Yet I have seen wing warps of 1/8 or more along the whole span. A simple way to check for wing warp is shown in **(RPMA pg 64)** where the finished wing is laid across the sides of an ordinary drawer. There is one warp, however, that is not only permissible but is mandatory. That is the warp or wing twist for **Washout**. Instructions for building in and holding washout are covered in the **Chapter 1, Tools and Construction.**

Washout puts a twist in each wing that lifts the rear of the tip above the rest of the wing. This put the tip at a lower incidence angle **Fig 14-2**. Incidence is the angle between a line parallel to the chord of the wing (or stab) and a "fuselage reference line" which would be considered a horizontal line through the center of the fuselage when the model is balanced horizontally (**RPMA pg 105**). This is not always the "thrust line" since down thrust may be built in or have been added. The wing is usually at some positive angle above the fuselage reference line and this is called "Wing Incidence". Washout places the *tip* of the wing at a *lower* angle of incidence than the center. As the model climbs and the wing reaches a higher and higher angle of attack, the center will stall before the tip. This keeps the model from falling off on a wing tip into a spin and leads to a more gentle, straight ahead stall.

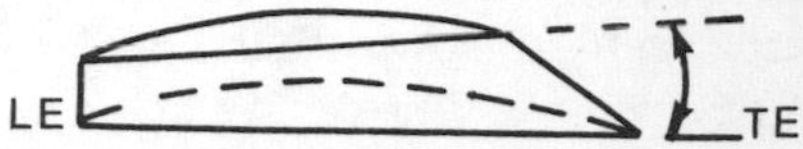

Fig 14-2

LE TE

Alignment

Along with warps, misalignment of flying surfaces causes the most trouble for beginners. It's obvious that a wing tilted down to one side will cause the plane to bank towards that side leading to a steep turn and maybe a crash. Many models have removable wings and tail surfaces for easier transport and shock response. Re-aligning wings and tail each time you fly or even after each landing requires patience and care. A better method is to add small "keys" to locate these surfaces (**RPMA pg 55**). These can be half dowels or strips of hard balsa glued to wing and stab so they "lock" on each side of the fuselage. Most fuselages are very narrow at the rear so a stab front stop and 1/32 ply platform are also helpful additions.

Balance

Balancing a model fore and aft is as simple as placing your fingertips under the wing at the approximate c.g.. I prefer a more accurate system using pencils inserted into a board with round erasers upward. But how often have you balanced your model side to side or weighed the wings individually? Since we are dealing with wood, glue and hand work, there is little reason why the wings would have identical weights. Once I got an electronic scale that could weigh within 1/10 of a gram, I started to weigh everything just for fun. I was quite surprised to find that wing spars could vary by 20% and the ribs for one side of a 36 inch wing could weigh two grams more than those for the other side. With this good tool I am able to arrange parts for better balance without having to add weights. A two gram difference in wing weight can cause a turn that needs a large rudder adjustment to correct.

For best stability, locate the c.g. 25% to 40% back along the wing chord from the Leading Edge.

How do you figure the c.g. when the wing has a tapered planform? You need to find **Mean Aerodynamic Chord (MAC), which is another name for the average chord.** It's an imaginary line along the chord (front to rear) of the wing that describes how the air sees the wing regardless of its planform. To find this **MA.C,** divide the wing area by the span. For a constant chord wing, take the number you just got for **MAC** and lay it out starting at the Leading Edge of the wing at the root. For a tapered wing, find the spot along the span where the MAC fits between LE and TE. You can find the approximate c.g. location by measuring 25-40% along the **MAC** back from the Leading Edge in either of the above examples. For a swept-back wing, add about half the sweepback to your distance from the LE. Remember, this is only an approximation to get you started.

With a movable wing, adjust c.g. by moving the wing back or forward. Keep the distance from the wing center to the nose about 1/3 the distance from the wing center to the stab center. Once you have located the CG, mark the spot with a tiny ink dot so future changes, if required, can be calibrated. Remember, the CG is the most important early adjustment. It's far better to add some nose weight to correct a rearward c.g. than to adjust something else, like warping stab TE down.

Control Surfaces

Before discussing "Incidence" we'll review *exactly* what the various control surfaces do to affect the flight profile. If you use tabs as control surfaces, keep them small. On any model under 36 in. span, tabs need not extend more than 1/4 inch or be more than 1 inch wide. You will be surprised at how much effect a small tab bent only 1/8 inch up or down can have during the power phase. If you have movable control surfaces (as on a scale model), restrict the movement even more because these surfaces will tend to be quite large.

Throughout this book all motion or deflections of controls on the will be considered as if seen from the pilot's seat. **Rudder** motion to the right, moves the model to the right. The movable part of the rudder (the stationary part is usually called the Fin) is typically near the top flattening the turn by injecting "opposite roll" . **Elevator** motion up at the rear moves the nose up. Deflecting the whole stabilizer up at the rear (as on a contest model) has the same effect and would be called **negative incidence**. Bending the **right aileron** down puts upward force on the right wing causing the model to tilt to the **left** (called a left bank - different from the one in Paris), which makes the plane turn **left**.

Already we see an interaction between adjustments. Left rudder and right aileron down *both* cause left turn. However, rudder alone will cause a skidding turn, the same as if you steered the wheel of a bicycle left without leaning a bit to the left side. This kind of "skid" reduces lift and can shorten the glide. On the other hand, too much bank in a turn also reduces lift and makes recovery harder. In a full-sized airplane with a pilot at the controls, we try to coordinate the turn by imposing balanced amounts of rudder and aileron. In a free flight model we tend to allow more "skid" to avoid a steep bank when we have no control input to use for recovery.

In scale models you may find that the tail tends to swing right and left a bit while the model "rocks" slightly from side to side. This is called a "Dutch Roll" and is caused by too small rudder and fin area. Add area to the top of the rudder a bit at a time using scotch tape or small scraps of balsa until the "wobble" disappears. An exact scale reduction of a full sized airplane would lead to rudder and stab areas that are too small for stability in an uncontrolled FF model. Most kits or plans expand rudder area to 10-12% and stab area to 25-30% of wing area. If you are scratch building or designing your own, use these figures as guides.

We can also adjust the **thrust line** of our model by various means as discussed in Chapter 1 **Tools and Construction** and Chapter 6, **Scale Models**. Even the full sized Piper Cherokee I flew had offset thrust and a bit of wing twist to counteract the high torque of the engine at full revs. Bending thrust to the right will turn the model right. Down thrust helps us counteract the engine burst at full power. Rarely, except in slow flying indoor models, is up or left thrust needed.

If you are a beginner, I strongly recommend that you read **RPMA** and experiment with control inputs on a stick model like the Canary or the AMA Racer <u>before</u> testing a heavy, large electric model that may have taken weeks to build. Though you may have a good technical understanding of flight adjustments, there's nothing like some real experience to give you a feel for when you are approaching a dangerous condition. Sometimes the adjustments that produce a fine glide will be just enough to cause disaster under full power. The rudder, for instance, is much more effective at high speed under power than in the glide. Too much left rudder can cause a "death spiral" near the ground at full power.

Decalage

This is another built-in adjustment, like washout, that adds stability. Decalage is the difference in Incidence between the wing and the stab. Using the same Fuselage Reference Line, the angle of the wing should be positive and the stab slightly negative. A total of four or five degrees <u>difference</u> between these angles normally does the trick. **Fig 14-3**. Usually, the wing is at three degrees positive. One degree is 1/32 inch at a distance of 2-3/4 inches. Simply extend the lines to measure incidence in degrees for wider chords.

The effect of Decalage is similar to that of Washout. As the model climbs in a nose up attitude, the wing may eventually stall as it reaches an angle too steep to maintain lift. Since the stab is at a lower angle, it will not stall, allowing the tail to continue climbing so as to level the airplane. The forces acting on wing and stab are shown in **Fig 14-3** and **(RPMA pg 105)**. Almost all flying models including R/C have both Washout and Decalage built in. Only small hand launch or catapult gliders and aerobatic R/C's have zero Decalage. In gliders, decalage would cause looping at high launch speeds.
In aerobatic R/C's, less stable (no decalage) means greater maneuverability.

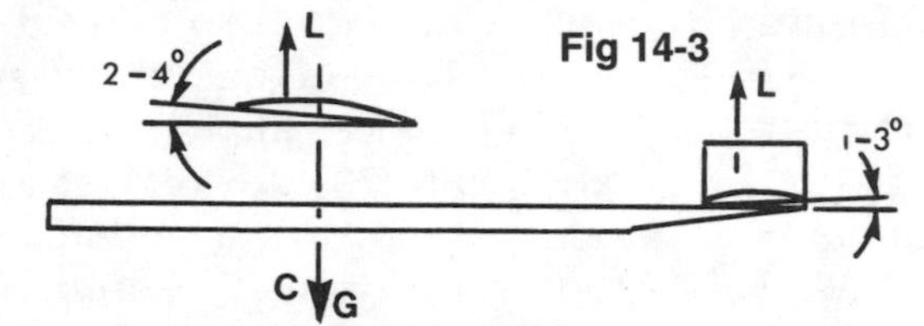

Fig 14-3

Dihedral

Here again we have to build something in to help the model recover by itself from banks and spirals. Dihedral is a bend along the span of the wing so that the tip is higher than the root. The effect of dihedral is to make the lower wing in a bank achieve more lift to return the craft to level flight. Most scale models have simple dihedral with a single break at the wing center or root. Contest models often have "Polyhedral" with another break out towards the tip. This helps the model "roll" into a thermal and increases endurance. Dihedral is typically an inch *at each tip* for every foot of total span.

Incidence

Once the model is warp free and balanced with Washout, and some Decalage and Dihedral are built in, we can proceed with basic flight testing to establish the rest of the control requirements. I believe **stability** is the very first flight requirement. Later we can work on flight profile and endurance. Although many kit instructions call for hand gliding to start flight trim, I disagree.

It's not easy to throw a model at exactly the proper glide speed. Too hard and you may force it to fly too fast close to the ground causing a stall and crash. Too soft and the model will simply fall out of the air with the same result. I suggest initial testing at very low power. With a rubber model, 20-40 turns will work. For electric use a 20 second charge. For CO_2, gas, or compressed air, use the lowest speed that will keep the motor running and hold the model until the motor run is almost ended.

Launch the model aiming at a spot on the ground 20-30 feet away and give it a very gentle push straight ahead. You are going for a controlled, straight ahead glide of about 5:1 ratio. The model flys five feet forward for every foot it descends.

If the model dives, you now have 3 interactive adjustments you can make. (I told you this stuff wasn't easy.) Move the c.g. back by reducing nose weight. You probably had to add some weight to the nose for primary balance. You can also move the c.g. rearward (with relation to the wing center of lift) by sliding the wing *forward.* Remember, the c.g. is found by balancing the plane on the wings. Therefore, moving wing forward has the effect of moving c.g. backward. In an electric model you also have the option of moving the battery pack front or rear. The second option is to add wing incidence by shimming up the LE of the wing. The same effect, and the third option, can be achieved by shimming up the rear of the stab which is the same as adding up elevator.

The trick here is to make *very small adjustments* and to make them *one at a time* and also to record each adjustment and its effect. This c.g., Incidence and recording system is the primary flight trim exercise. When you get this right, the future holds no fears.

It's preferable to move the c.g. first, then add wing positive, then stab negative incidence. Don't move the c.g. more than 1/4 inch from the basic location (1/3 of the chord from the LE) in either direction. If this doesn't cure the problem, start with wing incidence changes of 1/32 at a time, up to three degrees, then add stab negative 1/32", at a time up to three degrees. Remember, wing incidence changes are about *twice* as effective as stab incidence changes.

Thrust

By now, you have probably achieved a decent powered glide straight ahead. If you have a very heavy model, you may need more power or a harder throw to test adequately. Very tiny models, like Peanuts are difficult to adjust. Their wing loading is relatively high and they are very sensitive to even the slightest trim change.

Beginners should start with a model of 16 inch span *minimum*, two feet is better. If you still have a dive, recheck all your settings. If your model is a kit or a tested plan, it probably is flying by now. If it is an original design, some aspect of the proportions may be wrong.

Now you can begin to add power in very small increments to achieve the beginning of a climb straight ahead. With rubber, you add a few more turns each flight. CO_2 with its infinitely adjustable speed is also test friendly. Electric and gas require more care. There are some cute tricks you can use with motors. First, put the prop on backwards so it produces less thrust. Or, use a prop only 60% of the required size. Some flyers keep a few 1/16" ply disks in various diameters from 1" to 3" to mount behind the prop thus blocking some of its thrust. Any way you can operate at 1/4 and 1/2 power will help.

You want a very shallow climb , of approximately 15 degrees. If the model starts to stall when you add power, you can now begin with thrust adjustments. Down thrust can be added up to even 10 degrees to handle high thrust values but four or five degrees usually works.

As you add power or thrust, speed increases very quickly which makes adjustments very sensitive. Your model is climbing high enough now to be able to observe the glide and the "transition" phase of the flight where the power bleeds off and the glide begins. In transition you have a model that has climbed at an upward angle and now must change to horizontal flight with as flat a glide as you can arrange. With rubber power, this transition is a bit easier because power eases off as the rubber unwinds tending to return the model to horizontal flight during the "cruise". Electric and CO2 power also allow for some cruise but glo engines have an abrupt cutoff and most engines tend to "lean out" as the tank empties, increasing rpm. You may have to add down thrust as you add power until the model climbs out smoothly, even at maximum power.

Torque

Before discussing turn adjustments you need to know a bit more about this force. Torque is a "twisting" force that acts *opposite* to the direction of prop rotation. Most model props will turn clockwise (as seen from the pilot's seat) so the torque force tends to turn the whole model counterclockwise, initiating a left bank. The amount of the torque depends on motor power, prop rpm and prop size, to some degree. This means that most models will have the most torque when power is highest right at the launch when the model is also nearest the ground. High torque can flip a model right over on a wing tip during an R.O.G. The easiest way to handle torque is to add some right thrust. Really high powered contest models sometimes even twist the *inboard* section of the left wing downward to add some lift and counteract the left bank. Right thrust is usually achieved by tilting the nose block (on a rubber model) or the whole motor or engine to the right a degree or two. Counteracting torque with rudder or aileron deflection is not a good idea because the deflections on these surfaces would have to be large and would become dangerous at high speed.

Turn

Once you have achieved a basic, low angle climb, start to adjust for turn. Outdoor rubber powered contest models should turn *right* in the climb. This type of model has a large diameter prop (as much as 40% of the wing span). It develops high **torque** at high power and tends to turn the model sharp left so you need right thrust to counteract this tendency. Some scale, low wing types will need to turn left so be really careful adjusting these. Indoor models should turn left because almost all of their flight is under power at the cruise level and missing the walls is more important than climbing high. Depending on size, a turn diameter of 50 feet is OK for small models. At 25% of full power the model is probably continuing to climb while turning.

Don't start looking for a skyrocket climb. That's probably the worst way to get long, high flights. You want your model to "climb on the wing" where the lift of the wing does most of the work. With our light models and powerful thrust a model can easily be made to climb at a very steep angle but it won't be as high at the end of the motor run as the same model climbing at a more efficient, lower angle.

Your motor run at full power is of a specific duration. The goal is to get your model as high as possible by the end of that run. High performance gas models often climb almost straight up but they also have a timer that changes stabilizer incidence for climb and then glide. Without this "bunt" arrangement, you should not try for this kind of profile. A good climb angle for a FF model; is usually somewhere between 20 and 35 degrees. At that angle, you will have to "eyeball" climb angle and height but the difference in height attained with the best climb angle will be apparent.

You will notice when the model begins to "hang on the prop". This means the climb is too steep and more down thrust may be needed.

This is the point where all the interactive adjustments come into play. Turn in the climb can be accomplished by:

1. Thrust offset
2. Rudder offset
3. Aileron or Wing tab offset
4. Very small weight added to inside wing tip

Adjustments should be made in the order shown above with each up to the suggested limit of deflection and #4 reserved as a last resort. Record each adjustment and its effect as you add power up to maximum. *Remember* that under power, each of the above adjustments becomes *more* sensitive as power increases. Therefore, if your turn is a bit too wide at low power, don't make changes yet. The turn may well tighten as power increases. The same goes for climb angle. It may get much steeper and require more down thrust as power increases. The preferred profile under full power would include a climb at less than 35 degrees with the model seeming to rise vertically while also going up the climb slope. This is due to wing lift. The circle can be 50-100 feet in diameter while the transition "slides" the model over the top without a stall and dip. The glide should be flat while continuing to circle.

Stab Tilt

Here's a neat idea that is said to come from **Carl Goldberg**. Tilting the stab towards one side or the other causes the model to turn towards the high side of the tilt (**RPMA pg 112**). It's interesting that this adjustment only has effect in the glide. If you tilt the stab 1/8 in. high at the outside tip on the right side, the model will turn right in the glide.

Once you have established a good climb and transition, you need to start all over again to create the best glide profile. Of course, any glide adjustments also affect the climb, so you have to be very careful here. The same flying surface deflections work in the glide but they are less effective at the lower speeds. Don't be tempted to bend the rudder a lot to keep the model in a tight gliding circle. You may also cause a high speed spiral in the climb. Some flyers prefer to climb right, then glide left. This has the advantage of creating a very smooth transition because the model makes a neat "S"- turn at the top of the climb. This can be done with right thrust (which is only effective in climb) and *slight* left rudder and stab tilt (high on the left side). Aileron deflection is not a good idea for this type of trim. My Champion Upshot is adjusted this way and has had more than 100 good flights. The disadvantage of this profile is that you will need a much larger field. I have lost the Upshot twice so far.

Stop Watch

This is the tool you need to make those final, tiny adjustments that can help your model find a thermal all by itself and double or triple your flight time. Once you have established a decent climb, transition, cruise and glide, you can begin to adjust for best duration flight profile. The requirements are a calm, cool morning or evening with little or no thermal activity. Begin testing the model with max power while you time both the power run and the glide. Eyeball the height reached with the same motor run, observe glide attitude and timing. Porpoising in climb (up and down bobbing of the nose) can be corrected with thrust adjustment. Porpoising in glide needs *very slight* change in incidence and/or c.g. The glide should be just below stall attitude and as slow and flat as you can get it. Time the glide duration so you won't be fooled. A faster glide, if flat enough may keep the model aloft longer !

Keep your adjustments on the order of less than 1/64 inch at a time and with only one surface at a time. Keep a bunch of 1/64 and 1/32" ply strips in your field box. Remember to check alignment often as you adjust. A tilted wing can cancel all your work as the model finds the only strip of concrete or pile of rocks in the whole county as it crashes. Another neat way to make trim shims is to wind masking tape around the end of a pencil or dowel. Once you have 6-8 layers of tape, you can cut a slice along the axis of the dowel to give you a strip of masking tape up to 8 layers thick. Then just peel away the tape to get the number of layers you want. Each layer is about .005 to .007" thick (1/3 of 1/64 inch) and will stick where you put it, at least while you complete the trimming.

At first, you may find significant duration differences as you make final adjustments. These differences will become smaller and smaller as the flight profile approaches optimum.

Power Train Changes

I'll bet you thought you were all done. Not hardly. Once you have the best flight profile you can manage with the present power train, start thinking about how to improve the power phase by altering the entire power system. This stuff is not restricted to the serious modeler. Every beginner needs to at least experiment with some of the changes described below to learn what each factor can accomplish.

Rubber is the power system that allows for the most variety. You can easily change the number of strands and/or length of the rubber motor and even the location of the rear peg to affect c.g. Prop variety is almost infinite. Diameter, pitch and blade shape is easily changed by carving blades, forming them or cutting from a plastic cylinder. These methods are discussed in detail Chapter 15, **Props**. All these changes will affect your flight profile. If the prop is free-wheeling rather than folding, prop changes may even affect glide.

Start with the kit or plan recommended prop diameter. If you have a prop with replaceable blades like the **Superior** free-wheeler or folder, then change diameter 1/2 inch at a time while watching and noting duration and stability. You probably can't add more than 15% to the diameter. Next, try the same experiment by changing pitch. Start with a Pitch Diameter Ratio (Pitch divided by Diameter) of 1.5. For instance, if the prop diameter is 10 inches, then a Pitch of 15 inches will provide a P/D of 1.5. With a **Superior Pitch Gage**, you can make these changes right on the field.

With rubber power you can go down to a P/D of 1.2 or up to 1.8. Very light indoor models get to P/D of 2. The best way to evaluate each change is to time both climb and glide while observing the profile. Once you establish the best prop diameter and pitch, you might try a couple of different blade shapes. My Sparky (the original kit was designed in the 40's) flies a lot better with an old time wide bladed prop than it does with the more modern slim blades.

You may find that too large a prop destroys stability and leads to a violent stall. Remember that a model with a small diameter, high revving prop will usually be more stable than the reverse. To further complicate the matter, as you increase prop diameter, you may need to add more rubber to swing it, thus also adding weight in the glide. Although this may sound like the worst kind of compulsive behavior, some may actually have a lot of fun working with a stable, rugged model to find the very best combination of adjustments and changes. The neat part of this system is that you can stop at any point after you have basic stability, as long as *you* are satisfied with the flight profile. Note that *each* airplane is a unique system and even two supposedly identical kits may need different adjustments even if they were built by the same person in the same shop.

For electric, gas, compressed air or CO_2, there is much smaller variety of props available. These are higher rpm systems so the thin plastic coke bottle type blades you might use for rubber are not appropriate. In small models, you are stuck with formed plastic blades. Superior does make some small props for both direct drive and geared electric motors like the **Kenway** or the **HiLine**, and **K&P** also makes some neat props with replaceable blades for the 6-10 watt electric motors. A larger diameter prop will also act to slow down the rpm of any of these motors. Your best bet here is to acquire a large variety of plastic props from 2-8 inches in diameter. Get 20 or so different ones. Then you can try a succession of props with the same engine settings. With CO_2 you can make some very big changes by using larger props than those supplied with the engine. I fly my 30 inch span twin-Brown powered, CETO controlled R/C model with a 9-1/2 inch P-30 type plastic prop cut down to 8-1/2 inches. I get flights slow enough for indoors and long engine runs.

With motors that have speed control you may find that you will get longer flights with less than a top speed setting. At top speed, the climb may be too steep to get best lift from the wing. Again, the stop watch is your best judgment tool. Glow engines are the exception here. They work best when "leaned out" (run at top rpm) and the lower fuel use extends the power run.

Tiplets

As mentioned in the Chapter 4 "**Evolution**" , Tiplets are small rudders that are attached to the wing tips. They usually slant outward at an angle of 15 degrees and each has an area of 3 to 4% of the total wing area. Tiplets can be effective in three different ways. First, they add a tiny bit to the apparent wing area while adding very little drag. Second they affect the model as if it had extra dihedral which smoothes and flattens turns, last, they reduce some stuff called "tip vortices" which are whirling air currents that travel along the wing from root to tip and then stream from the tips. These reduce wing lift but affect mostly heavy, fast moving aircraft. You can sometimes see the contrails formed by high flying aircraft. These vortices are dangerous to small planes landing too near big jets. Obviously, these won't be a problem on your electric P-30 but the tiplets <u>can</u> add some endurance and smooth control of your micro R/C as they did on mine. You can easily tack glue or pin a couple on your model and observe the effect.

Turbulators

I am often asked if these devices will significantly add to flight duration. They can but almost always require *complete* retrimming of the airplane and they aren't easy to put on, then remove. Turbulators are thin, [1/64" (.015) or less], strips added to the top of the wing along the span. Their purpose is to help break loose the "laminar" layer of air that passes over the wing during flight. This laminar layer is a thin sheet of air molecules that travel right along with the wing instead of passing over it. If this layer can be broken loose from the wing top surface at an earlier point on the chord, more lift will develop. *However* this adjustment will also change the best climb angle and the stall point, so you need to go back to square one and start adjusting all over again ! Turbulators can be made from simple sewing thread glued along the span at the 5% and 15% chord points. I don't know of any way to temporarily attach turbulators since their very action depends on a close bonding to the wing surface. Therefore, once you attach them you may have to soften with thinner, then re-dope the wing to return to its original condition.

There is no doubt that in many cases high performance contest models show marked duration improvement with turbulators. Some builders also add them to the stab and Bob Hatschek has had some good results adding strips to his very large diameter rubber props. I think these are useful mostly for the serious competitor who is already beyond what this book can cover. Interestingly enough, models built the old time way with top and bottom wing spars covered with shrunk tissue often already have slightly raised strips on the wing top surface where the top spars push the tissue up after shrinking. This may have accidentally accounted for the terrific performance of the old timers.

If you want to really enjoy increasing model performance, then practice to enhance your flight trimming skills right along with building improvements. Don't treat flight trimming as a necessary delay between the final coat of dope and the first good flight. Consider it more as another enjoyable aspect of the hobby that you can take pleasure in as you advance. It's *really* fun to see what effect small changes may have and to rescue a hopeless model and turn it into a good performer. **Fig 14-5** shows Bill Hartwell launching his perfectly adjusted Jabberwock on another winning flight. Bill and other master flight trimmers would certainly agree that good building is only half the job.

A very important point about flight trimming is that you have to be able to clearly *see* your model through all parts of the flight. Since we fly on mostly sunny days, we all wear sunglasses of some kind and we all risk ultra violet ray damage to our eyes as sunlight slips in on the sides or over the tops of our glasses. A while ago I discovered the **NOIR** line of wrap around glasses intended to fit right over your regular glasses. These glasses have highly sensitive chemical filters built right into the lenses that absorb the harmful UV, infrared and blue light. They come in a wide variety of colors from pink through green and gray so you can easily find a shade that suits. They also come in yellow and orange types that shield UV and, at the same time, provide high contrast so objects, (like a high model against a gray sky) become more visible.

Once you master the basic elements of flight trimming, you will be able to handle larger models with more power. This is a very important prerequisite for radio control. I have seen too many new builders start with an expensive, large R/C model that they "re-kit" on the first powered flight which discourages them enough to never try again.

Even if you never intend to enter a contest, trimming your model to improve on last year's or last week's *best* flight is an achievement you will long remember.

Fig 14-5

15

PROPELLERS

I have saved this chapter for last because you can't really make much more than an approximate choice of prop before you have an airplane to use it on. (**RPMA pgs 67-85)** has a great deal of useful information on props so I won't repeat it all here,however I'll cover some of the basic theory and offer a few specific ideas for the models discussed in previous chapters.

Prop and Pitch Theory

Although it is no longer accepted as the theory of propeller operation, imagine the prop as a screw that moves through the air by "turning" or "screwing" itself forward. This will make it easier to understand **Pitch**. Just as the threads on a screw look like miniature inclined planes when viewed from the side, so would a prop blade **Fig 15-1**. If you attached a tiny light to the tip and exposed the system to film for several revolutions, the moving light would describe a shape called a "helix". This helix_is shown in **Fig 15-2.** The distance the prop would travel forward in one revolution is called the **Propeller Pitch**. In order to act as efficiently as practical, propeller blades have a pitch or tilt that varies from hub to tip. This is called "Helical Pitch" which simply means each blade has its lower "twist" at the tip which gradually increases towards the hub.

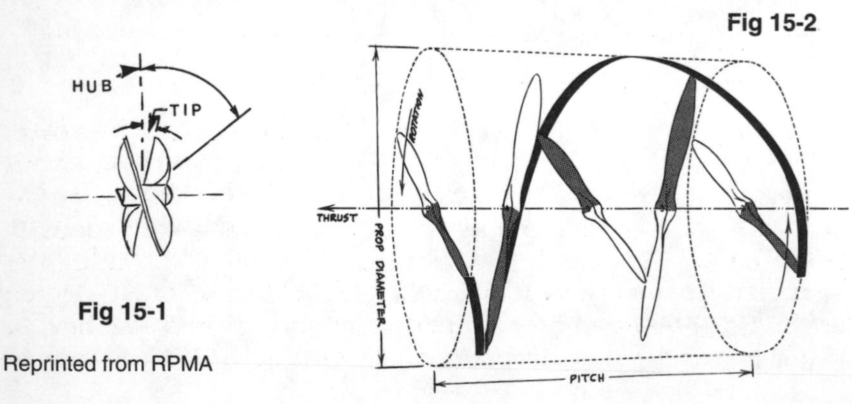

Fig 15-2

Fig 15-1

Reprinted from RPMA

If we picture air as a fluid through which the prop must force its way forward, then the larger the prop diameter and the higher the pitch, the more work the prop will have to do on each revolution. Wider blades with higher camber also require more work.

Let's leave the prop for a moment and consider what the prop does. Each *individual* model (even ones from the same kit or design) has *optimum* speeds for climb, cruise and glide. This means that the model will perform best at certain speeds throughout the flight profile. For instance, in the climb you want the very best speed that will generate the most wing lift. This is not (as discussed in Chapter 14, **Flight Trim**), the steepest possible climb angle. Rather, it's the speed that will get the model the *highest* by the end of the motor run. You can't really prove this out without wind tunnel data but your trusty stop watch and some eyeball height judgment will get you some surprisingly close estimates. In most full sized aircraft, the prop pitch is changed during flight by the pilot to accomplish climb and cruise (constant speed prop systems). For your model, you will have to find a prop pitch, diameter, blade shape and camber that provides optimum performance *throughout* the whole flight.

This isn't as daunting a task as you may think. There has been a great deal of work done to give you some close approximations. **(Fig 15-3, RPMA pg 73)** shows these factors related to scale, sport or endurance models. Again, these are guides not rules.

Fig 15-3 Basic Propeller Design Factors

Item	Scale	Sport	Endurance
Prop Dia.	.8 √ W.A.	1.1 √ W.A.	1.4 √ W.A.
Max Chord	15 %	12 %	9 %
P/D	1.4	1.3	1.2 - 1.5

Once you understand Pitch, you need to be able to measure, calculate, and build it into any prop system. If you could unroll the pitch path, **Fig 15-2**, as you might with a cardboard toilet paper tube, you would find that when flat it forms a right triangle, **(RPMA pg 75)**. This can be used to calculate pitch by finding the spot on the blade where it is exactly parallel to a 45 or 30-degree angle. **Fig 15-4** shows how to create a pitch gage and also how to calculate the various dimensions. For best accuracy, we want to use the angle gage that falls nearest to the center of the blade as measured from the center of the hub. That's why we have both 30 and 45-degree systems. Choose the one that intersects your blade nearest the center. A typical pitch gage is shown in **Fig 15-5**. Superior Props sells one that can be used right at the field.

Fig 15-4 **Prop Pitch Gage Settings**

Pitch	8"	10"	12"	14"	16"	18"	20"	22"	24"	26"	28"
45 deg	1.3	1.6	1.9	2.2	2.6	2.9	3.2	3.5	3.8	4.1	4.5
30 deg	2.2	2.8	3.3	3.9	4.4	4.9	5.5	6.1	6.6	7.2	7.7

You can carve a prop from balsa or hardwood to a specific diameter and pitch **Fig 15-12, Fig 15-12A. (RPMA pgs 78-79)** show in detail how to calculate and carve one .You can also form a prop blade to a specific pitch. The blade can be formed from balsa soaked in water and ammonia or a couple of layers of card stock wet with white glue. Using what you have learned in Chapter 8, **Vacuum Form** , you might even form blades from plastic. To form a prop blade you need a Forming Block that can also be carved from balsa or hardwood. The interesting thing about a Pitch Form Block is that it will form the proper pitch angles *for any diameter* prop that requires the same pitch! If you carve a block for, say a 12" diameter x 18 " pitch, that same block can be used for a 9 or 11 " diameter x 18 " pitch, so carve (or orderfrom Superior) a block for the largest diameter you might need. I haven't room here to repeat all the prop charts and drawings from **RPMA.** They show simple, clear methods for laying out rectangular blocks to carve the above.

Fig 15-5

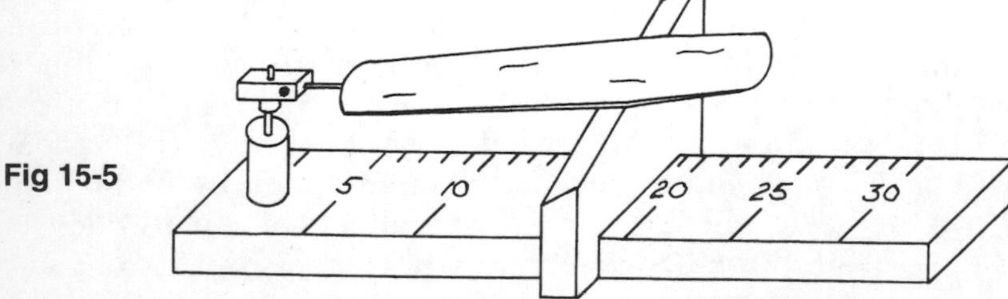

Laying out a Pitch Form Block is simple. (**RPMA Appendix A-1 pg166**) shows the Block Tip Angle in degrees. (The table was mislabeled in earlier editions. The1998 edition now reads "Tip Angle". Also the tip angle for a P/D ratio of 2.0 is shown as 33 degrees. The correct angle (1998 edition) is 32 degrees. To simplify your calculations and eliminate the need to choose a Tip Angle for each specific pitch, I have set up **Fig 15-6** which provides dimensions for 5 Pitch Blocks at P/D Ratios of 1.0, 1.5, 2.0, 2.5 and 3.0. The table also specifies a Block Width of 1.5 inches for all sizes. This will give you an arsenal of Prop Pitch molding blocks to cover most of your early requirements. As you progress, you may wish to study the tables in **RPMA** to form or carve props in finer increments. (**RPMA pg 76**) shows a typical Pitch Block.

Fig 15-6 **Pitch Block Dimensions**

P/D Ratio	Tip Angle (degrees)	Tangent	Block Width (inches)	Block Height (inches)	Nearest Fraction
1.0	18	.3249	1.5	.487	31/64
1.5	26	.4877	1.5	.730	47/64
2.0	32	.6249	1.5	.937	15/16
2.5	38	.7813	1.5	1.172	1-11/64
3.0	44	.9657	1.5	1.440	1-7/16

Fig 15-6A shows a carved Pitch Block for 1.5 P/D Ratio. This would fit a 19.5 in.dia, (9 in. blades + 1.5 in. hub) prop or smaller. The undercamber shim is optional.

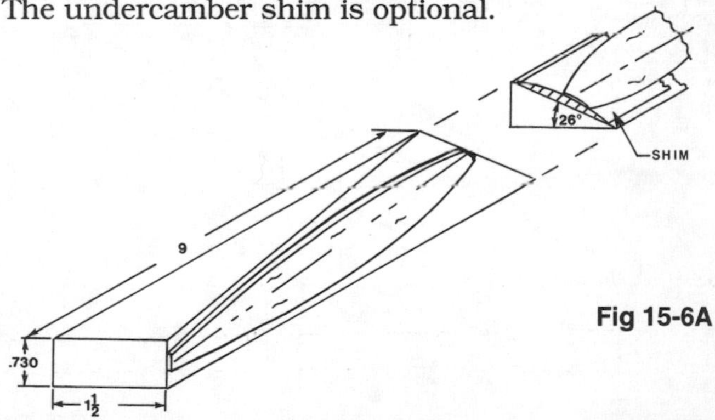

Fig 15-6A

Fig 15-12

Prop Carving Factors

Selected P/D	Block Width Factor Wb	Block Depth Factor Hb	Tip Depth Factor Ht
.9	.95	.45	.24
1.0	.94	.50	.27
1.1	.92	.54	.29
1.2	.91	.58	.31
1.3	.89	.62	.33
1.4	.88	.65	.35
1.5	.86	.68	.37
1.6	.85	.72	.39
1.7	.83	.75	.40
1.8	.82	.78	.42

Fig 15-12A

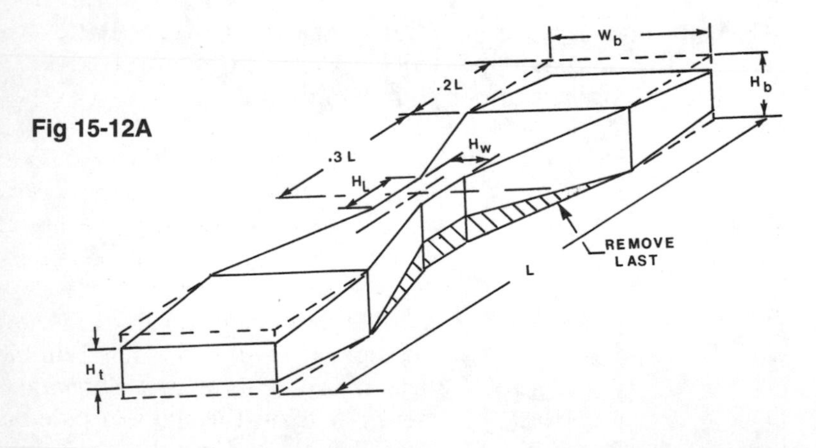

Reprinted from RPMA

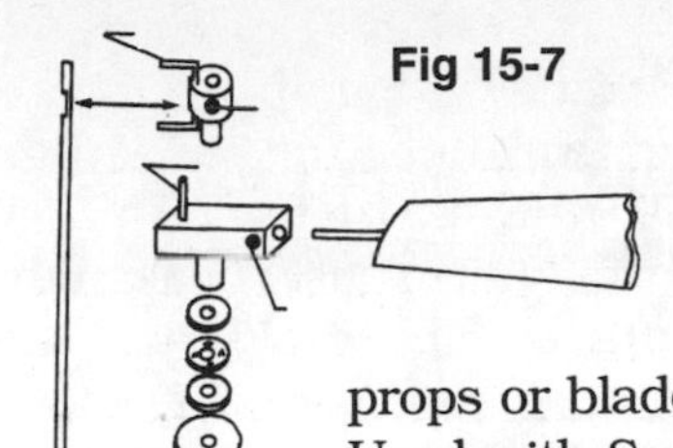
Fig 15-7

All the above is great to know, but **Superior Props** has solved most of our prop problems and, except for the "whittlers" among us who enjoy inhaling balsa dust, we can all just simply order form blocks or carved props or blades to almost any diameter or P/D ratio. Used with Superior's "Replaceable Blade and Adjustable Pitch Free-Wheel Hub" **Fig 15-7**, you can have a complete arsenal of props to test. Decide on the most efficient P/D ratio in a Free Wheel configuration, then order the same P/D with Ed's "Z"-wire folding hub or an Old Time solid balsa folder hub to get the best possible glide. Ed's folder blades are also replaceable by unscrewing a retainer knob and slipping off the blade. Cover your blades with silk and carry a spare set so you won't ever have to quit flying because of a broken blade.

Free Wheeling and Folding Props

Fig 15-8

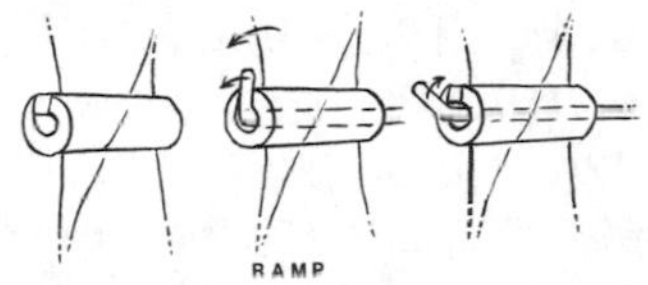

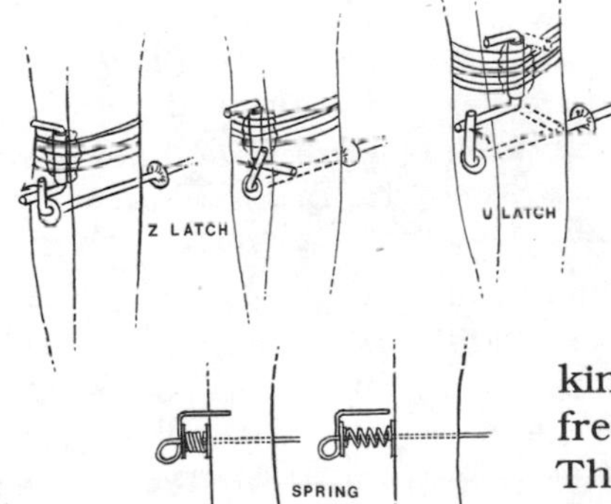

Reprinted from RPMA

A free-wheeling prop is one that releases itself from the shaft and rotates free after the power has run out. This is a big help in the glide. If the prop stays attached to the shaft, then it must drag the whole power train as the air forces it to rotate. This, as well as the extended blades, causes considerable drag. For rubber powered models, there are several kinds of latches that will allow for free-wheeling **(RPMA pg 8), Fig 15-8** These are simple to make but Superior's Free-Wheel Latch is absolutely foolproof and also allows you to replace blades. Many small electric motors (HiLine and Kenway) are set up to allow the shaft to slide back and disengage from the gear.

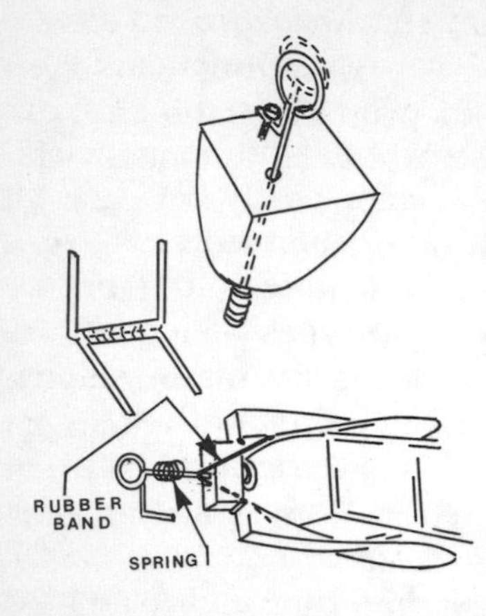

Folding props offer a big reduction in drag once the power has run out. Of course, they also allow the blade to fold harmlessly in a crash. Another feature of most folders is the spring and prop stop screw. **Fig 15-9, (RPMA pg 81)** shows a typical old time folder. The spring in front of the prop hub pulls the shaft forward against the rubber. As the rubber tightens, the shaft moves back towards the rear of the fuselage, thus freeing the hook from the screw and allowing the rubber to rotate the shaft and prop. As the rubber tension eases, the shaft moves forward until the hook engages the stop screw. At that point, the prop stops and folds while the rubber is still under slight tension. This keeps the rubber from unwinding fully and (since the rubber motor may be 1-1/2 times the fuselage length), stops it from shifting and disturbing balancethe glide.

A more modern type of folder hub **Fig 15-10, (RPMA pg 82)**, is the "Z"-Bar. You can make your own by bending and soldering music wire to shape, but **Superior** does it better. His "Z" Bar hub comes with replaceable blades and is bent to the exact angle for a flat fold against the fuselage sides. You can adjust the stop screw for different amounts of rubber tension. I like to stop the prop with about 20 turns still on the rubber. A good addition to the folding system is a small rubber band attached from one blade, across the hub to the other blade. This forces the blades to "snap" into folded position instead of flapping back and forth as the model turns in the glide. The band can be attached to the inside of the blade 3/4 inch from the hub. Run it over the hub to the inside of the other blade. Centrifugal force will extend the blade.

Fig 15-10

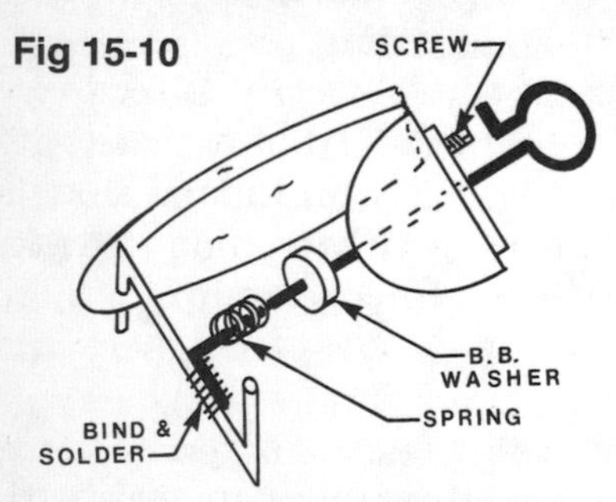

Reprinted from RPMA.

Some old time models (like the Korda Wakefield) used single-bladed folding props. The theory was that with two blades the air was disturbed and turbulent as the next blade entered that space so a single blade would run in more smooth air and be more efficient. This theory has been mostly discarded, partly because it's very hard to perfectly balance a single blade against vibration. Just adding the proper weight to the off side won't quite do the job.

Folders have been used on virtually all types of models including CO_2, electric, gas and compressed air. Evenlarge electric RC models use them with a rubber band to help fold the blades.

As you can see from the above, choosing the right prop can be a hobby in itself. With rubber power, you may choose a prop, then have to change all the parameters as you increase or decrease the rubber size. This is true with indoor models where a change from .060 to .075 rubber can *completely* alter the flight profile. Adding another cell to an electric system can require a larger prop for better climb. Three and four bladed props are almost never used on endurance or sport models since they are not as efficient and are harder to balance than the conventional two blader but they appear on WWII scale models. A three or four blade prop should have the same P/D, with 75% of the diameter of a two-blader.

Indoor Props

The world of indoor flying is quite different from the outdoor one. The flight profile is under power from launch to landing with the cruise as the longest element. Ceiling heights limit climb, and glides can end at walls. Best endurance, even with scale models, calls for a shallow, slow climb, a long cruise and a gentle descent. Flying speeds are much lower indoors, partly because there's no tall grass around and walls are quite unforgiving.

To meet these requirements, indoor model weight is far more critical. Almost every stick gets weighed to 1/10 of a gram and few models are doped. **Lew Gitlow**'s fine book on Indoor Models and **Ron Williams**' outstanding "Building and Flying Indoor Model Airplanes", can teach both beginner and experienced modeler alike how to build and fly indoors. I'll just cover the basic requirements for indoor props and power trains.

Indoor models should fly almost on the edge of a stall. As this provides the slowest flight profile. Longer rubber motors with smaller cross sections (sometimes 3 times the fuselage length) and a lot more turns will do the best job. Most indoor models fly

with a single loop of rubber. My Mini-Stick (7-inch span, 6-inch prop) flies with a *single strand* of .040 rubber wound to 1000 turns. Indoor props, therefore, are of larger diameter and higher pitch, with wider and more cambered blades.

Indoor models are divided into two major categories. The endurance type like the Easy B and Pennyplane are *extremely* light, with weights varying from under one gram to three or four grams. A flight time of ten minutes is quite normal. Simple endurance models regularly fly for 3-5 minutes and are among the most beautiful sights in the air. Flight speed is considerably less than that of a slow walking man (under 4 mph) and some models almost stand still in the air. These models usually have a very light stick, or even a rolled balsa tube made from 4-lb. stock less than .010" thick, to carry the rubber motor and act as a fuselage. Flying surfaces are single covered and construction would qualify as "ghostly".

Modern materials like carbon fiber strands to strengthen structure and Mylar less than .00016 (1/16 of 1/1000") thick for covering have reduced weight, added strength and allowed these incredible flight times. Obviously, props for models like these will differ a lot from anything described so far.

Since rpm on an Easy B can be less than 50, the prop needs to be very large with a high P/D ratio to produce adequate thrust. With an 18 inch span, the prop will often have a *14 in. Diameter* and a P/D of 2 or more giving a Pitch of 28-inches. This is far above the range discussed for outdoor rubber power. Props for this type of model vary widely with the design. Most are of thin balsa sheet (.010 to .020") with grain angled and a thin, hard Balsa stick hub. Blades are molded (two at a time with tissue in between), wet, on a Pitch Block and carefully glued to the hub using an accurate pitch gage. Bearings are a wire loop or thin aluminum sheet with a small hole for the shaft to pass through.

The stopwatch is king in flight-trimming or choosing a prop for an indoor endurance model. Certainly, most would fly adequately with a much smaller prop. IMS' "Slowpoke" is basically a Pennyplane for beginners with a 6-inch plastic prop and is capable of long flights. However, if you want to get the most out of an ultra light indoor model, you have to work towards a large prop with high P/D and the very lightest rubber motor you can use. A rubber stripper is almost mandatory here because a difference of .005 (1/3 of 1/64 inch) will affect flight profile. Both IMS and Micro-X sell rubber strip in .005 increments so, as a beginner, you don't have to buy a stripper.

I suggest you buy a simple Easy B or Pennyplane kit and experiment with rubber size and prop dimensions while timing and recording flight profiles. Once you have some experience, there are many Easy B, Mini Stick and Pennyplane plans available. If you like the idea of flying something silent, slow and gentle in a nice, warm gym, while a blizzard is blowing outside, then you can advance to some of the more sophisticated indoor competition types like Manhattan Cabin and Paper Stick. Some groups are even flying R.O.W. (Rise off Water) indoor models off 1-inch of water in a 1-foot square cake tin.

High level competition indoor models now use devices that actually vary the pitch of the prop as the rubber unwinds and the torque drops. These are torque actuated and are installed on models that *still* have an AUW of a gram or less. This stuff is definitely not for the beginner but is often described in NFFS or INAV reports. Probably the best way to get into indoor flight and learn which areas best fit your own profile is to contact AMA and join a local group.

The other general category of indoor models covers a wide variety of sport and scale types that weigh from about 5-grams to 30-grams. A few are listed and partially defined below:

Peanut Scale -	Fully shaped and covered 13 inch span or 9 in. fuselage max
Pistachio Scale -	9 in. span, condenser paper covered
Coconut Scale-	Large, up to 36 in span
Dime Scale -	16 in. span, single surface covered, approxi mate scale
Bostonian-	Scale like with Charisma, 16 in span, 6 in prop, wheels for ROG, windshield and minimum fuselage dimensions - This is a fun event
AMA Scale -	13 into 36 in span, scale documentation and judging
No-Cal Scale -	16 in. span, profile fuselage only, motor stick and single surface covering

These, and an almost infinite variety of sport indoor models powered by rubber, CO_2, and electric, use props similar to the outdoor variety. Tiny electric motors running on one or two 50 mAh cells use props as small as 2-inch diameter with P/D of 1 or a bit less. Unfortunately, the choice of props for these motors is somewhat limited. Many use plastic props intended for rubber models. Ed Wickland is making some very nice small wood props in various sizes that work well with HiLine Micro 4 and Kenway motors. Wickland's larger wood props for the HiLine Mini-6 and similar motors have proven to perform a lot better than plastic props. I have found that indoor flight with CO_2 requires a larger prop than those recommended by the manufacturer. I have gone as high as 8-1/2 in. diameter with a Brown B-100 or J-70 twin to get long, slow, flights.

Since rpm on heavier models is a lot higher (500-1200 rpm), the prop to span ratio is about the same as for an outdoor model. Many builders have experimented with various prop shapes and many have settled on rather wide blade shape **Fig 15-11** for Bostonian and similar models. Placing more of the blade area *in front* of the hub may allow the blade to flex and thus produce a slightly higher pitch at high torque as the flight starts. Again, I disagree with the experts here and would place more area *behind* the hub (before or behind refers to right or left of the hub as the prop rotates) so that pitch would be lower at the start of the flight when rpm is highest. This is more like how a full sized airplane with a variable pitch prop would work. Some high tech Bostonian models (**David Aronstein**'s "Lifting Body") even have tiplets applied to the prop to enhance efficiency.

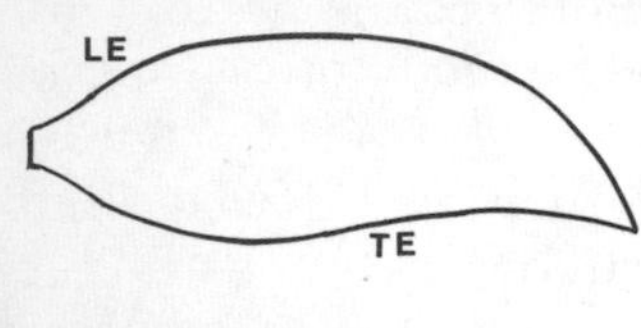

Fig 15- 11

Phil Alvirez of **Idealair Models** has done a huge body of work on "Props on a Can". This is a fine, 25 page book that describes in detail his methods for molding prop blades on various diameter cans.You can create true helical pitch in a wide range of P/D's without fancy trigonometric calculations. His charts allow you to simply choose a P/D and then pick off the appropriate can diameter and molding angle. With prop form blocks, computer carved blades, machined hubs for free-wheel or folder and pre-calculated carving or can molding charts, you can easily become a "gentleman farmer" and enjoy the flying or, if you like to carve, be assured that your work is producing accurate, efficient "airscrews".

All I, or any writer can do, is give you an overview and some approximations for the many systems involved in flying models. There are almost as many "best designs" as there are modelers. Rather than become discouraged because the rule book is vague and certainly incomplete, just enjoy the idea that with some dedication and experimentation, you may add significantly to the sum of modeling knowledge while having a wonderful time. I think it was Da Vinci who said, ***"Once you have tasted flight, your eyes are ever on the sky".***

Rubber Powered Model Airplanes, is the first in this series. It is not only a primer for beginners in rubber power but also a powerful tool for anyone starting out in this particular phase of the hobby. The book includes plans for simple stick models as well as a built up stick and tissue model with a 24 in. span and new construction methods.

Many radio control modelers are looking for a good entry model for a child or grandchild. Rubber power is an ideal way to teach building and flyingskills at low cost and in a short time.

The basics for much of what appears in this book are covered in extensive detail in RPMA. In addition, there is basic information to "Design Your Own" Conventional, Biplane, Canard and even a Flying Wing. RPMA (ISBN No. 0-93871619-0) is available from many hobby suppliers.

Oh! I have slipped the surly bonds of earth
and danced the skies on laughter silvered wings;
Sunward I've climbed, and joined the tumbling mirth
of sun-split clouds-and done a hundred things
You have not dreamed of-wheeled and soared and swung
High in the sunlit silence, Hov'ring there,
I've chased the shouting wind along and flung
My eager craft through footless halls of air...
Up, up the long delirious burning blue
I've topped the windswept heights with easy grace,
Where never lark, or even eagle flew;
And, while with silent, lifting mind I've trod
The high untrespassed sanctity of space,
Put out my hand and touched the face of
God.

" High Flight" by John Gillespie Magee, Jr. 1941

John Magee was a 19 year old American volunteer with the RCAF. He was killed in training December 11, 1941. He left every pilot, whether full sized aircraft or model something fine to look up to.

KITS - MATERIALS - SERVICES

A-J Funpak-PO Box 548-Oregon City,OR 97045- *OT AJ Catapult Gliders*
Ace-116 West 19 St-Higginsville, MO 64037 - *RC Supplies & Equipment*
Aero Composites-3400 Spangler Rd-Medway OH 45341-*Composite Materials*
Aerodyne-1924 E. Edinger- Santa Ana CA 92705- , *Many OT Kits*
Aeroloft Designs-2940 W Gregg Dr-Chandler AZ 85224 - *Panel Line Inks, Decals*
Aerospace Composites-PO Box 16621-Irvine CA 92714-*High Tech Materials*
Air Ace Models-700 Leader Bld-Cleveland, OH 44114-*Dennis Norman-Pre-printed Covering sSystem for Scale Models*
Airsail Intl.-P.O. Box 12723 Penrose Aukland NZ-*Inew line of kits(Hobby Supply South)*
Aircraft Spruce & Specialty-Box 424-Fullerton CA 92632-*Wood & Foam*
Allison, Mark-727 NW 16 St-Corvallis, OR 97330-*Gears for Rubber Power*
Alzart Originals-6871 Oakridge Ln NW-Alexandria, MN 56308-*HL Glider Kits*
American Fun Fly-7543 Maple Ave-Pulaski, N Y 13142-*Electric Power Systems*
American Gryphon Decals-4373 Varsity Ln-Houston, TX 77004-*Lozenge Patterns*
American RC-16181 Ganges Ln #3-Huntington Beach,CA 92647-*Small Electric RC Kits*
Amer. Science & Surplus-3605 Howard St-Skokie, IL 60076-*All Kinds of Surplus Stuff*
Americas Hobby Center-146 W 22 St-New York, NY 10011-*Mail Order Supplier*
Apple Rubber Prod-310 Erie St Lancaster NY 14086-*"O" Rings*
Applied Design-PO Box 3384-Torrance, CA 90510-*Sanders, Glue Tips, Tools*
Astro Flight-13311 Beach St-Marina Del Ray, CA 90292-*RC Electric Supplies*
BCI Enterprises-3142 S State St-Camden, DE 19934-*Special Large Sanding Blocks*
Balsa USA-PO Box 164-Marinette, WI 54143-*Balsa & Hard Woods*
Baltek Corp-10 Fairway St-Northvale, NJ 07647-*Wide Sheet Balsa*
Bell Model Aircraft-650 Pine Crest Drive-Largo, FL 34640- *FF Scale Model Kits*
Blue Ridge Models-Box 329-Skyland, NC 28776-*Fine FF Kits -P-30 & others*
Bradley Model Prod-1337 Pine Sap Ct-Orlando FL 32825-*Hi Tech Matls*
Brown Jr Motors-P.O. Box 77-Pine Grove Mills PA 16868-*CO_2 Motors*
Builders-53041 Fairchild-Chesterfield, MI 48051-*Vacuum Molding Materials*
C&G Balsa-2422 N Marks-Fresno CA 93722-*Balsa & Tools*
Campbell's Custom Kits-7233 Signature Ln, San Antonio TX 78263 -*FF Kits*
Campbell Model Supply-37742 Carson St-Farmington Hills, MI 48331-*Gampi Light Tissue, FF Elec motors & Supplies*
Champion Model Prod- See Aerodyne
Composite Structures Technology-PO Box 642-Tehachapi, CA 93581-*High Tech Matls, Carbon Fiber, etc*
Copter Concepts-832 Salem Lane-Carpenterville, IL 60110-*Rubber Power Helicopters*
Cox Hobbies-(see Estes)
DPR Models-Unit 9 Vanguard Way Essex SS3 9QY ENGLAND-*Many FF Kits-Foam*
Dare Designs-Box 521-Cumberland, MD 21502-*Wide Variety of kits, US & Imports*
Davis Diesel-Box 141-Milford, CT 06460-*Diesel Fuel, Supplies, Conversion Kits Gas to CO_2, Jet-X*
Dayton Plastics-2554 Needmore Rd-Dayton OH 45414-*Tghin Mylar*
Deppe, Joe-Box 185-Bolton Landing NY 12814-*Fine thin strip Spruce, Pine*
Diamond Machining Technology-85 Hayes Memorial Dr-Marlborough MA 01753- *Very Fine Blade Sharpening Stones*
Dicky Bird Models-PO Box J-Westminster CA 92684-*ARF Elec RC Scale Models*
Diels Engineering-PO Box 263-Amherst, OH 44001- *Rubber FF Scale Kits*
Dubois, Gene-PO Box 30053-Acushnet, MA 02743-*Rubber FF Scale Kits*
Du-Bro Products-480 Bonner Rd-Wauconda, IL 60084-*Metal Components & Matls*

Dumas-909FM, E. 17 St-Tucson, AZ 85719-*Laser cut scale kits 17-30 in. span*
EMPS-PO Box 134-Robeson, PA 19551-*Motors & Motor Systems, etc. for Electric Flt*
Easy Built Models-PO Box 425-Lockport, NY 14095-*Wide Variety Kits, FF & RC*
Edjer-PO Box 1775-Hemet, CA 92546-*X-Acto Blade Sharpener*
Edmund Scientific-101 E Gloucester Pike-Barrington, NJ 08007-*Scientific Equipment*
Estes-PO Box 227-Penrose CO 81240-*All Cox Products Plus Rockets & Materials*
Ewings-233 Windcrest Dr-Cecil, PA 15321-*Simple Rubber/Elec Conversion Kit*
FAI Model Supply-PO Box 3957-Torrance, CA 90510-*Tan Rubber & Other FF Supplies*
Fibre Glast-1944 Neva Dr-Dayton, OH 45414-*Foam block & Sheet*
Fiddler's Green-1960 W Ray Rd-Chandler, AZ 85224-*Card Models*
Flite Craft Models-1595 Victoria St N-Kitchener, ONT CANADA -N2B3E6-*Profile Kits*
Fly In Models-Lawrie Kelsall-POB 972 Murray Bridge S. Australia-*Down Under Kits*
Flying Start-10460 Ambassador Dr-Rancho Cordova CA 95670-*Beginner's Kits*
Free Flight Unlimited-6769 Angels Ln-Tucker GA 30084-*FF Kits & Supplies*
Golden Age Reproductions-PO Box 1685-Andover MA 01810-*OT Kits & Plans*
Great Planes-1608 Interstate Dr-Champaign IL 61821-*RC Kits & Supplies*
Gross, Art-12516 Maplewood Ave-Edmunds WA 98026-*Glue Dispensers, Belt Sanders*
Groth, Charles-604 Cleveland Ave-Batavie, IL 60510-*Timers for Electric Flight*
Guillow, Paul K-PO Box 229-Wakefield MA 01880-*Wide Variety of Scale Kits for Rubber, Electric or Gas. WWI, WWII, Golden Age, Multi-Engine*
Harlan, Ray-15 Happy Holow Rd-Wayland MA 01778-*Indoor Tools, Balsa Stripper, Scale, etc*
Helicopter USA-555 Sloop 9-Pittsburgh PA 15237-*Rubber Power Helicopter*
Herbach & Rademan-18 Canal St-Bristol PA 19007-*Surplus Catalogue*
Herr Engineering-1431 Chaffee Dr, Suite 3-Titusville FL 32780-*Rubber Scale Kits - Laser Cut Parts- Also for Elec.* CO_2 *Power*
Harry Higley-PO Box 532-Glenwood IL 60425-*Books & Tools of Many Types*
HiLine-PO Box 11558-Goldsboro NC 27532-*Motors, Elec Flt Supplies, Plans*
Hinson, Rex-1141 S Waterview Dr-Inverness FL 34450-*Torque Meters*
Hobby Club-931 Calle Negocio, San Clemente CA 92673 - *CETO System & Kits*
Hobby Hideaway-RR2 Box 19-Delavan IL 61734-*Kits & Diesel Motors*
Hobby Horn-P.O. Box 2212-Westminster CA 92683-*Kits & Matls*
Hobby Lobby-5614 Franklin Pike Circle-Brentwood, TN 37027-*small slow flite to lg R/C*
Hobby Supply South-1720 Mars Hill Rd-Suite 8365-Acworth GA 30101-*Wide Variety Dom. & Import Kits + Airspan & Litespan*
Indoor Model Supply-1887 West Haven NW-Salem OR 97340-*Indoor Wood, Kits, Matls*
JCI Intntnl-655 State College Unit 19-Fullerton CA 92631-*Many Colors of Tissue*
J'Tec-164 School St-Daly City, CA 94014-*Scale Instruments*
Jehlik, Don-Box 547-Crestline CA 92325- *ARF FF Helicopter*
Jones, Jim-36631 Ledgestone-Mt Clemens, MI 48043-*Balsa Stripper, Rubber Stripper, Rib Slicer & Other Tools*
K&S Engrng-6917 W 59 St-Chicago, IL 60638-*Tubing, Sheet Metal*
Kenway Micro Flight-PO Box 889-Hackettstown NJ 07840-*Small Elec Motor Systems, Plans & Supplies, Condenser Motor & Others*
Klarich Kustom Kits-2301 Sonata Dr-Rancho Cordova CA 95670-*OT Gas Kits*
Knight & Pridham-Castle Rd, Rowlands, Hants, PO96AS, ENGLAND-*Elec Motors, Propo & other unique FF Supplies*
Kress Jets-800 Ulster Lndng Rd-Saugerties, NY 12477-*Elec. motors,kits, ducted fans*
Lidberg, Al-1008 Baseline Rd-Suite 1074- Tempe, AZ 85283-*Kits & Plans for small Replicas of OT Models for Elec,* CO_2 *& Rubber Power*
Labco-27563 Dover-Warren MI 48093-810-754-7539-*Water Slide off Decal Material*
Lone Star Models-1623-57 St-Lubbock TX 79412-*Balsa 4-6 Density & Up*

MIA Designs-PO Box 34261-Chicago IL 60634-*Rubber Power Helicopter Kits*
Micro Air-PO Box 1129- Richland WA 99352-*Simple, Inexpensive Scale*
Micro Fasteners-110 Hillcrest Rd-Flemington NJ 08822-*Wide Supply of Fasteners*
Micro Mark-340 Snyder Ave-Berkely Hts NJ 07922- *ManyTools*
Micro-X-PO Box 1063-Lorain OH 44055-*Indoor Kits & Supplies*
Microscale-PO Box 11950-Costa Mesa CA 92627-*Lozenge Patterns*
Midair Models-97 Elmbridsge-Surbiton Surrey KT59HB-ENGLAND-*Foam Flyers*
Midwest Models-PO Box 564-Hobart IN 46342-*Kits, Beginner's & Gollywock*
Model Aircraft Labs-108 S Lee St-Irving TX 75060-*Small FF Kits for Gas, Elec or CO_2*
Model Research Labs-25108 Marguerite #160-Mission Viejo CA 92692-*Composite s*
Motion Ind-4901 W Van Buren-Phoenix AZ 85061-*Dow 33 Rubber Lube*
NOIR-PO Box 159-South Lyon MI 48178-*Special UVProof Sunglasses*
National Balsa-97 Cherokee Dr-Springfield MA 01109-*Balsa*
Nowlen Aero-139 Boardwalk-Greenbrae CA 94904-*OT Peanut Kits, Wright Flyer, etc.*
Old Timer Models-PO Box 7334 Van Nuys CA 91407-*OT kits & Supplies*
Oppegard, Robt-140 E. Golden Lake Ln-Circle Pines MN 55014-*Rubber Stripper*
Palmer, Fred-Rt 1 Box 151E-Baker City OR 97814-*P-30 Torque Meter*
Paper Airplanes-433 Nikoa St-Kahului HI 96732-*Widest Selection of Paper Airplanes*
Paper Models Intl-9916 SW Bonnie Brae-Beaverton OR 97005-*Paper Model Kits*
Papic, Ferrell-300 W Linden #82-Orange CA 92665-*Ducted Fan Construction Book*
Pasquet, Henry-HCR3 Box 224-Elsinore MO 63937-*CO_2 Supplies & Info*
Peck Polymers-PO Box 710399-Santee CA 92072-*Peanut & Larger FF & RC Kits- One Nite 28- Supplies, Tools, etc*
Penn Valley Hobby-837 Main St-Lansdale PA 19446-*Mail Order-Kits & Supplies*
PEP Aviation-111E Geneva Dr-Tempe AZ 85282- *Sky Shine Reflective Material*
Plan-It-15121 -62 Ave W-Edmonds WA 98026-*OT Kits & Gas FF Supplies*
Pond, Bert-128 Warren Terrace-Longmeadow MA 01106-*Compressed Air Motors*
Precision Molding-3591 Hearst Dr-Simi Valley CA 93063-*Sure Grip Pins*
RGOA-936 Hamal Dr-Littleton CO 80124- *Collapsible Poles*
Rocket City-103 Wholesale Ave NE-Huntsville AL 35811-*Pins, Clamps & Other Tools*
SR Batteries-Box 287-Bellport NY 11713-*Best Batteries, Chargers, Elec Kits etc*
SAMS-The Chapel Roe Green Sandon Buntingford Hertfordshire SG90QT ENGLAND- *Wide Variety Kits, Plans & Matls - Many Not Available in US*
Scale Flight Models-1219 So Washington-Bloomington IN 47401-*OT Kits*
Scientext-48 Whitney St-Westport CT 06880-*Elec Kits, Flying Boats & multi Engine*
SIG Mfg Co-401 S Front St-Montezume IA 50171-*Full House Mail Order, Kits-FF-RC, Matls, Tools, etc.*
Simple Simon Aircraft-P O Box 18-Longmeadow MA 01028-*Beginner's Stick Models*
Simplex Winders-John Morrill-143 Richmond St-El Segundo CA 90245- *Winders*
Skonk Works-1890 Forestdale Ave-Beaver Creek OH 45432-*RTP Kits & Supplies*
Small Parts-PO Box 4650-Miami Lakes FL 33138-*Small Plastic Screws, etc.*
Small Scale Custom Services-Spring Meadow Fyfield Andover Hants SP118EL ENGLAND-*Small Molded & Cast Parts for Scale Details*
Spin Master-205 Esplenade-Toronto, Ontario, CANADA M5A 1J2-*Compressed Air*
Starline-6146 E Cactus Wren Rd-Scottsdale AZ 85253-*Polyspan Covering*
Summerset, Wm-Rt 4 Box 365K-Canyon Lake TX 78133- *Timers*
SuperiorAircraft Matls-12020-G Centralia-Hawaiian Gardens CA 90716-*Balsa, Foam*
Superior Props-B. Gourdon-60375 W Spruce Ln-Lacombe LA 70445-*Best Props*
T&A Hobbies-3512 W Victoria Blvd-Burbank CA 91505-*Mail Order-Most Kits, Supplies*
Tipper, John-23 Green Ln-Chichester West Sussex PO194NS ENGLAND-*Indoor Matls*
Toms Model Works-1050 Cranberry Dr-Cupertino CA 95014-*Etched Brass Wheel Parts*
Transmotion-PO Box 160-North Hollywood CA 91603-*Small Parts, Screws, Washers,*

Unival-498 Nepperhan Ave-Yonkers NY 10701-*Special Solder Pastes*
VL Prod-7871 Alabama Ave #16-Canoga Pk CA 91304-*Elec Motors, Small Connectors*
Vacuum Form-Doug Walsh-2720 Morgan Hill Dr-Lake Orion MI 48360-*Book & Matls on Vacuum Forming*
Watts Up-PO Box 5702-Hamden CT 06518-*Motors, Motor Info*
Wells, Rob-1 Rockingham Dr-Wilmington DE 19803-*Lozenge Pattern Tissue*
Wickland-2412 Tucson Ave-Pensacola, FL 32526-*Wood Micro Props for small electrics*
Wilder Model Mach.Wks.-2010 Boston-Irving TX 75061- 214-253-8404-*Indoor 20:1 Winders with Torque Meters for Indoor Models*
Williams Bros-181 Pawnee St-San Marcos CA 92069-*Scale Plastic Pilots, Engines*
Wings & Wheels-PO Box 762- Lafayette CA 94549-*Badger Button DT Timers*
Woodhouse, Mike-12 Marston Ln, Eaton Norwich Norfolk, NR4 6LZ ENGLAND-*Many S Special FF Competition Supplies, Mylar Sheet*
Wycoff Assoc.-83 Flyers Dr-Norwich CT 06760-*No Cal Kits, Lozenge Patterns*

Publications & Organizations

Academy of Model Aeronautics-5151 E Memorial Dr-Muncie IN 47302-*America's Biggest Model Organization- Publishes Model Aviation Mag- Join It*
Aero Index-Mark Fineman-73 Charlton Hill-Hamden CT 06519-*Index of Mag Articles*
Aero Literature-PO Box 759-Ocean Shores WA 98569-*Books & Mags about aero*
Aeromodeller-Argus House Boundary Way Hemel Hempstead Herts HP2 7ST -UK-*English Model Airplane Mag - Very Good - Full Sized Plans*
Aircraft Data-Wm F McCoombs-PO Box 763576-Dallas TX 75224-*Good Book on Aerodynamics and flight Trimming Theory*
Aviation Bookmobile-12032 E Firestone Blvd-Norwalk CA 90650-*20000 Old Mags*
Aviation Modeler Intn'tl-(imported by Dare Designs)-*Fine all around Model Mag*
Bob Banka's' Scale Model Research-3114 Yukon Ave-Costa Mesa CA 92626-*Scale I nfo, 3 Views, Photo Packets*
Carsten's Publications Flying Models Magazine-PO Box 700- Newton NJ 07860-*One of the Better Model Mags with lots of FF and Many Full Sized Plans*
Cloud 9 RC-John Worth-4346 Andes Dr-Fairfax VA 22030-*Micro RC Newsletter*
Cottage Wings-Bill Warner-1310 Monache Ave-Porterville CA 93257-*Source Listing*
Flying Aces Club-(Lin Reichel) 3301 Cindy Ln-Erie PA 16506-*Scale Model Society*
Flying Model Warplanes-John Fredriksen-69 Flamingo Dr-Warwick RI 02880-*Pics & Sources of Warplanes, Kits etc*
Hannan's Runway-Bill Hannan-PO Box 210-Magalia CA 95954-*Series of Model Books*
INAV-444 Bryan St-St Louis MO 63122- *Indoor News and Views -Nat Indoor Newsletter*
Model Airplane News-Air Age Publishing-251 Danbury Rd-Wilton CT 06897-*Fine Model Mag- Mostly RC- Plans etc*
Nat. FF Society-Fred Terzian-4858 Moorpark Ave-San Jose CA 95129-*Publishes FF News- Worth Joining for FF Info World Wide*
O'Reilly, Jim-4760 N. Battin-Wichita KS 67220-*Cottage Industry List*
Society of Antique Modelers-Bob Dodds-209 Summerside Pl-Encinitas CA 92024-*Publishes SAM Speaks- All about OT Modeling - Join It*
NY Indoor Times-Ed Whitten-67 Riverside Dr- NY NY 10024 *Indoor Info*
Frank Zaic- *Zaic Yearbooks Carried by Many Supplier - Best Info in the Field*

Plans & Special Products

Aeromodeller Plans Service- *Plans From Aeromodeller Magazine*
Aero Plans-8931 Kittyhawk Ave-Los Angeles CA 90045-*OT Plans & Plan Books*
Airdevil Model Co-4304 Madison Ave-Trumbull CT 06611-*Scale Model Plans*
Ben Buckle-9 Islay Crescent-Highworth Wilts SN6 7HL UK- *Many OT Plans*
Brittains-500 Summer St-Stamford CT 06901-*Possible Source for Decal Matl*

Cardinal-RR1 Box 163-Cameron IL 61423-*Old Mag Plans*
Clary, Jim-3008 E Meadow Grove Rd-Orange CA 92667-*Tern Aero Plans*
Clements, Vern-308 Palo Alto Drt-Caldwell ID 83605-*Lots of OT Plans*
Cleveland Model Supply-9800 Detroit Ave-Cleveland OH 44102- *Vast Library of Cleveland Plans*
Clough, Roy-Box 150-Pittsfield NH 03263-*Electric Kits & Plans*
Cole, Brian-1312 NE 35 St-Ocala FL 32670- *List of Unusual Plans*
Conover Models-PO Box 628- Longmont CO 80502- *Project Grandpa Kits & Plans*
D. B. Enterprises- 5901 Wedgewood Circle N-Fort Worth TX 76133- *OT Plans*
DC Engrng-35218 W Pine Hill-Pinehurst TX 77362-*Exotic Model Plans*
Dinstbier, Steve-1159 Taft Rd-St Johns MI 48879-*Scale Plans*
Felix, Ron-PO Box 74-Soleburg PA 18963-*Text on Wakefields*
Fillon,Emanuel-60 Ru Du Bocage-83700 St Raphael-FRANCE-*Plans for most unusual models- Rubber Power Ducted Fans, etc.*
Flying Aces Models-1564A Fitzgerald Dr-Suite 118-Pinole CA 94564- *No Cal Plans*
Flying Scale-1905 Colony Rd-Matarie LA 70003- *Rubber FF Plans*
Friestad, Roland-2211 S 155 St- Cameron IL 61423- *Can Enlarge or Reduce Plans*
Gallant Models-34249 Camino Capistrano-Capistrano Beach CA 92624-*Model Builder Magazine Plans with Articles*
Gleason Enterprises-705-10 Ave SW-Austin MN 55912-*Vast Plan Catalogues OT Rubber, Gas Scale- Includes Beautiful Bess*
Grega, John-355 Grand Blvd-Bedford OH 44146-*Classic Era Plans*
Gregovsky, Radek-Svermova 1371-26601Beroun-2, Czech Republic-*WWI plans , kits & decals- Very fine Quality*
Gulf Coast Models-420 Lake Shore Dr-Hot Springs AK 71913-*Mike Midkiff Scale Plans*
Howard, Bob-519 N Youlon St-West Salem WI 54669- *Gliders from Beer Cans*
Hunt, Allen-Box 726-Dunbar WV 25064-*Large Plan List- OT-Scale- Unusual*
Idealair-Phil Alvirez-Box 44853-Detroit MI 48244- *Book-Props on a Can*
Midkiff, Mike-420 Lake Shore Dr-Hot Springs AR 71913-*Fine Scale Plans*
Michael Morrow--1327 44 Ave SW-Seattle WA 98116-*No-Cal Peanut Plans, Supplies*
Northrup, Bill-2019 Doral Ct-Henderson NV 89014-*OT FF Plans from Model Builder*
Patten, Jim-5646 S Rt 68-Urbana OH 43078-*Plans & Articles from many Mags*
Pond, John- PO Box 90310- San Jose CA 95104-*Has Most OT Plans*
Scale Model Research-3114 Yukon-Costa Mesa CA 92626-*Plans & Research Cards*
Scale Plan & Photo Serv-3209 Madison Ave-Greensboro NC 27403-*Scale Research*
Schultz, Charles- 910 Broadfields Dr-Louisville KY 40207-*Old Magazine Plans*
Smiley, Clarke-23 Riverbend Rd-Newmarket NH 03857-*Scale Plans*
Thompson, Bruce-328 St Germain Ave-Toronto, Ontario CANADA M5M 1W3-*List most plans in old mags*
Warner, Bill-1370 Monache Ave-Porterville CA 93257-*Cottage Wngs Supplier Listing*
Yesteryear Plan Service-3517 Kristie Dr-Erie PA 16506-*Scale OT Plans*

Videos

Harding Prod.-4787 Unity Ln Rd-New Waterford OH 44445-216-457-7352 - *How To*
Home Grown TV-94-20, 66 Ave. ForestHills NY 11374-718-275-6362-*Contest & Indoor*
Robin's View-Box 68-Stockertown PA 18083-610-746-0106-*How To*

For any of these services, send for a catalogue to get latest pricing.